THE WIZARD

AND THE
WITCH

EXPANDED SPECIAL EDITION
VOLUME I

"WE HAVE TO BELIEVE WE ARE MAGIC"

AN ORAL HISTORY OF
OBERON ZELL & MORNING GLORY

JOHN C. SULAK

Left Hand Press
Cincinnati, Ohio, USA

Reviews

I have found myself thirsting for information about those magickal pioneers who created the foundation upon which the current Pagan movement in North America was built. There are many names that those in the Pagan community are familiar with – those individuals who had the extraordinary spirit to explore that which was virtually unknown in North America in the 1960s and '70s. Oberon and Morning Glory are two such spirits. Their contributions to the current community are inestimable. Some of those contributions can be found in their other books which are also highly recommended. (Oberon's *Grimoire* is one of my favourites).

But there is very little out there which gives a sense of the growth of Paganism itself. To read about the lives of Oberon and Morning Glory and to get a sense of the background and history of the Pagan movement itself was exactly what I was looking for. My thirst was quenched. John Sulak (the Narrator) did a remarkable job of creating a seamless story from, what I can imagine, was a mammoth amount of life experience. I truly hope to see other such works. There is much to be learned from biography and this one, I definitely recommend. ~ **Beeavalon**

This is not a book about how to do magic for yourself. It is the story of two of the most extraordinary, yet ordinary, people to grace our planet. Two people who showed the world how to live a life of magic despite the odds of politics, finances, all manner of adversity and humanness. These two, as individuals and as a couple, altered the way thousands of people worship and live. Their love for each other, the Divine, knowledge, and people pours forth from the pages. It is a transformative tale and an inspiration to any who seek the courage to create their life the way they want to live it. ~ **Avilynn Pwyll**

Knowing only of Oberon Zell and Morning Glory Zell through their art and their reverence in the Pagan community, taking time to read through their lives together and from where they started in this unique book was truly an incredible experience. Through the many twists and turns in their lives it's amazing to see that through many difficult times, such beautiful experiences came through. In the end, it said that the original manuscript for this book was double what it came out to be. I honestly would have paid to read it in its entirety. I recommend this book especially for anyone within the Pagan community that would like to take a view into the lives of two incredibly influential people and their many friends and lovers and see the world as we know it shaped by their loving hands. I only wish that I had been there to truly experience it and I hope in my life to encounter a few of the wonderful people in this book. ~ **Cynthia A Rivers**

Books by Oberon Zell

1. *Grimoire for the Apprentice Wizard,* with the Grey Council (New Page Books, 2004)
2. *Companion for the Apprentice Wizard*, with the Faculty of the Grey School of Wizardry (New Page Books, 2006)
3. *Creating Circles & Ceremonies: Rituals for All Seasons & Reasons,* with Morning Glory Zell (New Page, 2006)
4. *A Wizard's Bestiary,* with Ash DeKirk (New Page, 2007)
5. *Green Egg Omelette: An Anthology of Art and Articles from the Legendary Pagan Journal* (New Page, 2008)
6. *Prophecy & the End of the World (as we know it): Apocalypse or Solartopia?* with Harvey Wasserman (TheaGenesis e-book, 2012)
7. *Barsoom: A New Map of the Mars of Edgar Rice Burroughs' "John Carter of Mars" Novels* (TheaGenesis e-book, 2012)
8. *The Wizard and the Witch: An Oral History of Oberon Zell & Morning Glory,* by John Sulak with Oberon & Morning Glory Zell (Llewellyn, 2014)
9. *Death Rights & Rites* with Judith Fenley (Llewellyn Pubs, 2020)
10. *That Undiscover'd Country: A Traveler's Guide to the Afterlife* (Black Moon Pubs, 2021)
11. *Song of Gaea,* with Kirsten Johnson & Pratima Sarkar (a children's book, IngramSpark 2021)
12. *Goodbye Jesus, I've Gone Home to Mother,* with Phaedra Bonewits (Left Hand Press, 2021)
13. *The Wizard and the Witch: An Oral History of Oberon Zell & Morning Glory* (special 2-volume expanded edition) by John Sulak with Oberon & Morning Glory Zell (Left Hand Press, 2021)

Books in Process from Oberon...

GaeaGenesis: Conception and Birth of the Living Earth
Creatures of Night Brought to Light
Legendary Journeys: Europe 1987, with Dona Carter
History's Mysteries
Grimoire for the Apprentice Wizard (special expanded hardcover edition)
Grimoire for the Journeyman Wizard
Walkabout of the Wandering Wizard (2018-2020)
A Wizard's Guide to Women
Wizards of the World, with Nikki "Solaris" Kirby
Unicorns in Our Garden, with Morning Glory Zell
Handbook for My Future Parents, with Cat Gina Cole

The Authors

Oberon, John Sulak, and Morning Glory at Azkatraz (Pottercon), 2009.

John Sulak (San Francisco, CA) is a storyteller, filmmaker, and the co-author of the book *Modern Pagans*. He is inspired by journalists like Studs Terkel, Hunter S. Thompson, Tom Wolfe, and Legs McNeil, and it was his idea to tell *The Wizard and the Witch* in the oral-history format and to get involved in the narrative as he was documenting it.

Oberon Zell (Redmond, WA) is a founding father of modern Paganism (and the first to claim that label in 1967), and one of the most respected Elders in the new movement of "green religion" that emerged in the latter half of the 20th century. Oberon is co-founder of the first Pagan Church of All Worlds, incorporated in 1968. He founded the vanguard Pagan journal *Green Egg* and served as its publisher for four decades. His book titles include *Grimoire for the Apprentice Wizard, A Wizard's Bestiary,* and many others. Oberon is also founder and Headmaster of the online Grey School of Wizardry, offering more than 500 classes in 16 Departments.

Morning Glory Zell (1948-2014) was a renowned Witch, Goddess Historian, Loremistress, and Ritual Priestess of the Great Goddess in Her many guises. Her journeys took her to the Australian Outback, the Coral Sea, the jungles of New Guinea, Greek temples and Hong Kong. She was a published poet, songwriter and author, with short stories included in two volumes of Marion Zimmer Bradley's *Sword and Sorceress* anthologies; and she was an acknowledged consultant for MZB's *The Mists of Avalon.*

Acknowledgements

We would like to thank the many people who
agreed to be interviewed for this book. These are:

Charles Zell (OZ's father)
Vera Zell (OZ's mother)
Barry Zell (OZ's brother)
Shirley Kaye (OZ's sister)
Alyce Mitchem Jenkins (OZ's 11th grade English teacher)
Lance Christie (OZ's first water brother, 1962)
Gale Fuller (OZ's old college professor and mentor)
Martha Turley (OZ's first wife, Bryan's mother)
John Brazelton (met OZ in 1964 as an impressionable teenager)
Bryan Zell (OZ's son by Martha, born 1963))
Tom Williams (CAW Priest & co-adventurer; joined CAW in
     1968)
Debbie Dietz (lived in the CAW temple on Gaslight Square, St
     Louis as a teenager in 1968)
Carolyn Clark (CAW High Priestess, St Louis)
Don Wildgrube (CAW High Priest, St Louis)
Ralph Metzner (psychologist, psychonaut, water-brother)
Laura O'Rourke Davis (lived with her mother and siblings at the
     Zell house in St Louis in 1971)
Michael Muddypaws Hurley (CAW Priest, St Louis)
Bobbie (Roberta) Kennedy (CAW Priestess)
Polly Love Moore (MG's mother)
Gary Ferns (MG's first husband)
Carolyn Whitehorn (MG's oldest friend from '60s)
Catherine Crowell (MG's friend since 1971)
Margot Adler (author of *Drawing Down the Moon*)
Robert Anton Wilson (author *Illuminatus,* water-brother)
Steve Frischer (old CAW member from St Louis days)
Pendragon Rashkiss (dear friend and lover from St Louis)
Cerridwen Fallingstar (lover, author, Priestess)
Anodea Judith (lover, CAW HPs, "Presitess," author, artist)
Anna Korn (close friend, met in Eugene, OR, 1976)
Alison Harlow (owner of Coeden Brith; invited OZ &
     MG to become caretakers & raise Unicorns)
Marylyn Motherbear (CAW HPs, early
     Greenfield pioneer)

Gail Salvador (MG's daughter)
Kirsten Johnsen (Greenfield neighbor)
Daryl Cherney (CAW Bard, Earth First!)
Elan Papa (met Unicorn as a child in 1980)
Farida Fox (CAW Priestess, friend and lover)
Eldri Littlewolf (lived with OZ/MG on Coeden Brith)
Ayisha Homolka (lived on Greenfield with Gwydion)
Artemisia (met as a teenager in 1982—longtime friend & lover)
David Hodghead (Alison's lawyer; agent for Living Unicorn)
Jeffrey Siegle (booking agent for Unicorn Ren Faire saga)
Daniel Blair Stewart (co-adventurer on Mermaid Expedition)
Diane Darling (3rd partner in triad marriage for 10 years, Editor
    Green Egg)
Zack Darling (Diane's son, OZ & MG's stepson)
Gary & Betty Ball (friends/partners in Between the Worlds)
Julie O'Ryan (OZ & MG's paramour since 1992)
Tom Donahue (MG's lover, HS teacher, best friend, helped
    launch Mythic Images; edited *Green Egg*)
Elantari Love (daughter of Aeona Silverson, and a dear friend
    since childhood)
Talyn Songdog (MG's lover)
Tam Songdog (Talyn's daughter, MG & OZ's water-daughter)
Kadira Belynne (OZ's lover)
Wolf Stiles (Ravenheart Family member)
Liza Gabriel (Ravenheart Family member)
Wynter Rose (Ravenheart Family member)
Ariel Monserrat (lived at Shady Grove for awhile; published
    Green Egg online)

And finally, Orion Morris, who joined CAW in 1969 and was
our co-adventurer for many years. Although he declined to be
interviewed, his delightful "Unicorn Song Part 2" charmingly
summarizes the great Unicorn Saga.

John Sulak would like to thank Elysia Gallo for her help in
shaping the many drafts of the manuscript. He would like to
thank Deborah "Oak" Cooper, Ken Montgomery, V. Vale
And Ron Ward for their friendship and support while he
was working on them. And, with love and
gratitude, John would like to dedicate this,
the completed book, to Alisa Highfill.

Foreword

by Carl Llewellyn Weschcke

HE SIXTIES AND SEVENTIES OF THE LAST century were very exciting times for Pagans and Occultists of all persuasions.

What had been repressed by Church and Society was suddenly being Born Again and the mood was revolutionary. We were discovering and recovering the Old Ways of Ancient Wisdom, but we were also part of the New Wave of Science and Political Liberation. The Old Ways and the New Wave fed into each other and inspired what we can still, legitimately, call the "New Age."

The New Age shook things up so much that it attracted as many crazy people as it did reformers and people wanting answers to old questions for which old answers were no long accepted. We invented new movements and new institutions, and found alternative ways to see the world. It was as if futuristic science fiction and medieval myths merged and came alive in our time.

Now, in 2008, I can look back over a half century of publishing for the New Age with astonishment and enjoyment for all we've done and for all the people that played active rolls in giving it birth. Today, so much of the New Age is part of the modern world that what was once strange and scary to mainstream America is now common culture in the newly forming global civilization.

Even the pioneers don't appreciate all that has happened. We planted the seeds that burst into New Life; we were the mid-wives to the birth of a New Earth; we nurtured a New Generation through childhood and adolescence; and now we watch as the Final Drama unfolds and the world-as-know-it ends and a New World Order takes its place.

In the Fall of 1973, Llewellyn sponsored an event called "Gnosticon," standing for *Gnosis*, or Inner Knowledge, in the New Age. Many of these pioneers came together ostensibly to learn from each other but more importantly to 're-birth' one another. The energy of the moment was astonishing and still brings a song to my heart.

At the 1973 Gnosticon, I introduced Morning Glory to Oberon, and sparks flew. Suddenly, where there had been a crowd milling about near the hotel swimming pool there were only two people. It was a timeless moment when two parts became a Whole greater than the sum of the parts.

It is said that True Marriages are made in heaven but we believe that the Kingdom of Heaven is within – in the Heart of each of us. The Kingdom of Heaven is forever and we can all enter in. A True Marriage is a fertile union that enriches the world around and gives birth to new ideas, new understanding, and renewed devotion to shared ideals.

The life of Oberon and Morning Glory shows all of this to be true, and therefore we can all share in the celebration of that life and the magic that they have brought into the world and are teaching to another generation.

~ Carl Llewellyn Weschcke
Planet New Earth, Fall, 2008

Preface:
American Lives

by John C. Sulak

HIS IS A BOOK ABOUT THE EARTH AND about people who love Her. Two of those people are Morning Glory and Oberon Zell. They live in America, and like a lot of colorful American characters that came before them, they are passionate and larger than life. They were pioneers, boldly going where no one had gone before. And like the crew of the Starship Enterprise, they had many adventures and made many mistakes along the way.

They are Pagans. The average American probably doesn't yet understand what a Pagan is. And, in fact, a lot of people who call themselves Pagans can't even agree with each other about what a Pagan is. But Morning Glory and Oberon know. They knew before they had a word for it, and they have spent their lives exploring and expanding what it means. It is their religion and their life, and it is as real to them as the Earth itself.

A lot of what they do is as corny as Kansas in August and as normal as blueberry pie: They dote on their granddaughter, they celebrate Thanksgiving and other holidays with big family dinners, and they love Disney animated movies. Oberon helps shoot off fireworks at his local community's Fourth of July celebrations!

Whatever they do that might not meet with public approval is not intended for the public anyway. MG and OZ are not looking to convert anyone. But of course if you want to learn about it, and ask politely, they'll tell you some good stories. And that's what this book is – stories about their lives, about what they've done in public and what they've done behind closed doors (or out of doors on private land!).

They believe in the power of myth. They are part of the ancient tradition of sitting in a circle around a campfire with family and friends telling tales. And you, dear friends, are now invited to join in the circle with Morning Glory, Oberon and those who have known them. Let the stories begin!

The Wizard and The Witch
Special Expanded Edition—Volume I
"We have to believe we are magic..."

Prologues: 2021 and 2009

By John C. Sulak

1: (Written in 2021)

I WAS STILL IN MY 40s WHEN I STARTED THIS book. It took almost a decade to finish the original, rough draft. When it was done we submitted it to our publisher, Llewellyn Worldwide, and it was rather swiftly rejected by our editor.

I was sent back to the drawing board with instructions to cut out more than half of the massive word count. It was also decided that I would need to write commentary for each chapter. I became the "Narrator." It took a few more years, but I got everything taken care of. The first edition of *The Wizard and the Witch* was finally published in early 2014.

And now here I am, almost 70 years old, and once again working on the project. This two-volume expanded edition is based on the original, unpublished manuscript. The narration that I wrote later has been edited into it by Oberon. (Perhaps a more accurate title for this book would have been *The Wizard, the Witch. and the Narrator!*) OZ has also added new material, some of which he wrote, and formatted both volumes.

The prologue that follows this one was written by me in 2009 but not included in the Llewellyn edition. Like a lot of what I did with that first draft it is raw and naive, but also enthusiastic. I have agreed to let it, and the rest of these two volumes, be printed now for historical purposes.

Many of the people that I interviewed for *The Wizard and the Witch* are no longer with us. I am grateful that I had the opportunity to document some of what they had to say. What is remembered lives.

~ John C. Sulak, Sept. 1, 2021

2: (Written in 2009)

NCE UPON A TIME THERE WAS A BOY WHO grew up in Illinois." Hmm, that could be either Oberon Zell Ravenheart or me, John C. Sulak. We're both listed on the cover as co-authors. And this is my part of the story, where you will learn some of my past, and about how and why this book was written.

The book was, in a way, begun in 1969. That was when I hooked up with the Church of All Worlds at the World Science Fiction Convention in St. Louis. I was 16 years old. I ended up getting a subscription to the *Green Egg,* which at first I thought was a science fiction fanzine. The whole concept of fanzines was, back then, pretty cool. You could do it yourself! They were mostly published on mimeograph machines. Those machines were usually used by businesses and schools. The idea of "desk-top publishing" did not exist then. If you wanted a copy of something at home, you had to use carbon paper. So the idea of taking that technology, and using it to publish your own personal magazine, was radical.

And a lot of really messy work. First you had to type up a stencil, then put the stencil into the machine, load it with ink and crank the thing by hand. It used a special kind of paper that had a distinctive smell when the ink on it was still wet. They don't make those machines or paper anymore. A friend of mine has a bunch of old mimeograph equipment in his basement which he keeps around for spare parts so he can keep printing that way. He also has a few cases of the paper in storage, and when they're gone, that's it. He works with computers for a living, and could easily publish with the latest laser printers, but he digs the romance of the old ways—just like Oberon and Morning Glory do!

I returned to my hometown of Rockford, Illinois after the convention, and started my junior year of high school. After having just met a bunch of science fiction writers, and since it was the first time I'd ever even talked to a professional author, I was pretty excited about the whole idea of being a writer. For the next two years I wrote for the high school newspaper. I tried my hand at writing fiction, but also developed as journalist. That seemed like maybe one path I could follow later on in life. The big challenge was actually finding something to write about, which was mixed in with the challenges of my adolescent angst and my self-destructive tendencies.

My freshman year of college I found some real inspiration when I read Tom Wolfe's book, *The Electric Kool-Aid Acid Test*. It was, and still is, amazing. It was written it in the style of a novel, but it was about real people. Wolfe was one of the characters in it, and he described things not just as an observer but as a participant. The Grateful Dead, my favorite band at the time, were also characters, and so were Ken Kesey and the Merry Pranksters. I thought that it would be really cool to hang out with a tribe like that and write a book like Tom Wolfe did. I wanted to get on Kesey's bus and ride off into the sunset!

...Acid Test was soon followed by Hunter S. Thompson's *Fear and Loathing in Las Vegas*. It took Tom Wolfe's style of writing to another, and much crazier, level. I wasn't sure if I wanted to live like Thompson did, but it did offer some new possibilities for how to be a reporter. It was called "gonzo," and the word seemed appropriate. A couple of years later I read Studs Terkel's *Working,* which was a collection of short interviews with different people about their jobs. Studs just let them talk, and it worked really well.

I went to college and studied psychology and philosophy. And I continued getting the *Green Egg* in the mail. I noticed that what Tim Zell was writing about in GE overlapped with what I was learning about psychology. I, too, was interested in the humanistic psychology of Maslow and Perls. "Self-actualization," as described by Carl Rogers, seemed like a goal worth pursuing, and that was the same goal being pursued by the CAW. I became involved in a number of cutting-edge psychological activities, including encounter groups, consciousness-raising sessions and feminist workshops. The format for all of these was the same that Zell was using in the CAW and that I later found being done in other Pagan groups.

So, some things that had started when I was 16 continued to expand. And so did my self-destructive tendencies. For some people, it just isn't a good idea to be taking any kind of drugs or alcohol, and I am one of those people. It never got to the point of doing any permanent damage, but what it did do was interfere with whatever else I was doing – it kept me from making any real progress with my life. It was easy to go into an altered state and think that I was accomplishing something, or doing something really important. It was also easy to call it "Dionysian," and that somehow justified it. But Dionysius, I learned much later, is a very dangerous God, and has to be dealt with carefully and treated with respect.

The *Green Egg* ceased publication in 1979 and when I went to science fiction conventions Tim Zell was no longer there wearing animal skins and a big snake. In his place, or so it seemed to me, were a new group of fans who called themselves "anarchists," and they were all dressed in black. They had read the same Robert Heinlein books that Tim Zell had, only instead of starting a church they had started a political sci-fi subculture. But the anarchists shared a lot of ideas with CAW Paganism. The anarchist fans labeled Heinlein's books as "libertarian." What that meant was that the characters in them took care of business themselves—they didn't ask any authority figures to help them, and they wanted the government to leave them alone. They believed that individuals had a right to make up their own minds, to control their own lives, and to do whatever they wanted to as long as it didn't interfere with anyone else's life.

Their fave Heinlein novel wasn't *Stranger*... but *The Moon is a Harsh Mistress*, which is about a colony on the moon that revolts against being ruled by the Earth. It is basically a fictional look at what a functional anarchist society might be like. Heinlein points out that being an anarchist is a lot of work. And so the moon colonists talk about "TANSTAAFL," which stands for "There Ain't No Such Thing As A Free Lunch."

Zell had picked up on Heinlein's politics when he was reading his books as a kid. The libertarian ideas are there in a lot of the early Heinlein books, including his juvenile fiction. They were stories that had shaped Tim Zell's thinking and behavior. As I went back and read all of those books myself, I discovered that they fit in with experiences that I was having.

Tim and Morning Glory went off into the woods, and I went to the city. It was there that I found the punk rock subculture. I felt right at home, and I saw a lot that I recognized: Punk fans connected with each other by creating fanzines, just as science fiction fans and Pagans had. And the punk philosophy was about anarchy – don't let anyone else tell you what to think or believe! Do it yourself! Control your own destiny! It was all very comfortable and familiar to me, and I found a home in the punk rock world for several years.

But there were the usual dangers there, too. Eventually I had to bail out and start over. I ended up in New York City's East Village, where I ran into an old friend that I had met at a science fiction convention years earlier. He was a Pagan, told me what had happened to Tim (now Otter) Zell, and directed me to a shop called "Enchantments," where I picked up *Drawing Down the Moon* and *The Spiral Dance.*

All this time I was working in restaurants, something I continue to do to this day. That was a way for me to earn money but also have the flexibility of schedule to write and to explore different things. (It also meant I could always get something to eat.) Another advantage of restaurant work was that if I wanted to pack up and move, I could usually find a new job in a new town pretty easily. And so I traveled a lot, and eventually I ended up in San Francisco. And that was where I found a good therapist.

Getting help from that therapist was, as OZ has often described things, a transformative experience. I finally learned what was at the root of so many of the difficulties I had been having with my life. I learned about being co-dependent and about the recovery movement. The important thing was that I was able to turn my life around and finally start living as a happy, healthy, sane human being. It was wonderful!

By this point it was the mid-'90s. I began to sell articles to magazines and to some of the first internet businesses that bought reviews. And a book came out that blew my mind: *Please Kill Me: The Uncensored History of Punk Rock.* It was written by Legs McNeil and Gillian McCain and it was amazing. It was written in the style of *Working,* and another book I had read called *Edie: An American Biography* by Jean Stein and George Plimpton. It didn't have a traditional structure or narrator, but it was epic! I had been at a lot of the events covered in the book, and I was impressed how *Please Kill Me* documented the history of what had happened, and yet also got behind the scenes and explained a lot of it. And it was an enjoyable book to read. I thought, "Wow. Someone should do a book like this about Pagans!" (And I also want to mention that Legs McNeil had been a punk fanzine writer and gonzo journalist extraordinaire from the day punk started.)

And I made a new friend named V. Vale. I already knew who he was because he'd published an early punk fanzine named *Search and Destroy.* I'd had a letter published in one of the first issues, but I'd never met him. Finally I was introduced to Vale by ex-lover of mine who was dating a friend of his. I am mentioning all of this because it is similar to things that have happened in the rest of this book: my fate was determined not just by my own work and ambition, but by chance and who I had slept with!

Vale and I got to know each other and, not surprisingly, found out we had a lot in common. Vale had, since his fanzine days, become an independent book publisher and done many excellent books about subjects I was interested in. I suggested to him that he should do a book about Paganism because it was an anarchist spirituality. Eventually we ended up doing that book together. We called it *Modern Pagans,* and looked at as a follow-up to his influential book about tattooing and piercing called *Modern Primitives.* (It's still available at www.researchpubs.com)

I became friends with the Ravenhearts while doing *Modern Pagans*, and even put Wynter Ravenheart and her snakes on the cover. And that lead to me and OZ talking about doing a book together. I thought the life that the Zells had lived was a great story, and it was not just a story for Pagans. I wanted to take the Zells out of their community and let the rest of the world know about them. I might not have been the most obvious person to work on such a book—I wasn't a member of the CAW or any other Pagan group. I went to rituals and took classes in San Francisco, but I usually didn't see anyone from the local community at any other times. And I was skeptical and cautious about a lot of things that I saw going on. But I think that was what made me qualified to do this project. I wanted to be objective about what had happened, and to document the truth as accurately as possible. Being something of an outsider helped me do that. In the end I got the gig because, as Woody Allen says, "Eighty percent of success is showing up." (And that, for me, is also one of the secrets of how to do magic!)

From the very beginning I wanted it to be an oral history, like *Please Kill Me.* The idea was that I would do interviews with the Zells and their friends and families, and then I would transcribe the interviews and edit them together. And that, dear friends, is what happened. I recorded all of the interviews on tapes and did all the transcribing myself. I spent many years interviewing people and preparing for this before we hooked up with a publisher. It was a lot of work, and I did it all while working full time waiting tables. There were many decisions to be made about what to include and what to leave out. My great role in this was to give it structure. I wanted the book to be historically accurate but also entertaining. So as I edited things together I tried to make sure that there was a clear narrative being told. As work on the book progressed and I put the chapters together, OZ, and then later MG, would go back and add to what I had done. Then I would do more interviews based on their suggestions. We kept the process going and worked well together as a team.

I would like to thank all the people who talked to me for this project. MG and OZ are used to giving interviews and telling stories about themselves, but some of the others had never talked about any of this stuff with a journalist before. I spent a lot of time getting to know people on the phone, and most of what we talked about didn't end up in the final draft. They were all awesome people, and I am sure each one of them could write their own book (and maybe some of them will). I tried to get different perspectives on what had happened, but it wasn't always possible to get all the points of view that I wanted to. Some people didn't want to talk on the record about what happened, and some didn't want to talk at all or we couldn't find them. And sadly, some people have already died. (We have a Facebook page under the name "OZMG Anecdotes" where anyone who wants to can go and comment online about this book and what is and isn't in it.)

I would like to thank Deborah "Oak" Cooper, who is a Pagan, a professional therapist and a good friend. She went out for lunch with me when I got a bit stressed out and needed someone to listen to me. My friend Ron Ward was always available to yak on the phone after a hard day work. He encouraged me to join a gym so I could get some exercise and take yoga classes. I did, and that was really helpful in getting me through the last six months of this project.

And so a project that began 40 years ago reaches its conclusion. Thank you for reading my book—I hope that you have enjoyed the experience.

Peace and blessings,   ~ John C. Sulak
                                                      San Francisco, 2009

Talking
my Walk
by Oberon

I've been lately thinking about my life's time
All the things I've done and how it's been,
And I can't help believin' in my own mind
I know I'm gonna hate to see it end.
~ "Poems, Prayers & Promises" by John Denver

S A YOUNG LAD GROWING UP IN "PLEASANT-ville," I enjoyed reading biographies of people who inspired me in various ways. With such sterling examples, I've tried to live a life that would be interesting enough so that others would like to read about it someday—or even watch the movie or mini-series version.

Early on I considered that my life was already getting so weird that any biography of me would have to be presented as science-fiction or fantasy! Indeed, much of my life has in fact been inspired and influenced by sci-fi and fantasy novels.

One aspect of my life which people often mention is my propensity for "thinking outside the box." However, I think this is a bit of a misapprehension. For me, it's always been more: "Box? There's a box?" Indeed, through sci-fi, fantasy, and mythology I have always lived amidst such a diversity of perspectives, opinions, theories, cultures and customs that any notion of the "One True Right and Only Way" which things are "supposed to be" has always eluded me. I have no idea what "normal" is; I've just gone along living my life as I've seen fit to do, blithely oblivious to the opinions of others.

And yet, people would often tell me, "You really should write your autobiography! I want to read it!" A few misguided folks have even said they wanted to be just like me—and I have had to try and dissuade them, telling them that my life has been shaped by too many mistakes that I wouldn't wish on anyone. And that rather than try to become me (or anyone else), they should devote their efforts toward discovering and becoming who *they* are. Just as I have.

In 1973 I found and subsequently married my soulmate, Morning Glory, and my story became inextricably merged with hers. And then there are all our family, friends, lovers, waterkin and co-conspirators along the way, who would also need to be included for the story to make any sense. As the years accumulated (nearly 67 of them now…), the prospect of attempting to write my own autobiography began to seem an impossible task!

Then, a couple of years ago, our friend John Sulak approached me with a proposal for writing what he called "a narrative biography." This would consist entirely of interviews—not only with me and Morning Glory, but also with many of the aforementioned "significant others" in our lives.

Remarkably enough, pretty much everyone—from parents and siblings to lovers over the decades—was willing to talk to John. And of course, Morning Glory and I also spent countless hours responding to his insightful questions. John has taken these many, many hours of interviews and edited them into sensible commentaries, and then integrated them all into this flowing narrative—as if we are all sitting around the campfire, passing a bowl and sharing our lives.

People often speak of the importance of "walking your talk," which I certainly agree is a good idea! But I've learned that it may often be best not to try and do so much talking before you've done the actual walking, and so I've tended to just go on ahead and do the thing, and then analyze it afterwards. After all, as the saying goes, "if you want to hear the laughter of the gods, tell 'em your plans!" So this isn't going to be a book elucidating my philosophies and principles for how to make this a better world. Rather, this is the story of the journey already taken thus far. Where it goes from here we'll just have to see!

~ Oberon Zell-Ravenheart
RavenHaven, Beltane 2009

Addendum 2021:

After a decade of lengthy interviews, transcriptions and editing by the redoubtable John Sulak, the First Edition of this book was published by Llewellyn in early 2014, just a few months before Morning Glory ("The Witch") died of cancer (multiple myeloma). Fortunately, she was able to read it, and share it with her friends, family, doctors and nurses. She loved it, as did everyone else.

However, as Llewellyn's Senior Acquisitions Editor, Elysia Gallo, stated in her "Afterword," the first draft was 370,000 words long, which would have come to 1,155 pages—plus six Appendices! Elysia said:

> "Here at Llewellyn it was agreed that we needed to have John and Oberon trim the book to 150,000 words or less; otherwise it would have become a prohibitively expensive, gargantuan doorstop that readers could neither afford nor lift. I advised Oberon to save that manuscript for his children and grandchildren because it truly is a treasure trove, but that we needed to seriously narrow our focus."

John labored heroically to trim the massive manuscript down to an acceptable size, writing a considerable number of personal narratives to bridge the gaps of deletions and relate the saga to what was going on at the time on the outer world. This was completed in early 2013, though my own account concludes in June of 2009.

Since Morning Glory made Her journey to the Summerlands, I envisioned adding an epilog for subsequent printings to fill in those last few years of Her life and Her remarkable death and green burial on our sacred land of Annwfn. I even considered publishing the original 33 long chapters as a blog series, but never got around to it.

Then, in the summer of 2021, Llewellyn decided to discontinue publishing the book, and turned over all rights to John and me. At that time, I was writing for another publisher—Black Moon/Left Hand Press—and they immediately offered to pick up the ball by publishing the full original text—including John's excellent narratives—as a two-volume Special Expanded Edition.

This time it fell to me to edit the vast amount of original material into a coherent story. Now you can all read our full, uncensored, unexpurgated behind-the-scenes memoirs of our crazy lives amid the emergence of the modern Pagan movement.

Since all too many of those interviewed here have also—like Morning Glory—since made their own passage to the realms beyond, their words here are all the more precious. And with the discorporation of all my own elders and most contemporaries from "those thrilling days of yesteryear," I have become pretty much the last man standing: "…and only I survived to tell the tale."

"In the end, it said that the original manuscript for this book was double what it came out to be. I honestly would have paid to read it in its entirety."   ~ Cynthia A. Rivers

"I've been hearing about "Oberon's memoirs" for years now and it's been well worth the wait, though I probably would have loved to read the 1,100 page version."

~ Jason Mankey

~ Oberon Zell
The Longhouse
Redmond, WA
Sept. 3, 2021

Living Out Loud

By Morning Glory

"Someday we'll look back on all this,
laugh nervously, and quickly change the subject."
~ Ashley Brilliant

THIS BOOK WAS IN THE WORKS FOR SOME time, but when I was diagnosed with cancer (multiple myeloma), it put an urgency to telling my life story and personal history that was never quite there before. Also, the birth of my Granddaughter added more importance to this effort to leave a written record that will help her make sense out of her wacky Grandma's life.

A lot of people have asked me while I was writing this book whether or not I was worried about exposing all these stories in my life, especially the ones that are outrageous or that show so many of the mistakes that I have made in my past. Believe me, it's something I certainly have considered. But in the long run, I made the decision to tell the story of my life in a straightforward manner and let people make up their own minds about me. I have never been of the same opinion about writing that H.W. Longfellow ventured when he said: "Write not a word that your daughter should not read." Not that my daughter won't be reading this—of course she will, and she will probably give me a lot of hell about it too; that has always been a big part of our relationship.

People have always said to me: "Don't you care what people think of you?" Of course I care, I care passionately. But what matters more to me than people's good opinions is their genuine informed opinions and their understanding, for those are a far rarer commodity than just good opinions alone any day.

I guess it's just that I have spent most of my life with people shushing me. OK, I know that I talk too much and often about things that might be better left unsaid. I know my big mouth has gotten me into loads of trouble ever since I was a kid. Both my mom and my girlfriends would beg me not to talk back to my dad so I wouldn't get a beating; but on some weird level I always felt like I loved him enough that I owed it to him to be real with him and not just put on an act to stay out of trouble. It might have earned me some bruises, but it also earned me a kind of respect from him in our relationship. My loud mouth has annoyed a lot of people, but it has also made me a lot of friends as well, because I am of the opinion that more problems seem to arise when people try to keep things secret.

Most of the plots in everything from Shakespeare to soap opera revolve around mistaken impressions that are deliberately or inadvertently allowed to persist between people who should be communicating better. Even in Science Fiction some real tragedies are played out between lovers who are telepathic, for heaven sakes! This is not to say that I can't keep a secret; there are things I will go to my grave without ever telling. But I have to have very compelling reasons for that kind of silence, and usually it is because it has been asked of me by someone else.

Because on the whole, I think I would rather just tell the truth and let the chips fall where they may. Besides, there are already plenty of dreadful rumors about me floating around in the world which I could never track down and lay to rest. People who are bent on casual character assassination are far too numerous to ever be squelched or even slowed down by the truth. "A lie can run around the world before the truth can get its boots on." Nevertheless, this is my chance to set the record straight on a number of issues for better or for worse and I wouldn't miss it for a gold clock.

I have lived my life pretty much in public. I have given more interviews to media than I could possibly remember. Why have I done this sort of thing? Do I crave attention that badly? Not really. Am I just a media slut? Well, maybe. Do I think I am so cool that I just have to see my face on camera? Hardly. The reason that so much of my life is an open book about subjects that are controversial or even downright forbidden in some places, is that I genuinely feel that I have something to contribute—especially in the area of changing public opinion in important areas. These areas include freedom of speech, freedom of religion (most especially unpopular religions like Witchcraft and Paganism), and freedom of choice around sexuality—to choose who and how many my lovers will be and to let them all be known to each other so that there are no shady secrets that can bring a love life crashing down around my ears. Not that

that doesn't still happen occasionally anyway, but where sex is concerned, honesty is really the best policy and in this day and age it can save your life. Besides, it makes you a lot harder to blackmail!

I have deliberately built my life in such a way that I can afford to be public about it. I own my own business so I don't have to worry that my boss will fire me if he finds out my religion or personal habits. I live in Northern California so I don't have to fear that my neighbors will come after me with torches and pitchforks. These are choices I have made that limit my successes in some ways, but open them up in others. And so it has come about that I'm in a position to speak for a lot of people who don't have the freedom to speak for themselves; who don't live where I do or work how I work, but who are just as passionately devoted to a Pagan lifestyle and/or juicy polyamorous sexuality. I've been willing to be the front person and take the heat for others who can't do that. I grew up being the unpopular kid who was willing to speak up for myself and for other unpopular kids like me. And the weirdest thing of all was that somehow, in the end, I won a sort of popularity out of that strategy.

I have given a lot of thought about whether or not I will succeed in leaving any "footprints in the sands of time." I have always seen myself first and foremost as a living flame on the wind—where will she go and what will she leave behind? Everyone has their issues about mortality and nothing brings them to the surface faster than a cancer diagnosis.

I have had lots of amazing adventures (chasing mermaids) and done things that no one else has managed to do for a very long time (raising unicorns); I have even coined a word *(polyamory)* for a lifestyle that lacked a satisfactory name for itself, and seen it adopted—not only by the movement but also by the *Oxford English Dictionary*. I, along with so many of my other brothers and sisters, have left legacies in the form of political and religious activism that will make it harder to persecute my people in the future and will lead to the hope of a living planet for our great-grandchildren to live on. I have written lots of articles and even a book or two, and I am determined that there will be more in the future. I have also led with my heart, taking risks and making huge and tragic mistakes, which people can point to as lessons about what not to do. After all, how can you grow if you don't admit your mistakes?

How else could anybody leave their mark on an ever-changing world? At this point I can only point to the words of Sappho, a far greater writer than I will ever be:

"Although they are only breath, words which I command are immortal. Gifts that the golden Muses gave me were no delusion: dead, I will not be forgotten, someone in some future time will think of us..."   ~ Sappho, Lesbos, 630-570 BCE

~ Morning Glory Zell-Ravenheart
RavenHaven, July 20, 2009

PART ONE:

A Changeling Child

CHAPTER 1:
A Changeling Child
(1942-1951)

~ "The Stolen Child," by William Butler Yeats, 1886

ARRATOR: IN 1942 PAGANS WERE A THING of the past. Gods and goddesses were what people had believed in centuries earlier; wizards, witches and unicorns were found in the fiction section of the library, magic was just a stage trick, and fairies lived only in fairy tales.

And in 1942 many Americans were as just as indifferent to the future as they were to ancient history and mythology. Science fiction authors were writing about space travel, atomic power, computers and other upcoming wonders but they weren't being taken seriously. That kind of stuff was considered to be, in the real world, centuries away or impossible.

The United States had just endured the Great Depression and was entering World War II. All that really mattered to most people was the present, and it was bleak. It was in that world that Charles and Vera Zell met and began a family together. Their first son was born on November 30, 1942, and they named him Timothy. He would grow up to be a Pagan and a Wizard, raise unicorns, marry a Witch, and change his name to Oberon Zell-Ravenheart.

OZ's FATHER, CHARLES ZELL: My Dad, Charles Francis Zell, was of German descent, but his forefathers also had some Swiss blood. My great-great grandfather, John Zell, migrated from

Germany around 1800 to settle in Churchtown, Pennsylvania. Zell is a German-Swiss name, like William Tell. There is a town in the Rhine Valley in Germany named Zell. In Switzerland, there is a Zell Lake and, oddly enough, *zell* is sometimes attached to a word to denote small or little. The Zells remained in Pennsylvania right up to my time. My Dad was born in 1886 and had no brothers or sisters.

My mother's maiden name was Mary Elizabeth Bitner, one of nine children—five boys and four girls. Her parents were born in Germany and came to the United States around 1875. Mother was next to the youngest child and was born on January 10, 1888. On my mother's side, I had lots of aunts, uncles, and cousins but seldom saw them except at funerals. And all of my grandparents had died before I was born.

I was born at home on Labor Day, Sept. 7, 1914. Since it was customary in that era to name the firstborn son after his father, I was named Charles Francis Jr. Prior to my arrival, mother had given birth to three girls, Dorothy in 1908, Irene in 1910, and Myrtle in 1912. (Dorothy died in 1912, and I was never told the cause.)

We were poor. I had to put cardboard in my shoes in the winter when there were holes in them. My father was a barber, and when the depression hit he was out of work for seven years. I determined when I was quite young that I didn't want to be poor the rest of my life. I wanted to go to college. I graduated from high school with honors. I was very active in Boy Scouts, became an Eagle Scout, and met a chap who helped me get into Lehigh University. I got a scholarship, and I got a job waiting on tables in a fraternity house for my meals. I played football, basketball and tennis, all varsity.

I graduated from college in June of 1938 and took a job as a salesman with Rust Craft Greeting Cards. On July 28 my father died in my arms of lung cancer. In December, Rust Craft sent me to St. Louis, where in June of 1940 I met my first wife, Vera. We were married that October 15. When the war broke out, I enlisted in the Marine Corps. That was in September of 1942. My wife was pregnant. Tim was born on November 30. When I got the news of his birth, I was so excited that on the obstacle course that day, for the first time I scaled the wall!

OZ: My mother's family was mostly Irish, with a bit of French, English, Scotch and German thrown in. Her mother was a McClarin and her father was a Bedell, and their families had been here since before the American Revolution. In the musical "Brigadoon," which is about a mythical Scottish village that only appears once every hundred years, there is a clan named McClarin. So I can claim a semi-mythical ancestry!

According to family records, my mother's great-great grandmother, Eulalie DeGascon, came over to America from Marseilles, France, with her family on a small ship in the late 1700s. Her brother Pierre later went back for their papers and personal belongings, but the ship sank and he was lost at sea, along with all the family documentation. Eulalie married Dr. Millington from England, and they settled in St. Charles, Missouri. Their son Jerome became one of the early riverboat captains on the Mississippi, with his own boat.

In 1830, their daughter Emilie married Robert McClarin, son of William and Isabelle McClarin of Plumbridge, Tyrone County, Ireland. Robert had run away from home at 14 (allegedly to escape prosecution for deer poaching) to come to America with his cousins, Robert and Hugh Campbell, who became famous fur trappers and traders. (The Campbell house at 1508 Locust St. in St Charles was eventually bought by the Historical Society as a museum, with furniture and other belongings kept the same as when the Campbells lived there.)

The Millingtons were related to the English Stewarts, and the DeGascons were members of the French nobility. When Robert and Emilie were married, the Millingtons gave them a wedding present of $40,000 and 40 slaves. They bought a very large estate, but the house later burned to the ground. They freed their slaves and bought another home, in which Emilie died at the age of 35, after giving birth to eight children. In 1889, Emilie's and Robert's daughter Isabelle (better known as Belle) married Albert C. Glenn.

My mother's great-great grandfather, James Glenn, came from the north of Ireland in about 1770 as a young man, and settled on a farm in Venago County, Pennsylvania, north of Pittsburg. In 1776, he joined the Revolutionary Army and went to war for the United States, fighting alongside George Washington. In 1812, James bought a 320-acre farm in St Clair Township, PA, and married Janet Buchanan, who was aunt to James Buchanan, our 15th President. Their first son, William, inherited half the farm, and after he died, it was passed on to his son James. James was elected Colonel of the Militia about 1840, and afterwards was always known as Colonel J.B. Glenn. His son, William Jr, enlisted in the Union Army in 1861, and fought in the Civil War, becoming Colonel of the regiment. In 1889, William's brother Albert C. Glenn married Belle McClarin, who bore them five children. One of these, Rebecca (my grandmother, called Reba), married Dr. Charles Thomson Bedell.

The Bedell side of my ancestry seems to comprise a long line of dentists, beginning with John Enzelie Bedell, born Jan. 17, 1838, who first took up the profession. He was one of nine children. The Bedells came to St Louis from Mt Vernon, Ohio, in 1889, but the family history goes back to around 1750 in New York, and takes in a mixture of French, Irish, Scotts and German. Along with his six brothers, John joined the Union Army to fight in the Civil War. But with his beautiful handwriting, he was not sent to the field, but rather assigned clerical work. His son, Charles Thomson Bedell, born in 1875, was my grandfather. My given middle name, Thomson, is a tribute to him. He graduated from Washington University in 1898 and joined his father and brother, Orion Willis, in dental practice. Orion's son Evert Willis (born 1895), and his grandson Robert Evert (born 1921), also continued the family tradition of dentistry.

Albert Glenn died on Feb. 10, 1938, at the age of 88. My great-grandmother Belle died on Nov. 14, 1946, at the age of 84. I was four at the time, but I never knew her.

OZ's MOTHER, VERA ZELL: My father, also named Charles, was a dentist. And he was a naturalist. He knew the names of birds, insects, and flowers and that sort of thing. He would take yearly ten-day fishing trips that Tim would have enjoyed. He had a flower garden and a fruit tree orchard in the back, and he grew asparagus and tomatoes. He died in our home of coronary thrombosis on November 17, 1941, a week after Veteran's Day. He was 66. Tim was born a year later, on November 30, 1942. He was the most beautiful baby in the nursery. Even the nurses said so. It wasn't just my opinion.

Tim was born two years after Charlie and I were married, and two weeks after his father left for Officer's Candidate School. Charlie finally found a house for us in Dumfries, about six miles from the Marine base. When Tim was six weeks old, my mother and I drove out to Virginia with him. It was the middle of winter—ice, snow, and cold. Our home was an old farmhouse with a pot-bellied stove in the middle of the living room for the only heat. Charlie had to stay at the base and only got to visit us a few times. After OSC he went on to Reserve Officers' School. So we were in that house until Tim was about five months old.

With Charlie in ROS, I flew back to Kirkwood with Tim. Later, when it was time for him to report for duty, Charlie drove the car to San Diego, where he soon found a place for us. I took Tim out there by train. It was a hard trip because we had to change trains twice and the trains were full of service people. I had to make formula in the train kitchen where soot kept falling down from the ceiling. But Tim was a very good baby and adjusted to the inconveniences very well.

The house in San Diego was a little cottage in a tourist court called Paradise Court where all the tenants were service people. Tim was the only baby and everybody thought he was soooo cute. We had a great time there for several months until Charlie's unit was shipped out to the South Pacific. We were just a block from the beach so I could wheel Tim down in his buggy every day for a nap and a little suntan. Shortly before Charlie shipped out, my mother came out on the train (with a load of servicemen) to be with us all for awhile, and to help us on our train trip back to St Louis. (We sold the car in San Diego because gas was rationed and Charlie didn't think we should make that drive.) This was the first week in October, 1943, when we left.

CHARLES ZELL: I was sent to Officers' Candidate School in Quantico, Virginia, and became a second lieutenant. Tim's mother and grandmother drove out and stayed with me for six weeks in Dumfries. Then I went to Camp Elliot in San Diego to teach machine guns for six months. Tim and his mother went with me. We were together 'til he was nine months old, then they went back to the Midwest. I didn't see him again 'til November, 1945.

I went overseas with my battalion. I was sent to Guadalcanal in the South Pacific to join the Third Marine Division regimental weapons company as a machine gun officer. I was in on the invasion of Guam, and survived that. I was in on the invasion of Iwo Jima where they raised the flag. I survived without being wounded, but most of my buddies were either wounded or killed. I was with my

very best buddy when he got hit by a mortar shell and lost his arm.
I got him down to the beach and evacuated him.

NARRATOR: While Charles Zell was in the South Pacific fighting
the war his wife moved back into a big, old Victorian house with her
mother and sister in Kirkwood, Missouri—a suburb of St. Louis. At
that point in American history it was not uncommon for extended
families to live together. Their living situations were comparable to
the way the Addams Family lives in the TV show and movies, with
the grandma, uncle, cousins and assorted oddballs who just happened to drop by all under the same roof. (This was how Tim Zell
spent his first few years; and since growing up and leaving his family that is how he has lived most of his adult life.)

Households of this kind were often immigrants. They had come
from countries where deep-rooted traditions, customs and folktales
had been handed down from generation to generation. But things
like that were being lost, or left behind, as people become assimilated into the new world. Tim Zell's family traditions (known as
"fam-trads" in the Pagan world) were passed on even more directly,
since he considers himself to be the reincarnation of his mother's
father.

OZ: My mother's father had died of a heart attack the year before,
and his room was made into my nursery. My earliest memory is of
awakening in my familiar room, and there was my family gathered
around me. I looked up at them, and they were all looking at me kind
of funny. I tried to say something, but I couldn't articulate what I
was trying to say, and I got more and more upset. Finally I raised
my hands in front of my face, and they were little, tiny baby hands.

I freaked out and started screaming. I had awakened in the room
that I had died in. I went straight from one life into the next one. It
was a direct transmigration. Obviously there was a time gap of a full
year, but I have no memory of any of that. It was like I had gone to
sleep the night before, and I awakened the next morning with the
same people around me.

As I became more verbal as a child, they would often tell me
"that's just the kind of thing your grandfather would say!" I always
felt like, from the time that I was able to talk, that I was somehow
older, wiser and more mature than they were. I never quite could get

it that I was the child and they were they adults. It always felt the other way around.

For my first three years the only people in my universe were my grandmother, my mother, and my aunt Betsy (who never married). So my whole life revolved around the Maiden, the Mother, and the Crone—the Triple Goddess of Celtic lore.

My mother's folks were Presbyterian, but I don't recall ever being taken to church in those early years. But I was baptized. I remember that distinctly because I didn't want it to happen. I screamed and fought it, but they did it anyway. It was very traumatic.

My early years were haunted by recurrent nightmares of dying. I remembered time and time again in my dreams the sensation of dying. It was like falling down a well. The world got smaller and smaller and disappeared. Sometimes I would even get that feeling when I was awake, and I'd have to kind of blink and shake myself.

I was very telepathic. A lot of the time I heard their thoughts as clearly as words. And I just took that for granted as perfectly natural. They didn't have to speak directly in order for me to understand them. I did not distinguish between spoken words and articulated thoughts.

When I was around two or three there were some women over visiting. I was upstairs in my room, and I remember hearing this commotion of voices. I came down the stairs, and I looked at all these people that I didn't know. There was this noise that hurt my ears. I put my hands over my ears but it wouldn't go away, because I was hearing it inside my head as well. And I yelled out, "Be quiet!"

All these faces turned and looked at me. They stopped talking, but the babble got louder. I looked at them and for the first time understood that their mouths weren't moving, and therefore they weren't speaking, and yet I was hearing them.

I ran back upstairs, hid under the covers, and tried to shut out the commotion that was inside of my head. And that was the last of that. I learned the difference between a thought that was in my head and a thought that was coming into my ear.

MOTHER: He talked very early. He was walking when he was seven months old. He didn't like to get down and crawl. We just thought he was absolutely the bee's knees. He was very well-behaved and active. And not hard to cope with at all.

OZ: My grandmother was very intellectual, so reading was valued highly in our family. I was probably about three when I started being able to read for myself. My mother had been reading me these books, and she would trace her finger along as she was doing it and I would learn it. At first I was just kind of recognizing words but before long I could read them myself.

NARRATOR: Timothy Zell's religious education after that point came not from his elders, or from other people he knew who were in a position of authority, but from books and direct observation of nature.

OZ: When I was very small my mother got me the *ChildCraft* books, which were put out for kids by the *Worldbook Encyclopedia*. There was a whole series of them on different themes. My favorite was the one on world mythology. The very first things I read were Roman versions of the Greek myths from Ovid, before *Dick and Jane* or anything else. I'll never forget reading about "Pluto and Proserpine" as children. These stories introduced me to lots of important concepts, one of them being that there were multiple deities, gods and goddesses of all kinds. So I didn't start off with the assumption that there was only one God; I started off with the assumption that there were many deities worshipped among many people. Later on, when I learned about Christianity, it was not like, "this is the only God." It was just one more story, about one more God.

FATHER: After three years on active duty, mostly in the South Pacific, I returned home and back to civilian life. It was late November, 1945, when I was reunited with Vera and Tim, our three-year-old son who had been nine months old when I went overseas. After the war I resumed my pre-war job as a salesman for Rust Craft. I worked my way up and became the national sales manager.

Tim was already talking very well when he was only three years old. By the time he was five he was drawing like somebody who was 15 or 20 years old. He drew pictures of deer and animals that looked like they had been done by professionals. He carried on conversations at five that would do credit to a child who was ten or twelve.

OZ: My father came home from the war in 1945 and became a traveling salesman with Rust Craft Greeting Cards. After four months, he was transferred to Pennsylvania. We moved into a not-quite-finished home on 110 Hill St., Clark's Green, Pennsylvania. It had a big backyard with a swing set, slide, wading pool, and a little terrace where we could slide down on a sled. We lived there for five years, and that was where I started school, taking the bus to kindergarten.

Clark's Green is where I really came into my identity. We had this little house and I lived upstairs, where I had my own room and my own desk. My dad and I were very close during that time—he used to tell me wonderful bedtime stories. He'd say, "What do you want to hear about tonight?"

And I'd reply, "How did the giraffe get such a long neck?" And he'd just make up a marvelous story along the lines of Kipling's "Just-So" tales.

We even had a young governess I loved named Catherine, whose family lived on a farm. Sometimes I got to visit there—I remember riding a cow and fishing for bluegills in their pond.

And there were woods and fields all around us that I used to spend much of my time exploring. I would go hang out with animals and climb trees. I would merge so totally with the place that the animals came to accept me. I would just sit at the base of a tree for hours and hours 'til the deer would come and graze right next to me without being alarmed. I would climb up into the branches of a tree during the bird nesting season and just sit and watch them lay their eggs and raise their babies. And they wouldn't be disturbed by me. Those years were very happy times.

VERA ZELL: Tim could spend hours watching a little bug crawling up a wall. Literally. He would go out under the porch and follow the bugs or ants.

FATHER: One episode I vividly remember occurred when Tim was six or seven years old and had visited a neighbor who had a few pigs in a pen. It was early spring and the pigpen was a gooey mess.

Somehow, Tim got in the pen, slipped and fell in the slush and when he came home, you could smell him before you saw him. We had him completely undress outside the house, then rush to the bathroom to shower. The clothes were destroyed!

OZ: Deep in the woods beyond Clark's Green, there was a monastery that I discovered while I was out exploring. I didn't know anything about monks, so I didn't realize what they were, but I'd sneak to the edge of the woods and watch them. There were these strange buildings, like a castle, and guys wearing medieval robes. It was all very arcane and mysterious. I discovered their trash dump in a canyon behind the place, and I would look at the junk and try to make sense of it. It all seemed magickal—like they were an order of Wizards or something. Sometimes I would arrange objects in patterns, or fill bottles with different fluids and place them around. When I returned, I'd check to see if they had been noticed and rearranged, as a way of communicating, but they never were.

I never made my presence known to the monks. I was afraid that it was like spying on the Faeries, and I didn't know what they'd do to me if they caught me. It was my little secret world that I never told anybody about, and nobody ever mentioned the place to me. I went back to Clark's Green 50 years later to check it out, and it's still there! It's St Gabriel's Monastery, at 631 Griffin Pond Rd. But to me, it was this strange, mysterious, mythic world. It did not exist in the suburban reality that was around me, but it was real. This was something really different. It was a part of my discovering other realities that were not part of the mundane reality. And this validated my sense that there might be even more magical realities.

My lifelong interest in magick and Wizardry had been ignited when I first read stories of magick as a child—such as in fairy tales and the Greek myths. In particular, I was deeply imprinted by the early animated Disney movies featuring magickal characters and happenings—a later favorite being the tale of Merlin and young Arthur in "The Sword in the Stone" (1963). Throughout my life, I've tried to never miss a movie with magickal elements. Presumably most kids identify with the young heroes in such stories, but I've always identified with the Wizards!

"Fantasia" in particular (which had come out in 1940—two years before I was born) had a huge impact on me. Of course, I loved the whole "Rite of Spring" evolution sequence, with the dinosaurs. But it was the "Pastorale" that really captured my soul. The final scene, when Nyx draws a veil of night like a blanket across the Arcadian sky, and we see a crescent moon which, as we zoom in, resolves into Diana drawing her bow and releasing a meteoric arrow…well, that arrow plunged straight into my heart, where it has lodged ever since! (Many years later, I did a poster based on that image; and later, a statue and a jewelry pendant—all of which have been very popular.)

I didn't have any social sense at all as a kid. Not with people, anyway. I got along great with animals, but I never really formed close friendships with other boys. I just didn't understand them—or trust them. And this was reciprocal; I was like a "pink monkey." One time, in second grade, the kids were all coming in from recess, and I was holding the door open for them. And this kid whipped out a pocket knife and slashed the back of my thumb. He came very close to cutting it off. I have no idea what provoked that. Things like that have always shocked me. I have never been able to comprehend why anyone would do such a thing. And it was a serious injury that never quite healed right; I still have a big scar there, and my thumb has been double-jointed ever since.

The lesson I got was that there were bizarrely cruel people in the world that I would somehow have to deal with.

I always liked hanging out with girls more than boys. They were nicer and more interesting, and they didn't want to pick fights with me. I understood them better—and I still do. In second or third grade I had two girlfriends, which was the beginning of my lifelong polyamory. They were both named Carol. One of them (Carol Jones) lived at the bottom of the street, the other (Carol Arcure) lived at the top, and I lived in the middle. I kept trying to get them to be friends so that we could all three be together and do things. But they didn't want to do that. It was a constant power struggle. I didn't want to have just one girlfriend. I wanted both of them.

My brother Barry was born almost on my fourth birthday, Nov. 25, 1946. He and I had kind of an odd relationship. I had no idea how to be a big brother. I was really awful to my little brother, but he absolutely worshiped me and followed me around all the time.

Once, when I was being pummeled by a bully, Barry grabbed a 2x4 and knocked the kid unconscious. Gave him a concussion!

My sister Shirley was born about 2½ years after Barry, on March 27, 1948.

FATHER: He was the oldest of the three children, and the other two looked up to him like he was some kind of god. Because he had them mesmerized with his knowledge and his ability to express himself.

NARRATOR: The three Zell siblings were "baby boomers," and they all grew up in a time of prosperity and economic growth. Women who had worked in manufacturing jobs during the war were replaced by men and sent home to raise children, and the men made lots of money and spent it on new consumer products (televisions, refrigerators, washers and driers, etc.) for their new homes that were being built in the new "Levittown" suburbs. Extended families were being split up as every couple had to have a house of their own, and a garage with two new cars in it. Older relatives had to live alone and take care of themselves.

It was also a time of conservative politics and conformity. America's allies in WW II quickly became its new enemies as politicians began talking about the threat of communism. Any American who had left-wing or liberal political views was perceived as a possible danger to national security, and freedom of speech and thought were actively discouraged.

While the Zell children were still in grade school US Senator Joseph McCarthy began what became known as a political "witch-hunt" against alleged Communists and sympathizers that would ruin many careers and lives. In 1953 playwright Arthur Miller wrote *The Crucible*, a dramatization of the Salem Witch trials that was actually an allegory for "McCarthyism," the House Committee on Un-American Activities, and the resulting blacklisting by the government. Citizens were encouraged to act and think alike, dress alike, and move to identical cookie-cutter homes in the suburbs.

OZ: I had my tonsils and adenoids taken out in 1946, when I was about 3½, and an appendectomy in 1956, at 13½. In those days the anesthetic they used was ether, which was horrible. Some people of which I was one—never entirely lose consciousness under ether but remain aware while immobilized in a paralyzed body. For me, this was the most awful nightmare imaginable—it felt just like dying (which I still remembered).

With the tonsillectomy, the only thing that got me through the experience was the thought of the ice cream the doctors had promised I could have all I wanted of when it was over. So as soon as I was able to speak in the recovery room, I croaked: "Ice cream!" They brought me a big bowl of chocolate ice cream (my favorite). But when I swallowed the first bite, it felt like molten lava was flowing down my ravaged throat (they'd scraped it raw to get out all the infection).

From that time on, the smell and taste of chocolate was forever associated with that trauma. And so I have never liked chocolate to this present day.

Somewhere around third grade or so I saw a boys' movie called *My Dog Shep*. After that I just had to have a dog. My dad let my brother and I both pick puppies from the same litter on Catherine's farm. Of course, I named mine Shep. He was a shepherd and looked just like the dog in the movie. We became utterly inseparable. He'd walk me to school every day, and when I got out, he'd be waiting for me to walk me home. We'd explore the woods and fields together, and he'd sleep at the foot of my bed. And since the two dogs were brothers, they got to hang out together when I was at school.

And then one day my brother's dog got hit by a car. He managed to crawl back to our front porch and died there. Shep was inconsolable. He cried and howled, and my mother just couldn't stand it. So she wouldn't let him come into the house. After that he had to sleep out in the garage.

But Shep would still walk me to school. And then one day when I got out of school he wasn't there. When I got home, I asked my mom, "Where's Shep?"

And she said, "We had to have him put to sleep, because he made too much noise." And I knew this didn't mean she had tucked him into bed and kissed him goodnight after a glass of warm milk and a nice bedtime story. I may have been a kid, but I wasn't a complete idiot. My mother had my best friend killed because he grieved over the death of his brother! And then she tried to dismiss my anguish with a euphemism.

MOTHER: The dog kept following him to school, and I got calls from the school complaining that it was causing traffic problems. It was barking at cars and chasing them. I couldn't handle it. His father was out of town a good deal of the time. He traveled regularly. That was his business. If he had been at home more maybe we could have built a higher fence so the dog couldn't have gotten out, or maybe he could have trained it. I took the dog to an animal shelter. Hopefully he was adopted. I don't know what happened after that. I hated to do it. He was a beautiful dog.

OZ: I learned a profound lesson then: grief is a capital offense! So I couldn't grieve for Shep, because I was afraid that I might be "put to sleep" too! Of course, as an adult now, I know that would never have happened (though I do read of such cases in the papers…). However, as a child, I had no context for such an unimaginable thing, and it shattered my innocent faith in my parents. And I have never been able to grieve since, to this day. Even when there are times I really ought to, I just can't.

That traumatic experience as a child really alienated me from my mother in particular. I felt it as a deep betrayal, and that I could no longer trust her. I retreated from both my parents and shut down any real communication. I'm sure this inability to trust anyone was also a factor in my never making any close friends until college—or ever getting another dog.

But my suppressed anger at my mother over Shep manifested in many confrontations from then on. I learned a word from her that I came to detest so much that I have never used it since in any context other than in recounting this story. That word was "impudent." I got to asking annoying "why" questions about pretty much everything—sometimes out of simple curiosity, but also, I'm sure, as a subtle form of defiance. My mother would randomly (it seemed to me) react by slapping me across the face, saying "Don't be impudent!" I hated this, and over time I developed really fast reflexes to block her blows with my forearm. Finally, when I was 16, I slapped her back, then locked myself in my room crying. She never struck me again, and we never spoke of it afterwards. And I vowed that I would never, ever, hit a child of mine, nor use that hated word. And so it has been.

CHAPTER 2:
A Boy Comes Out
to Wonder
(1951-1956)

Yesterday a child came out to wonder
Caught a dragonfly inside a jar
Fearful when the sky was full of thunder
And tearful at the falling of a star
~ "The Circle Game" by Joni Mitchell

Z: IN THE SPRING OF 1951, WHEN I WAS 8, MY father got transferred to the Midwest. They had a nice big home built on a large double lot on Riverside Drive in Crystal Lake, Illinois—a bedroom suburb west of Chicago. We moved into the new house in July of 1952, and I lived there from 4th grade through high school. Our house was only a couple of blocks from the lake, and each of us three kids had our own room. And this place was exactly like the neighborhoods where families that were on TV lived, like "Ozzie & Harriet," "Leave it to Beaver," and "Father Knows Best." I was in high school during the exact same era and setting that all those 1950s high school movies were set in.

My parents joined the Congregational Church, which is a very easy-going white-bread-Protestant kind of thing. It seemed mostly to consist of social clubs, bake sales, potluck dinners, youth groups, retreats, and things like that. Although my folks were evidently quite active in the church, I don't recall them talking about religion at home. However, I got really into Sunday school. I took confirmation, and I still remember the most important lesson: *Christian* means "Christ-like." So Christians are supposed to be like Christ. The question then becomes, what was Christ like? I took that in rather deeply, and I think I have actually lived in a very "Christ-like" way, even though I eventually came to identify myself as Pagan!

Unlike my parents, who joined the country club and had many friends and parties, I wasn't much of social person. But I was definitely into the religious thing. I read the Bible as mythology—like the legends of Jason, Heracles, Odysseus, King Arthur, and all the other stories I had been reading. I got involved in the pageants they would put on for Christmas and Easter. I usually got the part of narrator, and I loved it. This is where I discovered that I had an aptitude for theater—which I really got into in high school and college.

I had a perfect Sunday school attendance record every year 'til I moved away for my senior year of high school. But I never went to the actual church services unless I was in the pageant. I never heard a sermon or saw a funeral, baptism or other ritual. I never saw a marriage until years later when I started performing them.

I read the Bible from beginning to end. There were all these things in there that I thought were really bizarre, but fascinating. But since I'd started out reading Greek myths, it never occurred to me that this was any different, and was supposed to be the one true right and only way. And eventually I had this major epiphany—I realized that the entire Bible, from Genesis to Revelations—was the story of a specific people—the Jews. This was all about *them* as the "Chosen People" of their tribal God, Yahweh. Their origin mythos; their history; their commandments and rules; their kings, prophets, and prophecies; their messiah; their redemption.

But *I* wasn't Jewish! My ancestors were Celts and Teutons. The Bible was not the story of *my* people or history at all—and thus it simply was not relevant to me. Indeed, I realized that *my* people were the ones continuously mentioned throughout the Bible as "the other people" that the presumed Jewish readers were not supposed to emulate. This realization precipitated my liberation from Christianity, after many years of total immersion in it. And eventually, of course, in seeking my own ethnic religious heritage, I came to identify as a Pagan.

As a kid, I read everything I could get my hands on. I was a totally voracious reader. My folks subscribed to *National Geographic, Time, Life, Reader's Digest* I read 'em all, cover to cover. I'd even read the backs of cereal boxes! I also loved comic books, which I first discovered at the barber shop when I'd go in for my monthly haircut. They had stacks of EC comics around—horror and science fiction being the main categories—and I simply devoured them. The horror comics were always about "grisly justice," and invariably featured a final panel in which someone would exclaim: "Good Lord! *Choke*" (Today Morning Glory and I often refer to "Good Lord Choke, the god of grisly justice.") Later I subscribed to a few favorites, including Jesse Marsh's *Tarzan, Tom & Jerry, Little Audrey,* and Carl Barks' *Uncle Scrooge.* When I got old enough to go the library, I haunted it.

In school, every classroom had shelves along the window side. And on these shelves they kept the *World Book Encyclopedia.* This was the same encyclopedia that was associated with the *ChildCraft* books that I had read before. So I would always come in and take a seat right next to the bookshelf. And so, one volume at a time, I read the entire *World Book Encyclopedia.*

I would read the textbooks for the class first. And then I was done with that. I wouldn't have to worry about it. We'd be assigned a chapter or a page to read before the next day, but I didn't need to do that because I had already read the whole thing. So I could always answer the questions that came up about the textbooks and I didn't have to waste my time re-reading them anymore.

So I would take one volume of the *World Book* at a time and I would hide them behind my textbooks in the same way that other kids would hide comic books. When I got to volume "D" there two things in it—one was dragons and the other was dinosaurs. I'll never forget my reaction on opening up that two-page spread of Charles Knight's famous mural from the Field Museum of Natural History in Chicago of a triceratops facing off against a tyrannosaurus rex.

And there it was—Wow! Suddenly a major leap epiphany occurred to me: *Dragons were real!* Once upon a time real dragons ruled the Earth! That was really profound, and it's only gotten better over the years as we've discovered that dinosaurs were not reptiles at all, but warm-blooded and intelligent, and related to birds. It's made the dragon stories even more fascinating. The existence of dinosaurs validated the stories of dragons in a sense. This was the reality behind the myth. At least that's how I felt as a kid. Now, I think there is actually a lot more to the dragon legends. But nonetheless, this was a significant epiphany.

So, from that point on, I saw all myths through a double lens.

One was the story itself, and the other was the reality behind the story. I became like a "myth detective," trying to ferret out the truth behind the mystery. Eventually, this led me to recreate living Unicorns, dive for Mermaids…and write *A Wizard's Bestiary.*

But the most immediate effect of the discovery of dinosaurs was that I became a total dino kid. I obsessed over learning all their names, translations, dimensions, habits, when and where they lived, etc. I read all the books I could find on dinosaurs. And I started collecting dino figurines and models, which I would paint realistically and arrange in dioramas. At Christmastime, when we would set up a little village with a crèche around the Christmas tree, I would include my little dinos, with a brontosaurus peering into the manger at the baby Jesus. (I have continued adding to this collection to this very day, and I now have a *lot* of dino models!) When my parents had company over, they would often bring me out and ask me to tell 'em all about dinosaurs—especially the names, which the grownups seemed to find utterly unpronounceable.

From wanting to learn all about the different kinds of dinosaurs, I branched out into natural history with the intention of learning the names, habits, habitats, properties, and means of identification of all creatures, plants, minerals, etc. In 1949, Simon & Shuster published *Birds,* the first in an ongoing series of little hardback "Golden Nature Guides" edited by Herbert S. Zim. This was followed by *Flowers* (1950), *Stars* (1951), *Insects* (1951), *Trees* (1952), *Reptiles & Amphibians* (1953), *Mammals* (1955), *Seashores* (1955), *Fishes* (1956), and many others throughout the '50s and beyond (*A Golden Guide to Hallucinogenic Plants* was published in 1976).

I got every single one of these the moment it came out, and devoured them avidly—learning everything they had to offer about everything described therein. I still have these books, and today, Morning Glory and I have a continuing little contest to see who can be the first to identify any creature—living or extinct—that we see in Discovery Channel documentaries. We're both pretty good!

NARRATOR: Tim Zell discovered science fiction at an early age and looked to the genre for inspiration. While at that point it was still mostly considered to be low-brow entertainment, for Tim, the sci-fi library books he was reading weren't merely imaginary tales but visions of possibilities. (He also had a crush on the local librarian-lady, which helped to keep him going back for more.) He read the "juvenile" novels of author Robert Heinlein as they each came out, and Heinlein became a significant childhood mentor, teaching what it means to be human.

OZ: Cheap pulp paperbacks were offered through a special subscription program to get kids interested in reading. This was in the late '40s-early '50s. I encountered Robert Heinlein's juveniles just as he was writing them. I also discovered the sci-fi adventure tales of Edgar Rice Burroughs, H.G. Wells, and especially Jules Verne.

Verne's *20,000 Leagues Under the Sea* was my favorite book. And so I was very excited to learn that Disney was making a movie adaptation! This was released in 1954, when I was 11, and for the weeks leading up to it my anticipation could scarcely be contained. However, my mother—always trying to figure out ways to control me—told me that I could only go if I got home on time every day. And on one of those days, I got chased by bullies and came home late. So I never got to see the movie in its first theatrical release. And of course in those days there was barely even TV, let alone DVDs! I had to wait until it was re-released in theaters many years later.

I totally fell in love with the submarine Nautilus, and tried unsuccessfully all my life to find a model kit of it to build. I even got some plans, and began making my own model out of balsa wood—which I never finished (I now have a 31-inch commemorative replica). The attack of the giant squid also inspired a lifelong fascination with cephalopods, which was later reinforced by the life-sized *architeuthis* model still hanging from the ceiling at the Field Museum of Natural History in Chicago.

I've always loved science fiction—especially stories of space travel. I followed avidly the early sci-fi TV shows, such as *Tom Corbett: Space Cadet, Captain Video, Flash Gordon,* and *Space Patrol. My* mother taught me how to sew, and I made a space suit based on the ones in the movie *Destination Moon.* Then I built a spaceship control room set and got my father to film a sci-fi movie I wrote involving a journey to Venus. I created all the costumes, sets, props, backgrounds, miniatures, and special effects. I recruited some other kids and dressed them up as crewmen and monsters. It was a lot of fun! I was about 12 at the time, and I still have the film on VHS.

BROTHER BARRY: Tim has a photographic memory. I remember testing it once. While on a family vacation, I came across a display of posters. I showed him one with a lot of verse. A half hour later I asked him if he could recall the verse on that poster. Indeed, he was able to recall it—word-for-word!

I also remember having to write a paper in high school. I selected dinosaurs as my topic. My entire research consisted of a half-hour discussion with him! Tim saved me a trip to the library. I've always been awed by the number of topics with which he is extremely knowledgeable. The list includes world religions, world history, astronomy, geology, archaeology, anthropology, medicine, zoology, paleontology, psychology, mythology, and sociology! Add to that his genius IQ, his sculpting and painting artistry, his speaking expertise, and his writing ability, and you have quite a unique person.

OZ: It's interesting that my brother was so impressed by my memory and artistic skills. I've always been amazed at the truly remarkable gift that he and my father share. They are both math savants, and you can rattle off any string of numbers and ask them to add, subtract, multiply or divide them by any other set of numbers, and they can do it instantly, in their head, without any obvious process of calculation. And they are always completely accurate! This remarkable talent has served them both well in business—my father becoming a successful executive, and my brother an accountant. I could have really used that ability, but the genes passed me by. I've often felt that my other skills are merely in compensation.

FATHER: When he was in fourth or fifth grade he was doing very well. And he didn't have any homework. And I said, "Tim, when do you do your homework—in the study session?"

And he said, "No, I go to the library then."

And I said, "What do you do in the library?"

And he said, "Oh, I read medical books and stuff like that." If he read it or heard it, he remembered it. So he didn't have to cram.

OZ: In 1953-'55, when I was 10-12, I had to go back and forth from Crystal Lake to Kirkwood, Missouri, for months at a time. This was for extensive orthodontic work, as I had really bad buck teeth. I lived with my maternal grandmother, whom I called "Gogi," and my Aunt Betsy, both of whom I loved dearly.

In Kirkwood, I befriended an old lady who lived down the street. She had a talking parrot—and the first TV I'd ever seen, with a small round screen. I'd go there every day after school to watch *Tom Corbett: Space Cadet,* based on Heinlein's 1948 juvenile, *Space Cadet.* The very popular show (an early precursor of *Star Trek*) ran from 1950-1956, and was a pop culture phenomenon, with comics, toys, trading cards, lunch boxes and other collectibles; but I never got to see all the episodes.

One summer in Kirkwood I had a pet rabbit; another time a kitten—but I always had to leave them behind when I went back to Crystal Lake. Many years later, when I was in grad school in St Louis, I visited Gogi and Aunt Betsy, and noticed a print of my high school yearbook senior photo on the mantle. I turned it over, and written on the back were the words, "Hope of the World."

But my memories from those times are quite confused with memories of my former life as my grandfather in that same house and yard—such as that of the giant alligator snapping turtle I recall befriending, who hung out in the asparagus patch. I named him "Rastus," and at the end of the summer, we took him down to the St. Louis Zoo, where I would go to see him every time I went back— even into the 1970s, with Morning Glory. I would identify him because he was the biggest turtle there, in with the alligators.

But a few years ago, when I asked my mother about this, she told me: "That never happened to you. It was your grandfather who brought home a big snapping turtle from one of his fishing trips, and kept it for awhile in a big tub in the back yard, before giving it to the zoo. He called it 'Rastus.'"

I also dearly loved my other grandmother—my father's mother, Mary (Gramma Zell to me). Making the rounds of staying for periods of time with each of her several children, she would come and spend a few weeks with us every year, which I always looked forward to. She was a great cook, and turned me onto what became one of my favorite foods (and still is!)—fried oysters. But sometime during high school, she disappeared out of my life; she just stopped coming for visits. 50 years later, my father told me that she had been banned from our home by my mother. I never saw her again.

Tim's maternal grandparents:
Reba & Charles T. Bedell
(1875-1941) Tim's previous
incarnation

Tim's parents, Charles & Vera Zell.
Wedding (Oct. 18, 1940)

110 Hill St., Clark's Green, PA.
March 1947.

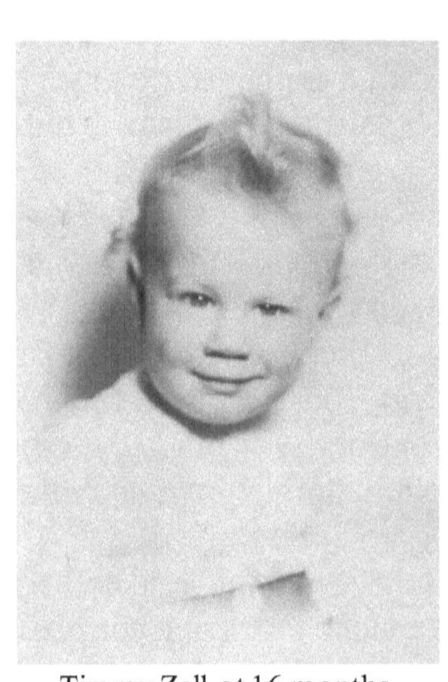

Timmy Zell at 16 months.

Barry, Shirley & Tim in
Crystal Lake, 1953

CHAPTER 3:
Pleasantville High
(1954-1961)

Sixteen springs and sixteen summers gone now
Cartwheels turn to car wheels through the town
And they tell him, "Take your time, it won't be long now
'Til you drag your feet to slow the circles down"
~ "The Circle Game" by Joni Mitchell

OZ'S FATHER, CHARLES ZELL: TIM WAS VERY bright. His problem in school was that he was so bright that he often corrected the teachers when they were wrong, particularly in English. His mother had been an English major, so he was very well-versed in correct English. The only problem I had with Tim in school was not his grades—those were fabulous. It was his conduct as a student.

OZ: One time my dad got called in because I had disputed something the teacher had said. The problem had been that I was correct. The reason I was being punished was for pointing this out and making the teacher look bad. I always thought that was my job. If the emperor has no clothes, somebody has to point it out!

I would argue with people about pretty much anything, and I was almost always correct, because I read and studied. And I wanted to show off my knowledge. I must have been a very difficult kid to deal with. In my younger years, I was not physically strong, having been through all those childhood illnesses. So I asserted myself through my vocabulary and intellectual dominance, which was really infuriating to the teachers, as well as to the other students.

FATHER: One of his tricks he did when he was maybe 10 or 11 years old. It was the middle of the winter, and when the teacher opened the desk drawer a mouse jumped out at her. Of course all the kids knew it was Tim. I was called to school, and I said to him, "Where did you find a mouse in the middle of winter?" There was two feet of snow on the ground! He said it was easy. He knew so much about nature, even at that age.

OZ: When I walked to school I went across-country through the fields and woods rather than taking the roads. I was always catching critters on impulse, but I never thought about what to do with them at the time. (This is still true, and has resulted in us having owls, snakes, lizards, turtles, possums, deer, and even wild pigs in our homes over the years.) One time I caught a squirrel by the tail, and it promptly whirled around and bit my hand. Another time I saw a couple of field mice running across the snow, so I just grabbed them and stuffed them in my pocket. When I got to school there seemed only one logical thing to do with them, and that was to put them in the top drawer of the teacher's desk. What I couldn't figure out was how they knew it was me!

OZ's BROTHER, BARRY: I recall one winter day when my dad received a phone call from the school principal about a field mouse which was found in Tim's teacher's desk drawer. My dad asked the principal why he thought Tim was responsible. The principal said, "Who else would know where to find a field mouse in the winter!"

FATHER: My two other children are completely different. My daughter and my other son were born after Tim was and they exactly fit the mold of what a normal child is supposed to be when they're growing up. Whereas Tim was always surprising.

When his brother was six or seven years old I'd be tossing the ball with him and Tim wouldn't toss the ball with us. He'd be looking at the insects or the birds. He wasn't interested in team sports. But he was a very kind person. He was always interested in animals. He was interested in many things a lot of other kids weren't interested in. Therefore he was kind of a loner. He never had a lot of real close friends that I knew of. He had friends but not anybody that he could hang out with on an intellectual level. Whereas his younger brother Barry had quite a few friends, but most of them were involved in sports.

Tim was very strong. He didn't look strong but he was. He spent one summer at the Carson Military Institute in Indiana and there they had to engage in sports all the time. I went down there to visit one weekend and he had broken his hand hitting a guy while he was boxing. Sometimes kids would pick fights with Tim because he was different and, strangely enough, he would always come out on top. So after that they left him alone.

OZ: Bullies used to keep trying to beat me up. I can understand their point of view. They were large and dumb, and I was a small, brainy, smart aleck who made them look bad in class because I always knew the answers to the teachers' questions. In a later era I would have been known as a nerd. And at one point I just snapped. They were teasing me. One of them took my sweater and wouldn't give it back. I went into a complete berserk rage, grabbed hold of him, knocked him to the ground, and started pummeling him. They had to drag me off of him. I had tears streaming down my face. It was like that scene in the movie, *A Christmas Story,* where Ralphie snaps and whups the bejeesus out of the bully who'd been tormenting him.

After that the bullies never bothered me again. And I started working on my body and my physical capabilities. I lifted weights, and got into school gymnastics, fancy diving, and trampoline. I took wrestling, joined the team, and later studied judo and karate. I went out for track and became a long-distance runner.

This was quite a job, because I had to overcome physical weaknesses to do these things. When I was younger I had several serious childhood illnesses, including chicken pox (1944), whooping cough (1944), measles (1948), mumps (1951), German (3-day) measles (1952), and even the early stages of polio—just before the Salk vaccine became available in 1956. But by the time I finished high school I was a pretty good wrestler and diver, and the second-place cross-country runner on the track team.

But competition itself has never been my motivation. I have always just wanted to be really good at whatever I decide to do. We get certain mandates from our fathers, about how they want us to be. One will say, "I want you to be happy." Another, "I want you to be successful." My father told me, "Whatever you do, be the best. I don't care if you grow up to be a garbage collector; just be the best garbage collector in town!" He also often quoted Davy Crocket's father: "Be sure you're right, then go ahead!"

So whatever I've tried to do in life, I've tried to be the best at it. Sometimes that's been difficult for others to deal with. For instance, my whole family played golf, but I only caddied. They paid me to carry the bags, which seemed a better deal to me. Playing golf just didn't strike me as being something I cared to try and get good at. So I didn't bother to do it at all. Same for skiing—after my father spent the winter of 1959-'60 laid up with his leg broken in four places from a skiing accident, I decided that I didn't want to go there!

My father used to take me out on week-long camping and fishing trips, and I loved those. I remember trips to the Flambeau Flowage in Wisconsin, when I was 13 and 14. We'd be gone for days in re-mote places full of Nature, with no other people. We'd catch some fish in the morning, then put into a rocky island and fry them up for lunch. I'd get to explore wild islands and shores, and one time, when I was 15, we got caught in a terrible storm out on the huge Lake of the Woods in Canada, and were in real danger. To keep the boat from swamping, I had to ride high on the bow, which was really exciting! Those were wonderful adventures!

FATHER: It wasn't so much catching fish as it was being together. We were bonding. He was a good swimmer. When he was 11 I trailed him in a boat across a lake that was a mile wide. He was swimming like crazy. He even taught himself to SCUBA dive. By the time he was 15 he could dive to a depth of a hundred feet under Navy Seal instruction and supervision.

OZ:Science fiction took me to the next phase of my magickal train-ing, providing many different scenarios of imaginative possibili-ties—including those of psychic abilities, and the future evolution of humanity. Books like Olaf Stapelton's *Odd John* (1935), Arthur C. Clark's *Childhood's End* (1953), and Theodore Sturgeon's *More Than Human* (1953) were particularly influential—but I voraciously read hundreds of others in those days, and gradually assembled an enormous paperback sci-fi/fantasy library.

Regarding psychic abilities, Robert Heinlein wrote a short story called "Lost Legacy" (in *Assignment in Eternity*, 1953) in which he mentioned specific techniques for developing these. So I started doing some of those exercises. I read about psychokinesis and started using that as a focus. At that time my family was into playing board games together. I spent hours of practice trying to control dice and coins as they were tossed. I got to be so good at it that my brother and sister complained that I was cheating. I guess I was, technically, although I was using a skill that I worked hard to develop. But it was a skill that went beyond the parameters of the game. I thought it was like somebody being really good at shooting hoops after a lot of practice.

I started doing lots of stuff like that. I'd focus on just refining some minute little skill that involved a psychic component. I would spend hours and hours doing it, 'til I would get to where I could feel the difference. I got to know when I was right in the groove. I made a set of Zener cards for telepathy experiments, and got really good at calling them—so much so that I freaked out a girl I was seeing who was a Christian Scientist, and probably thought I was in league with the Devil!

In high school I studied hypnosis and self-hypnosis, and practiced these on myself and other kids. I came to the conclusion that hypnosis could be used to enhance one's psychic and other abilities, because you could tell someone when they were hypnotized that they could do something, and then they could do it. I got to point where I could control pain and didn't need anesthetics.

But there are side effects to these things that you don't necessarily realize at the time. For example, the control over pain that I mastered severely reduced my empathy. I didn't experience other people's pain any more than I did my own. Later I went through a long period of having to re-learn a sense of empathy.

So I'm still capable of controlling my own pain, but I don't tend to do it much anymore unless it's really necessary—like the time at a nudist resort many years later that I nearly got my foot cut off when a kid crashed through a glass door right in front of me. Mostly now I tend to just experience the pain, and let it wash over and through me. It's not something I'd necessarily recommend to anyone else, but it's one of those odd lessons I had to learn. I feel, in some mythical sense, that things like this should only be used when absolutely needed or appropriate.

FATHER: When Tim was 15 I had him tested at the Illinois Institute of Technology. They didn't even want to test him. They usually didn't test anybody that young. But I had some contacts and I called in my chips. I wanted to see what was happening. They tested people who had high IQs, and I knew he was brilliant. For three days he not only did very, very well at it but he knew which test he was taking and why. So I'd meet with him for lunch and say, "How are you doing?" And he'd tell me all about the test. And I'd say, "How do you know so much about the test?"

And he'd say, "Oh, Dad, I read about that years ago!"

When it was all over the head of the school called me and said, "You have a very interesting son. His tests are just off the chart!"

And I said, "Well, what should I do?"

And he said, "Just stand back and let him go. Don't interfere with him. Just understand that he is one of a kind." And he is.

OZ: From then on, if I wanted a chemistry set, a microscope, or a telescope, I got them. It never occurred to me that this was unusual. I also really got into model-making. First balsa-and-paper airplanes with rubber band motors; then later plastic model kits—which I still enjoy. I particularly focused on spaceships and other science-fiction models, but I also built a lot of planes, anatomy models, and even "Famous Monsters of Filmland." I entered some of these in model contests, and won several trophies.

But my best model was certainly the "City of the Future" that I made out of shirt cardboard, covering an entire desktop. It had futuristic buildings, elevated roads, and even tiny cars and aircraft—all completely my own designs. To enter it into a contest (where it won first prize), my dad had to load the whole desk into a truck!

One model, however, was particularly special. I had seen an exhibit called "The Transparent Man" at the Museum of Science & Industry, and I was inspired to create a small replica. I drew a series of anatomical diagrams of skeleton, organs, blood, nerves, and muscles using the same outline, which was of a 15"-tall man with legs slightly spread and arms slightly out to the sides. I'd gotten as far as carving some of the skeleton from balsa wood, when Renwal came out with their wonderful plastic model kit of "The Visible Man." It was 15 inches tall, in the exact same position as my drawings, and was exactly what I had been trying to create. When I showed the kit and my drawings to my folks, they were as amazed as I was. Did I imagine that kit into being?

Another elaborate model I made in my junior year of high school was my own design for my ideal house—donut-shaped around a central swimming pool. I built the model of balsa wood, to a ¼"=1' scale. All the doors and cabinets could be opened. I used pinheads for doorknobs, and nylon stockings for door and window screens. It was quite a piece of work, and I managed to hold onto it for many years, though it got rather mangled after college when our cat made a nest in it.

I seem to have always had an ability to create whatever I could imagine. I always say that the secret of being an artist is that you start with a blank sheet of paper, and then you put anything you want on it! The same applies, of course, to a block of wood or a lump of clay. I entered many art contests, and always won prizes. I did anti-smoking and other posters, and one year got to paint a large down-town window for Hallowe'en. While for my own enjoyment I mostly drew dinosaurs and spaceships, I also did portraits of anyone who asked, and I even drew paint-by-number pictures of horses for the girls in my classes, and cartoons for the school paper. In college, I learned about oils and acrylics, and created a number of paintings in my dorm room—mostly with apocalyptic themes of a nuclear hol-ocaust—a great concern at that time! I gave away or sold all of them, and I have no copies.

I loved music, and took music classes at school. I learned to read musical notation, and I even took up the accordion for a few years. I figured it was like Latin—if I could learn to play the accordion, then I'd be able to play almost anything! I learned songs easily, and loved to sing when I didn't have anything else to occupy my mind—such as when I was mowing the lawn.

Sadly, this was the one area where my general giftedness did not apply; it seemed I was tone-deaf, and couldn't carry a tune in a bucket! I had no idea until my mother told me to stop singing when I mowed the lawn, because it was so awful. And although I learned to read the notes and press the right keys, with my tin ear I could never quite just play music on the accordion. I've often thought that developing my artistic skills was an attempt to compensate for not being able to do anything musical.

When I was 16, I got a summer job working as a clerk at my Uncle Ed's souvenir stand ("Zell's Cards & Gifts") at the top of the Prudential Building—at the time, the tallest building in Chicago, with a fancy lounge, restaurant, and observation deck on the top floor. To go into the big city, I had to take a commuter train, so I had a monthly pass. But I didn't have to work on the weekends, so I used my pass to go in and spend as much time as possible in the several world-class museums there; especially the Field Museum of Natural History, the Museum of Science & Industry, the Shedd Aquarium, and the Adler Planetarium. I was really inspired, and at one point I managed to befriend a curator at the Field Museum, who took me into the back rooms of the fossil collection, and even gave me a few small fossils to start my own collection!

I've always wanted to have a museum, and I made collections of seashells, minerals, bird's eggs, fossils, insects, butterflies, and stuff like that. A great mentor to me in all this was Capt. Bennings, the curator of the little museum collection at Camp Culver, who taught me how to prepare and display specimens. I got really into insect and butterfly collecting, making my own net, cyanide killing jar, and display cases out of cigar boxes and picture frames. This ended after a couple of years when I finally caught the "holy grail" of collectors: a male Luna moth. The most beautiful and ethereal of all Lepidoptera, I learned to my chagrin that—unlike any other butterfly or moth—its unique luminous green color fades to that of dry straw after it is dead. So after that, I gave up bug collecting.

Fairly early on in my childhood, I discovered animal skulls and I became really fascinated by those. I decided I wanted to collect the whole set. The easiest access to skulls were road kills, so I started working with road kills initially just to collect the skulls. I'd cut off the heads and boil the flesh away and clean them up. In the process of doing this I soon became interested in the rest of the anatomy as well. I was taking biology classes in school, so I started doing dissections. And as I learned to dissect various critters in biology class, I applied those techniques to roadkills. This was a precursor to the idea that I would someday become a surgeon. I had excellent hand-eye co-ordination and got extremely good at being able to tease out the blood vessels and the nerves from the flesh.

I dissected everything I could get hold of. Then I preserved the skins, saved the bones, and cleaned the skulls. Each one was like a unique vessel for the soul of the creature. I was more intrigued by the skull structure than I was by the external appearance.

These were what I would now call "Wizardly Studies"—the study of arcane, obscure, little-known, forbidden, and esoteric knowledge. The stuff that other people didn't know about has always fascinated me, even if the "other people" were just other kids my age. I've always collected old maps, and the part of the maps that most intrigued me would be the blank spaces where it said, "Here be dragons!"

I was fascinated with the stars, and I'd often lie out on the ground (or on the roof) at night studying the constellations, spotting planets, watching shooting stars, etc. I read all the books I could find on astronomy, and visions of future space travel.

I would shine a flashlight up into the sky to try and signal the flying saucers to come get me and take me home. I felt like an alien in human society—a "stranger in a strange land." The weird thing about this was that I did feel I belonged to the planet. I felt totally at home in Nature and with animals. But I did not feel as comfortable with people, and didn't really feel like I was one of them. Today I would say that I was a "Changeling."

Our house was on the periphery of town. Nearby there were fields, a marsh, a lake, and a forest. There was a big sprawling golf course a block away that had lots of woods in it. When everybody else went to sleep, I would sneak out of my bedroom window late at night, especially if there was a full moon, and go running around in the dark. And no one ever caught me doing this. Sometimes I would even leave my pajamas behind and go naked in the dark. This was a whole world that was mine alone—totally unpopulated by humans. The animals that would come out at night were unafraid. (Morning Glory says that Witches are not afraid of the dark—the dark is afraid of us!) There was something totally magical about that—my "secret life."

This was when I when I found a lot of critters, because they too were "children of the night." I was always dragging in strange new "pets." I brought home a screech owl that I called "Archimedes"—after Merlin's owl in T.H. White's *The Sword in the Stone.* I had a white rat, lizards, salamanders, toads, frogs, box turtles, water turtles, crayfish, a possum (which I named "Pogo"—the first of many possums I've had in my life…even to now), and a little brown bat I called "Boris." And my mother let me keep them all in my bedroom—everything but snakes. She was remarkably indulgent about that, I eventually came to appreciate.

MOTHER: His grandfather once caught a little squirrel out in the garden. We kept it for awhile in the house as a pet. It would jump from the curtains onto your shoulder. Tim was always bringing home snakes, which I could not stand. One time Tim's father was cleaning out the garage, and he picked up a hatbox and it was absolutely writhing with snakes. Tim was taking care of them and feeding them. We were not too happy about that.

He had a terrarium full of praying mantises, and an ant colony. And he had a whole beehive that he had ordered by mail. He took it to school for show and tell, and they all got loose in the room. You can imagine the chaos that caused!

OZ: My mother would have bridge club meetings at our house. We always had a housekeeper so my mother didn't have to clean house. I did not want the housekeeper coming into my room and cleaning it up, but my mother insisted. The housekeeper would break a delicate model, and then throw away the pieces! This was a constant battle. One time the housekeeper left my bedroom door open while the bridge club was in the living room…

MOTHER: All of a sudden the girls started screaming, and here was this bat flying around the room. They were all crawling under the tables. Another time they went to use the powder room that was closest to where we were playing bridge, and there was a screech owl in it. They came screaming out of there fast!

ALYCE MITCHEM JENKINS: I had you in 11th grade English. I've wanted for a long time to apologize to you for giving you a failing grade on a very creative book report on *Intruder in the Dust* written in Faulkner's style. As a young teacher, I felt bound by the English

Dept. rules concerning fragments and run-ons. But I recognized your intelligence and creativity and talent, all of which have served you well in your ministry. Please forgive the failing grade.

OZ: I have no memory of this book report or the failing grade you gave me, but it's certainly true that I've always taken a rather novel approach to my writing. And I was given Faulkner, Twain, and Joyce to read, so naturally I had to try out their various unconventional writing styles—which I know didn't set well with my more conventional teachers. Y'all would have certainly failed them too! Anyway, that was long ago, and all is forgiven. I'm truly amazed that you have been following my career and ministry over all these years. And it just amazes me that you've thought about that book report for more than 50 years! It musta been a helluva report!

ALYCE JENKINS: I am relieved to be forgiven. I'm sure you were upset with me at the time – glad it didn't scar you for life!

Yes, it was a very special report, written in Faulkner's style, quite a task in itself. If, indeed, you'd read everything at the beginning of the year, then you were probably bored to death in class. I don't recall your participating much. You sat in the back of the room, but I realize when I think about it that that probably wasn't from choice. I usually seated students on the first day so I could learn their names – and your name started with Z.

OZ: Yes, having a last name beginning with "Z" in a situation where everyone was ranked in alphabetical order, whether it was for seating in classes or position in lines—was a constant irritation and source of resentment to me. It seemed like blatant arbitrary favoritism, which all kids instinctively resent.

ALYCE JENKINS: Thanks for the update on your life. I am a bit more conventional in my religious activities, but you are absolutely amazing. We go to Chautauqua Institution in upstate New York, and a couple years ago I was standing in a line for an author's book signing with a religion student from Oberlin – and he knew about you right away when I mentioned you.

I knew you by reputation before you were in my class. I knew you were very bright and very much a nonconformist. I'm not sure why you weren't in an advanced class – you surely belonged there to be challenged. Perhaps your nonconformity meant you hadn't met the arbitrary "requirements" and jumped through the proper hoops to be where you belonged – and where you might have thrived. You were probably dealing with astronomy or astrophysics or botany when I was expecting you to participate in a discussion of Emily Dickinson. I hope the private school experience your senior year was better for you.

OZ: Well, it's certainly true that in my youthful arrogance I had little patience with teachers who I didn't think had anything to teach me. And there were a lot of those. I appreciated most the teachers who challenged me to go further and expand my horizons, rather than trying (as I saw it) to cram me into a Procrustean box.

I know from stories like yours and those told me by my parents that I was a very difficult student, and totally exasperating. I must have made your life miserable, as I'm sure I did with many teachers until I got into college, where I could finally stretch my wings. My belated and most humble apologies!

It's funny, but I never really thought of myself as a "nonconformist" exactly. I mean, I didn't go out of my way just to be different. The thing was, I just had no idea what I would have had to do to fit in! No one ever really explained this to me in a way I could get it. Somehow I missed out on normal socialization. I never had any real friends among my contemporaries, as I just didn't find any common ground with them for conversation, interests, or activities—and thus no role models I wanted to emulate. So I just went my own way, and immersed myself in books and Nature.

NARRATOR: The adolescent Tim Zell was what today would be called a science geek, though the word "geek" didn't mean the same thing then as it does now. American life was changing rapidly, and the changes included what it meant to be a teenager, and how to describe the way teens behaved and interacted with each other. What was happening with Tim and people his age was a new cultural phenomenon. As the baby boomers grew up they found themselves in the unprecedented position of not having to go directly from childhood to assuming adult responsibilities. They were the first generation of American teenagers to have their own culture, their own music, movies and a new form of entertainment called television (with lots of new shows for adolescents with time on their hands).

But Tim Zell was different from other teenagers. He was 13 when Elvis Presley first appeared on the Ed Sullivan Show—the perfect age to be when rock and roll was being invented—but it meant nothing to him; He didn't listen to Buddy Holly or Little Richard, he didn't go see James Dean movies, and he hated *Catcher in the Rye.*

Tim was, instead, the kind of student who joined the debate team, did all of his homework on time, excelled in his lab classes and created his own science projects. One winter Tim built an igloo in the back yard of his home based on reading he'd done about the Inuit (Polar Eskimos,) and it was so authentic teachers would bring their classes for tours.

OZ's SISTER, SHIRLEY: In my opinion it was perfect—exactly the way the Eskimos would build an igloo.

He was always doing cool stuff like that. In the front of our house we had this planter, and in the winter we would get these huge icicles hanging from the roof down to it. And one winter he colored them all with food coloring. So we had these beautiful blue, green, red and yellow icicles all across the front of our house. We had a large home on a corner lot, so they would have been very noticeable to people driving by. He was always very interesting and fun to hang out with. He had a great sense of humor.

OZ: Another year I built a sod house in the field in back, like the pioneers used to build out on the Great Plains. I built tree houses and forts. I would totally get into these things. I would read about something and then I would want to do it. I read about Stone Age technology and learned wood-carving and flint-knapping to make and use spears, atlatls, arrow points and stone axes.

MOTHER: He wasn't one to follow rules. He walked a different walk. I can't explain that at all. I'm the most conventional person there ever was. So he didn't get it from me.

FATHER: He has been a blessing and a joy. He has been a problem at times. Not a bad problem, but I didn't know how to get along with him. There are lots of things about Tim I still don't understand. I told him one time, "I love you dearly, but I don't always like you."

OZ: I know I was an extremely weird kid. But hopefully, at least interesting. For many people that phase of their life is a fairly short period of time. But mine goes on for my whole life. My parents thought I was a rebel, but that wasn't really the case; I just went along my own way, oblivious to what others may have thought about me. I have never sought the approval of others, nor do I feel it is up to me to approve or disapprove of them. As for my "thinking outside the box," it's really been more a matter of: "Box? There's a box?"

Insofar as I hung around with other kids at all I mostly hung around with girls; especially when the girls and boys became more differentiated. I had very few male friends, and none of them really close. I was oblivious to peer pressure, and never got into the guy culture thing of sports, cars, rock 'n' roll, and stuff like that. Since that wasn't my crowd, I never had the slightest interest in doing any teenage drinking or smoking cigarettes. All the adults I knew who smoked were always trying to quit, so I figured I could save myself a lot of trouble by never starting! I just never felt any particular desire to be like other kids, which is unforgivable in teen culture.

My father got me into Boy Scouts and I really enjoyed that. I got really good at woodcraft—things like tracking, trapping, fishing, building fires, camp cooking, making shelters, and how to survive in the woods. I learned to identify all the local plants and animals. Many years later I went on a two-week vision quest in the Oregon woods with only a pocketknife and I survived just fine using my Scouting skills.

The Scouting went on for many years, and it only ended because of a bizarre situation at a Boy Scout Jamboree. That was a big thing, where different troupes from all over the country would come together for a mega-campout. I was maybe 14 or so and we set up our pup-tents. Somehow I ended up in a tent with an older camp counselor and not another scout. And when we were in the tent together and I was getting ready to go to sleep this guy made sexual advances towards me. His attempts to fondle me seemed very weird and disturbing. I had no idea what that was all about. My whole awakening concept of sexuality was totally oriented towards girls.

I was just a kid and didn't know how to deal with it. That kind of thing wasn't discussed back then. Homosexuality? Pederasty? Never heard of 'em. I managed to brush him off, but it really creeped me out. I never went back to Boy Scouts after that.

Insofar as I hung around with other kids at all I mostly hung around with girls. Especially when the girls and boys became more differentiated. I had very few male friends, and none of them really close. I was oblivious to peer pressure, and never got into the guy culture thing of sports, cars, and stuff like that. Since that wasn't my crowd, I never had the slightest interest in doing any teenage drinking or smoking cigarettes. All the adults I knew who smoked were always trying to quit, so I figured I could save myself a lot of trouble by never starting! I just never felt any particular desire to be like other kids, which is unforgivable in teen culture.

FATHER: He had the measles when he was six or seven years old, and as a result of that he started stuttering. When he was in high school he taught himself to stop stuttering by enrolling in debate and drama classes.

OZ: From being in church pageants I'd learned about drama, so I then began to try out for the plays in high school. And I always got accepted. One of my favorites—in which I had the title role—was a comedy called "I Was a Teenage Vampire," and I got to speak with a Transylvanian accent! I also played Action in "West Side Story," and a lovesick teenager in "Nuts in May." I got into all other aspects of theatre in addition to acting—working on sets, props, costumes, and makeup. This was the best possible preparation for eventually becoming a priest and ritualist, where I still apply those skills.

That put me in a very different social context. I was now hanging out with the theater crowd, which led me into becoming a teenage Beatnik (in all those old '50s high school movies and TV shows, there's always one—that was me!). It also introduced me to some really neat girls. Intellectual types. I was never particularly attracted to any specific physical type; girls had to be smart, or I wasn't interested. I'd strongly imprinted on the town librarian, so I've always had a particular "thing" for archetypal women librarians, big glasses and all!

Our librarian was for me the ultimate ideal woman, and I had a big crush on her. I spent so much time in the library that she got to know my tastes quite well. When I discovered science fiction, she turned me onto the juvenile novels of Robert Heinlein, and as each new one came out each year (with kid protagonists about my age) she would reserve it for me to be the first to read it! This was the Heinlein saga of teaching boys to become men, and waiting for the next installment became a very important part of my life. Thus Mr. Heinlein became my most significant childhood mentor, as his stories were always about what it means to be a true human.

Another important mentor in those years was my junior high biology teacher, Mr. Teske. He was one of the few teachers who really gained my respect, and he encouraged me to study and explore outside of class, such as with my roadkill dissections.

Early in high school, I got into the old black-and-white Hammer horror films, which were being shown every Saturday on a late-night TV show called *Shock Theatre,* with a suitably fiendish comedic MC named Marvin. I created my own little fanzine for the show, which I called *The Cool Ghoul.* I did all the writing, art, and cartoons, ran copies off on the school ditto machine, and handed them out for free. This was the beginning of my lifelong career as an editor and publisher! I also worked on the annual high school literary anthology and the yearbook.

Another thing I got into in high school was learning Latin and German. German because I wanted to learn the language of my father's ancestors. But I especially loved Latin, and was very involved in the Latin Club, where we would dress in togas, and have Roman feasts reclining on cushions around low tables. Many years later, in my own home in St Louis, I set up a similar dining arrangement.

Hallowe'en was my favorite holiday of the year. I've talked to lots of magical folks who say that. We're the kind of people who like to leave our Hallowe'en decorations up all year round! I loved costumes, and my mother taught me to sew so I could make my own. When I was a junior in high school I created a costume based on the human fly character that Vincent Price played in the horror movie "The Fly." I made a giant fly-head with big bulging paper mâché eyes, and movable antennae and mandibles.

Hallowe'en came and my folks went out, leaving me at home to dispense the trick-or-treat candy. So I covered all the furniture with sheets, put colored light bulbs in the lamps and hung up cobwebs so it looked like a haunted house. I answered the door in my fly costume, and the kids wouldn't come in. They would take one look at me and start crying. I'd thought my costume was really cool; I didn't realized how terrifying it would be to little kids. Half of them dropped their bags of candy and ran away screaming.

Shortly after this I began seriously dating two girls simultaneously, Kathy (whom I called "Kitten") and Nancy. One night the following spring my parents were out at a party, and I thought it might be fun to go visit Kitten in the fly costume, which she had never seen. So I put it on and set off to walk over to her place.

The first couple of miles were mostly through woods. I got over to her neighborhood and walked the rest of the way down well-lit suburban streets. I wanted to go to her bedroom window and surprise her, and in order to do that I had to go around to her back yard. So I went to the back of the block, down an alley, and climbed over a fence. Suddenly a bright light was shining in my face and I heard a muffled voice, and then a loud bang which sounded like a gun shot. And it was.

I realized there were cops in front of me, shining spotlights, firing a warning shot, and ordering me to halt or they would shoot me. At that point I froze. I never really thought I would get into trouble, and this was a major flaw in my thinking when I was a kid. I would just do these things spontaneously. Even now I still may anticipate lots of things, but the idea of "getting into trouble" is so vague that it just doesn't register and compute when I'm analyzing things.

Any effort that I made to try to speak came out muffled, which is what it were supposed to do. It was hard to take the costume off. Finally I managed to do it, and I saw quite a scene. The entire neighborhood must have been there. They had flashlights, rakes, shovels and crowbars—it was like the mob of peasants storming Frankenstein's castle! I never did get to visit my girlfriend. I was taken to the police station. They didn't press charges but they called my parents and the pictures ended up in the paper.

FATHER: He wound up in jail, and I got a call from the police. I knew them. It was a small town. They said, "Charlie, come down here and pick up your son." I asked Tim why he did it, and he said, "I made this costume and didn't know what to do with it. So I decided I'd scare people." That wasn't serious. He wasn't hurting anyone. There wasn't any intent for physical harm. It was just for fun.

ALYCE JENKINS: What fun if it would be made into a movie! You seem to have very unusual abilities and powers. I'm amazed. As your "old" English teacher, I like your writing a lot – and how great to have the comments of others. Believe it or not, I remember hearing about the night in the fly suit when the police came. I am amazed and in awe of your powers to read and remember.

OZ: I went back many years later and checked out the old haunts. I went to the police station and there, on the bulletin board, was an old yellowed newspaper clipping about that night, with my picture.

Nancy and Kitten got into considerable rivalry, as often happens. And it started really escalating. This culminated over who would be the first one to actually have sex with me. That turned out to be Nancy, and it happened right after the end of the semester, at the beginning of summer vacation, in the back seat of the car. I was 16½, and I thought this was the best thing in the universe! That summer we made love all the time—every place we could find. We'd drive out into the country and make love in the corn fields. I got a job mowing the lawn in a graveyard, and we'd make love behind the gravestones. I still have her picture in an old wallet.

I just absolutely loved sex—and still do. And I determined from the very beginning that this was something I wanted to study and practice as much as possible and get really good at! It totally transformed me in so many ways. Nancy said she'd "made me a man," and I think that was so. Up 'til that point I'd been obsessively body modest around other people. And that all just disappeared. In fact, years later I got into nudism.

NARRATOR: The fun came to a quick halt in the fall when Charles

Zell sent his son to an all-boys college prep school for his senior year. Once again the teenage Tim found himself with no friends and no love-life.

OZ: I think somewhere during that summer my folks must have figured it out. So that fall, my senior year, they sent me away to a boarding school in Beaver Dam, Wisconsin. I regretted that I would have to leave Nancy, but I couldn't really complain to my parents about that. So I looked forward to Wayland Academy as a new adventure. It was my first time being away from home. I kind of embraced it once I got into it, and tried to do well.

FATHER: Wayland Academy was a terrific, well-known prep school. I picked it for him because he was having problems in his high school—he was smarter than most of his teachers. I was trying to get him more disciplined and more in line with the other kids. I'd sent him to military camp for six weeks one summer, hoping he would go on to military school. But he didn't like that, so I sent him to Wayland instead. And it wasn't because of him dating anyone.

OZ: But it was still more of the same kind of control thing. It was a very structured finishing school where they did not allow any opportunity for the boys and girls to get together unsupervised. The dances were carefully chaperoned. Boys and girls couldn't even go to town on the same day! There was a girl there whom I was mad about. I spent all the time I could with her, and even wrote her poetry. But after graduation I lost contact with her and everyone else at Wayland, and I never returned for any reunions. And since I didn't graduate with my class at Crystal Lake High, I never went back there for any reunions either. That phase of my life was over.

However, it was at Wayland that I first became an entrepreneur. I liked to munch Sunshine Cheez-Its crackers as I read in bed before going to sleep. They were my favorite "comfort food." So once a week, on my town day, I would buy up a whole case of them for 19¢ a box. I would later sell them to the other students for a quarter a box, keeping one or two for myself, and coming out ahead in the deal. Cheez-Its became a permanent part of my life—and eventually, a "snackrament" in the Church that I would later found.

NARRATOR: The future Tim had grown up dreaming about was rapidly approaching. As a result of the space race against Communist Russia, the United States began to emphasize science education and Tim would get a scholarship to the college of his choice when he graduated from high school. Other "science-geeks" and science-fiction fans like himself would receive similar opportunities, and they would go on to help create the computers, cellphones, and internet that are in use today. And Tim Zell would go on to create his own church.

Barry, Tim & Shirley in Crystal Lake, Christmas, 1960.

The Fly costume (with cousin Nancy)—Halloween 1959

Tim Zell, high school graduation, 1961

Tim working at Zell's Card & Gift Shop in Prudential Building, Chicago, Summer, 1960.

PART TWO:

Sharing Water

CHAPTER 4:
Sharing Water
(1961-1965)

Then two college boys thought it would be a joy
To try and start livin' like Martians in their dorm. (In their dorm!)
So they shared a glass of water and they did what they oughter,
And the Galloping Garrulous Grok-Flock was born!
~ "The Galloping Garrulous Grok-Flock"
Chorus by Adam Walks-Between-Worlds

ARRATOR: TIM ZELL'S FRESHMAN YEAR began at Westminster College, a small school in Fulton Missouri, in 1961. Westminster was a men's college and there was a woman's college across town called William Woods. He chose it because he intended to become a surgeon, and the school was well known for its pre-med program.

1961 was the year that John F. Kennedy was sworn in as president. Unlike his predecessor, Dwight D. Eisenhower, JFK was young, charismatic and had a beautiful and charming wife. Eisenhower had been an army general in WW II, and during the eight years of his presidency, kept his strict military attitude and maintained the national status quo. At his inauguration Kennedy declared a "New Frontier" and began working to create positive changes.

This was also a time when the first baby boomers began to mature and, inspired by President Kennedy and Dr. Martin Luther King, got involved in politics and social issues like the civil rights and free speech movements. Liberal college students graduated from rock and roll to folk and protest music and were soon singing along to songs like Bob Dylan's *Blowin' in the Wind* and *The Times They are a Changin'*. And, following the example of the Beat poets and their interest in Buddhism, they began to explore Eastern religions and other alternative forms of spirituality.

Tim Zell's mystic path would soon take him in a direction much different from even his liberal peers—as usual he was following his own muse. His life was about to be changed by a friend he would meet and the science fiction novel they would both read.

OZ: In my final year of high school, my dad took me on the classic road trip to check out as many promising colleges as possible. Although I had written my high school "Vocational Notebook" based on a career as an astronaut, by that time I was thinking I wanted to be a brain surgeon, so I was looking at colleges that had a good pre-med program. Here's the thing about college in those days: A few years before that the Russians had launched Sputnik. And the immediate response of America was that we needed to turn out our own brilliant people who would be able to compete in science and the space race. So scholarship programs were created, with tests to determine the brightest and most promising students. I was in the first generation of kids to be given those tests, and I passed with flying colors, qualifying for an academic scholarship.

Initially, I wanted to go to Duke University, to participate in their work in psychic research which I'd read about. But after a visit there, I ended up choosing a small school in Fulton, Missouri, called Westminster College. Its main claim to fame was that it had been the place where Winston Churchill had delivered his famous "Iron Curtain" speech that heralded the Cold War. There were less than a thousand students and some really marvelous professors. It was a men's college, and there was a woman's college (actually, a 2-year girl's finishing school) across town named William Woods. Coincidentally, William Woods was where my mother had gone to college back in the late '30s!

The summer between high school and college turned out to be a wonderful adventure, as I got a summer job working at Grand Lake Lodge in Rocky Mountain National Park. I bussed tables, washed dishes, cut firewood, and did various odd jobs…with plenty of time off for hiking, canoeing, and mountain climbing. It was glorious, and I returned for two more summers in later years: 1962 and 1965.

So I started college in the fall of 1961—the dawning year of what would eventually become known as the New Age "Psychedelic Psixties." At Westminster, the first-year students stayed in dormitories, but for your second year you had to live somewhere else, so I decided to join a fraternity. The first week I was there they had the pledge parties. Nobody had explained the concept of the college fraternity thing to me, and, as was so often the case, I didn't quite get it. I didn't understand that the purpose of the fraternities was to make connections with people who will help you in your future career. Eventually I accepted a membership in the Phi Kappa Psi fraternity, which was, as it turned out, the lowest one on the social scale. Social status was something I've always been pretty oblivious to…even to this day.

And at the very beginning of all this I met Lance Christie.

LANCE CHRISTIE: I ran into Tim Zell during the pledge week. We were in the anteroom of one of the fraternities. One or the other of us, I don't remember which, made some sort of wisecrack about the strange customs of the natives. The other one of us responded, "Ah! Somebody else who has the same view of things that I do." Later on he told me that I was the first person he had ever met who seemed to be a member of the same species that he was.

OZ: Lance was the first real peer I had ever found, with the most brilliant mind I have ever encountered. A fellow "alien anthropologist." We immediately became fast friends for life, and stayed up late at night talking.

LANCE: We discussed the whichness of what, and how to unscrew the inscrutable, and we were excited about all the information that we were coming across. We realized that there was a gigantic, wonderful picture puzzle out there, that could be put together, that formed a road map to how to build a hopeful and enlightened future. Every time we came across another piece that seemed to fit into the puzzle, or at least told us where to look for the next piece, we would recognize it and be all excited about it. It was very emotional – this stuff was coming from the heart. It wasn't just an abstract intellectual exercise.

From reading science fiction authors such as Olaf Stapleton and Arthur C. Clarke, we had acquired the concept of the human race evolving. And there being subgroups within the race that were actually different subspecies. We concluded that we were members of a different subspecies than the mass of people. Of course in *Atlas*

Shrugged Ayn Rand described these people as being the innovators, the creative thinkers that the majority of people will then attack because they are different, and they feel threatened by these people operating outside the bounds of safe conventionality. We obviously could identify with that.

I was not pledged by any fraternity. I was one of the rejects. I had gone through the pledging process, but it was apparent to them that I was not someone who would respond to their social norms. There was a building on campus that had a second floor that was a dormitory for non-affiliated students. I ended up there.

NARRATOR: During all this, and for years to come, the most important woman in Tim Zell's life was someone he had met right at the beginning of his freshman year at Westminster College.

OZ: The first Friday there was a mixer with the William Woods girls. At that time I was trying to re-invent myself. I didn't want to be a nerdy, non-social kid like I had been in high school. I took James Bond and Hugh Hefner as my role-models, and I showed up looking very dapper. There was this gorgeous redhead there named Martha McCance. We danced and fell head-over-heels in love.

MARTHA: It was love at first sight. We were inseparable after that. We did everything together. We used to call each other Prometheus and Gaia. I thought he was very handsome and intelligent. I was majoring in journalism and drama. In high school I had been the editor of the student paper.

OZ: Martha and I continued to date, and it got more and more intense. We discovered a great trysting place on the girl's campus. There was a Gothic-style chapel that had a little prayer room in the top of a tower that nobody ever went to. I made some adjustments to the lock so that we were able to slip in when no one was watching, and make out. We did that a lot.

As it turned out, Martha had grown up on a family farm only about 25 miles from Crystal Lake, so I was able to visit her when I came home for breaks. I loved the farm, and I got along great with her parents. One time they even took me along for a family vacation to Arkansas to visit their relatives. That was a very strange and spooky experience, given the racial tensions of the time.

In college, I was like a kid in a candy store. I signed up for everything I could—I took the maximum number of hours I was allowed, and continued doing so every year. The first year I took all the pre-med classes, statistics, etc., and I encountered the psychology department. There hadn't been anything like that in high school. I was fascinated by it. It was a brand new field with lots to study. The head of the Psych Department, Gale Fuller, became one of the great mentors of my life. He was interested in things like the beginnings of the psychedelic movement, and the transcendental psychology movement that was just being started by Abraham Maslow, Karen Horney, and Eric Fromm. He refused to wear a necktie, asserting that it was a "symbolic yoke of submission; a hangman's noose."

The concept of the self-actualizing person, to me, played right into the idea of the next step in human evolution. That was a strong part of the science fiction vision that I had been exploring. There was a lot of that kind of stuff going on at that time. Gale Fuller was a very impressive mentor. He was brilliant, insightful, funny and wise. He had a big house and grounds on the edge of town, and he invited some of us to an occasional pig roast there. We spent many hours talking around the fire, and it was his influence that really inspired me to shift my major from Pre-Med to Psych, Soc, and Anthro. My folks never quite understood. They had envisioned having a son who was a successful brain surgeon, and they didn't get it that my destiny lay along a different path.

GALE FULLER: Tim obviously was a very bright young man. He seemed to live in a sci-fi world much of the time. He was not an ordinary person or student in that respect. He didn't seem to spend much time studying. But he knew what was going on and had answers to the problems. He was bright.

Westminster was associated with the Presbyterian Church. When Tim was going there they had required chapel for all of the students. They had assigned chairs in the chapel where they were supposed to sit. If they cut so many times they'd lose credit towards graduation. It was a pretty stuffy place at the time.

It was a liberal arts college of rather high standards. It required that you had to take a certain number of specific courses during your first two years. He griped about having to take the religion classes. He was more willing to challenge the instructors.

Just about everything he did was contrarian. I don't think that has changed over the years. If we were going up the steps he was going down. He was a nonconformist. Even if he agreed with your belief system, he'd challenge you just to see if you really knew what you were talking about.

I think he lived a lifestyle that many of the other students wished they could live. But Tim was independent enough, and self-assured enough, to go ahead and do what he chose to do. He didn't pay much attention to what other people thought or said.

OZ: That fall the October selection of the Science Fiction Book Club was a new book by Robert Heinlein called *Stranger in a Strange Land.* Lance was a subscriber and he got the book. He took it home and read it over Christmas vacation. When he got back he handed it to me and said, "You have got to read this!" So over Spring vacation I did. I felt an incredible sense of recognition—here was someone who understood us and was talking to us. And the ideas that he was putting forth were ones that we already resonated with on so many levels.

Coincidentally, ten years later, Mr. Heinlein wrote the following to me:

So you went to Westminster in Fulton? "Small World" note: One of my aunts had the history department there many years ago (she would be more than a hundred now, were she still alive). I have a brother living about twenty miles from there—Major General L.L. Heinlein, Retired. I was born in Butler, south of Kansas City, grew up in K.C., and was appointed from there to the Naval Academy, and have hardly been in Missouri since—save for quick trips to act as a pall-bearer; my contemporaries are dying off.

(~ Robert A. Heinlein to Tim Zell, Jan. 20, 1972)

Having been an avid reader of Heinlein's juveniles all through high school, I was really ready for SISL. As the protagonists in his previous works had all been my age progressively, so it was with the newest one: Valentine Michael Smith—as an infant, the sole survivor of the first attempted manned expedition to Mars, which crashed upon landing. The baby is rescued and raised by native Martians, in their ancient and wise culture—with no idea of his human heritage. 25 years later, a second expedition succeeds in reaching Mars intact, and brings Michael back to a homeworld he's never known…with his Martian-trained mental abilities and alien cultural perspective. A perspective uncannily like that of Lance and myself.

Well, the saga started in '61
When a man named Heinlein began the fun
When he wrote a sci-fi book about another man

That man was Valentine Michael Smith
And he was born on a one-way trip
To the planet Mars, where they crashed the ship
And all the men and women in the crew were killed.

But the baby was saved by the Martian race,
The wisest beings in outer space
And they brought him up to think and grok like them.

25 years later another ship
Arrives on Mars on a second trip
And they find our boy and bring him back to Earth

And he views our world with alien eyes,
And through him we have a big surprise
As we find that all we take for granted just ain't so.

Sex and love and politics,
Religion especially needed a fix;
So Mike creates the Church of All Worlds to make a go.
~ Oberon Zell, "The Galloping Garrulous Grok-Flock"

In the novel, Valentine Michael Smith establishes the "Church of All Worlds," built around "nests"—a fusion of congregation, group marriage, and intentional community. A key concept is *grokking* (literally, "drinking"), i.e. the ability to be fully empathic, taking another into oneself. Thus the sharing of water is the most profound act of communion between two people—or a group.

Heinlein's SISL introduced us to the ideas of immanent Divinity ("thou art God"), pantheism ("all that groks is God"), sacraments (water sharing), priestesses (only Pagan religions have priestesses), social and ritual nakedness, communities of intimate extended families; and, of course, open, loving relationships without jealousy, and joyous sacred sexuality as Divine Union ("Great Rite"). By defining *love* as "that condition wherein another person's happiness is essential to your own," SISL changed forever the parameters of our relationships with each other—especially in the sexual arena. And all this in the context of a legal religious organization—a "church"—which could have all the rights and privileges granted to the mighty Church of Rome! This was heady stuff, and we drank it up.

LANCE: We talked a lot about the possibilities that were available to human beings to take a different path, in respect to the way society was put together and the premises on which it was founded. That's where *Stranger* had such a powerful affect. Heinlein constellated the idea of trying to work out and install a different set of cultural premises, to develop an alternative human civilization based on more enlightened concepts about human beings, their relationships to each other, their relationships to the natural world, and the purpose and conduct of life, what constitutes right livelihood, what constitutes right action and so on.

We didn't have those terms at the time. OZ and I were very early in receiving this impulse from the collective unconscious, and we were more cognitively differentiated and sensitive to it than the other people around us at the time. It doesn't mean that we were superior in some sort of cosmic sense. We were just able to receive the signal at an earlier time than a large number of other people who have since started to receive the signal and recognize it.

OZ: In *Stranger,* sharing water, and saying "Water shared is life shared," is the fundamental ritual of the book. So on April 7, 1962, Lance and I sat down in a field, shared water and became water brothers, dedicating ourselves to creating a life based on the insights and principles that were in this book—and to trying to actualize them and manifest them into reality. That was essentially the founding event of what eventually became the Church of All Worlds—as well as the Association for the Tree of Life.

When our girlfriends (and future wives), Martha and Penny,

returned from Spring Break, we turned them onto SISL and shared water with them, too. That was on May 25. And so it began…

LANCE: So what we then tried to do was recruit people into a water-brotherhood.

Our collaboration was such that I cannot remember who thought of what first, because we were playing off of each other. I think that what I'm describing now is a fairly accurate account of our bumbling intuitive impulse at the time. The vision inside of us that was not formed, that was not clear, did permit us to recognize stuff that fit and stuff that didn't.

I had no idea how well it would work as a vehicle for meme propagation, but it was certainly the most suitable vehicle I could see. I knew it would involve ritual, religious celebration, and that it would hopefully induce progress towards self-actualization on the part of individuals, and would also be a direct and uninhibited vehicle for pushing people towards the transcendental religious experience. Most churches appear to be quite concerned that people might actually have one, because such experiences tend to completely blow anybody's idea of "line up behind our orthodoxy and send money."

OZ: Lance and I were both in the psychology dept., and the big thing there at the time was the brand-new field of Transpersonal Psychology, inspired by Abraham Maslow's concepts of self-actualization. He listed a hierarchy of 15 basic needs of self-actualizing people, which became the basis of a nifty psych survey called the "Edwards Personal Preference Survey" (EPPS). Our entire freshman class was given the EPPS upon enrolling. Because I was taking Statistics, I needed a project of some kind to do statistical analysis. And Gale Fuller, the head of the Psych Dept., needed student assistants who would score all of the test results. So Lance and I volunteered.

Naturally, we looked up our own scores first, whereupon we immediately noticed that we shared a unique profile that was very different from that of most other students—an "M" in the middle five criteria (respectively, Affiliation, Intraception, Succorance, Dominance, and Abasement), where most other students had a "W." So we flagged every other student whose EPPS profile showed that special "M," and we looked them up, and turned them on to SISL (we bought a bunch of paperbacks and handed them out). Those who came back saying "Wow! This is fantastic! I wanna live like this!" we took into our confidence, and offered them water.

Thus began our first water-brotherhood, a "secret society." We called it *Atl,* which is the Aztec word for "water"—with the esoteric meaning of "original lost home of our ancestors."

LANCE: The prefix "Atl" was chosen because it appears in "Atlantis," the "Atlas Mountains" of northwest Africa, and the "Atlantic Ocean," all of which derived from the Greek mythological Titan Atlas who bore the heavens on his shoulders. Our attention had been directed to the use of Atl to indicate a founding intelligence, synonymous perhaps with "grok," by Ayn Rand's book *Atlas Shrugged.*

OZ: Eventually Atl grew to about a hundred people, many of whom had grown up in different religions. We had come from Episcopalian, Baptist, Congregational, Catholic, Jewish and other backgrounds, but none of us really felt like that was the one for us.

We wanted to create an affiliation that was based on cherishing diversity, and a deeper level of bonds between the people, one that we really felt a natural affinity to. None of us felt like we quite belonged to the families we were born into, but we wanted family! We wanted a tribe. The only way we could get it was to come up with different criteria. The old saying was that "blood is thicker than water." We created a family in which water is thicker (or at least deeper) than blood. And the sharing of water became a stronger bond to us than the blood relationships that formed the basis of all families prior to us. And in our new tribal family, we all took initiatory names—usually from Greek mythology. I was Prometheus, the fire-bringer who defied the authority of almighty Zeus to bring enlightenment to humanity; and Lance was Chiron, the wise centaur and mentor of heroes, such as Heracles and Jason.

And right about then I formulated my lifelong Mission Statement, which has remained unchanged ever since: "To be a catalyst for the coalescence of consciousness."

LANCE: Something that was very fundamental to our intuitive take on the world, that we still have, is that instead of the paradigm in which you have a prophet, or authority figure of some sort, or intellectual leader reveal or dictate a religious system, we instead had absorbed the concept that the only way of doing things was individually. We were definitely into the Gnostic tradition of, "go get your own experience, goddamit! We will be happy to tell you what we know about the tools for getting there, but you have to do the journey yourself." What we were trying to do was to get people to take responsibility for themselves, to pursue self-knowledge and self-actualization. We didn't want to teach a rigid body of revealed doctrine. That's where the patrist religions went wrong, so to speak. (I picked up the term "patrist" from feminist literature. It is used as a modifier for "system" to describe a civilization or institutional structure in which males are considered to be superior and/or the only persons qualified for positions of authority.)

What is essential to that process is that the individual actually breaks free of adherence to the normative values of their culture of origin and develops a highly individualized set of tastes, ethics, and understandings based on their particular characteristics of character. Self actualization involves coming to understand who you are, what your skills are, what your proclivities are, and how to utilize those to both satisfy yourself and benefit the world.

The impulse to benefit the world seems to be a part of the package, because otherwise we would have a bunch of extremely effective raging sociopaths running around. That right there underlines the inherent optimism that you find in Oberon's and my take on the world and its potential. What we both perceive is that when you actually get all the cultural craziness out of the way, and you have people develop and become this integrated human being that is not neurotic, not psychotic, that is not dragged down by all these shoulds, oughts, and weird cultural control mechanisms, then what you end up with, except for people that have a wiring defect and are sociopathic from the get-go, is a person who is, in fact, beneficent. Their instincts are to help the world and to help others. The enlightened person wishes the world to be a better place.

With the water sharing ceremony we were recognizing people who seemed to have the ability to look at society from an outsider point of view, and that were not inferior to the demands of society. Although some mistakes were made there, too. George Bernard

Shaw, describing the early Christians in his commentary on "Androcles and The Lion," observed that any progressive social movement attracts not only those who are superior to the demands of the contemporary society, but also those who are inferior to it. And we did acquire a number of people in the water brotherhood that proved to be outcasts from society not because they were superior to it in the sense of being more intellectually, morally or creatively developed, but in fact were people that had psychiatric issues that made them unable to function in society. And of course the natural tendency of all human beings is to come up with rationales for why that they're being cast out. That was a lack of differentiation that we had at the time. We didn't really understand the difference between an intelligent but damaged individual versus a person who is more advanced ethically and socially

OZ: With Martha's expertise as a journalism major, and my experience in high school with *The Cool Ghoul,* we started putting out a newsletter called the *Atlan Torch,* which became the first "underground" paper that the school had ever seen. It was secretly subsidized by some of the more radical teachers, who supplied us with paper and let us use the school copy machines. We tackled provocative issues like student rights and free speech, and poked fun at the campus socialists. I drew all the cartoons and wrote a column called "Tilting at Windmills." Martha and I did all the typing and formatting—typing everything twice to produce justified margins. It was quite exciting!

LANCE: The *Atlan Torch* made comments on things that were happening. It would have articles on things we had read which made some of the points that we were trying to get across to people. Along with humor and good old college hijinks. Because, after all, we were adolescents. After we got the *Atlan Torch* going one professor at the college wryly remarked, "The *Torch* is coming out more regularly than the school newspaper, it's longer than the school paper, and certainly more widely read."

OZ: As we were putting out *The Atlan Torch,* I also began designing and compiling the *Atlan Logbook.* It had five sections: "Dreams" (our statements of principles, history, symbolism, etc.),

"Voices" (quotes we considered inspirational—many from SISL) "Dreamers" (1-page personal bios of each Atlan), "Roll" (listing all Atlans and their basic data), and "Chronicles" (collected editions of *The Atlan Torch*). Two editions were eventually produced, and I still have both of them.

One of our Atlans was a streetwise New York Hipster named Pete F. He was from a different culture than the rest of us. He had been a part of the Greenwich Village Beatnik scene, and he introduced us to pot. It was an elaborate ritual—we pulled down all the shades, stuffed towels in the cracks under the doors, lit candles and incense, sat in a circle on the floor, and ceremonially passed the pipe. That really imprinted me. You only get one first time. From that time on, my use of any kind of mind-altering stuff has always had to be done in a ritual setting of some sort—as a sacrament. Nothing else ever seemed right. And thus I never really did that much of it.

But this sort of ritual became a part of our lives. The whole format of sitting around in a circle and passing the sacred sacraments started with that particular event. After that we added wine to our rituals, but I never just opened up and drank a bottle of it on my own or even with a meal. It was always part of a ritual. And so I never got into beer or hard liquor. They just never appealed to me.

NARRATOR: Across the United States young people were beginning to explore rituals like this. In the newfound freedom of their dorm rooms or apartments, away from home for the first time, they were discovering what opportunities awaited them in the brave new world in which they were becoming adults. They had read books like Aldous Huxley's *The Doors of Perception*, and wanted to open those doors for themselves. There were those who had grown tired of their family churches and were trying, on some level, to make a direct connection with what they thought of as "God." They were hoping to do it with drugs, and their number were growing.

And Tim Zell was not the only one who would go from this kind of ritual to what is now known as Paganism. What the Gardnerian Witches were doing in England at this same time was not known to him or almost anyone else in America. But there was a growing awareness of what shamans were, and of Native American spirituality. Indeed, anyone who had grown up playing cowboys and

Indians in their backyard knew what it meant to "pass the peace-pipe." And for them, this was just a taste of what was to come.

And this was all happening simultaneously with the beginning of the feminist movement, which Tim and Lance incorporated into their early church philosophy.

LANCE: We intuitively understood very early on that in order to get the world fixed, we had to reassert the importance of the feminine principle. Through reading history we realized that the Christian church, as an institution, was largely in competition with the Nature religions that preceded it. Those religions, of course, worshiped both the male and female principle. But they put emphasis on the female principle as the foundational principle of generativity.

We also realized that society had made the repression of sexuality a major part of its control mechanisms.

One tends to rationalize something that one's hormones are driving one to do with what one's philosophies are recommending. So mistakes were made. I'm sure that there were times when we acted in an exploitative fashion. I know I did. But the thing that would happen with us was that if we were getting out on a limb, most often times we would realize it. Because we would start to see the gap between what we knew we believed in and what we were doing.

OZ: The summer of 1962, I returned to Grand Lake Lodge with a pile of new books to read—especially, those of Ayn Rand: *The Fountainhead, Atlas Shrugged,* and my favorite: *Anthem.* In my off hours from work, I'd go out into the woods, climb a huge rocky outcropping, and sunbathe, read, and meditate. By doubling up shifts and trading with other college kids there, I was also able to arrange enough sequential days off to hitchhike down to Tulsa, Oklahoma, where Lance lived. There he introduced me to Lynne and Ralph, other members of his high school chess club, and they too joined Atl, taking the names "Dagny" and "Hank" from *Atlas Shrugged.*

I returned to school in the fall all fired up with visions and ideas of where we could go with all this!

LANCE: I was working full time and going to school full time. And, in addition to the Atlans, I constructed a satirical fraternity called "Mu Omicron Alpha," MOA—a flightless, extinct bird. It was mostly unpledged oddballs. We did not have a residence hall or meeting place. Instead, what the participants did was to take on the fraternities at Westminster in such competitions as community service projects and the float parade. MOA, which had an active "membership" of about eight at best, kept ending up winning these contests against established fraternities with circa 60 resident members. We were deliberately flipping the bird at the Greek system.

OZ: I hung with them a lot. There were foreign exchange students, there were people who had strange physiological characteristics. One guy was a Thalidomide baby and his arms and hands were like flippers. Another was a tall thin albino who looked almost spectral. There was a Masai exchange student from Kenya with ritual scarification who had had to kill a lion to become a man growing up in his culture. There was a lovely Hawaiian *wahini* named Karen-Lei. Some became Atlans, and some didn't.

(When *National Lampoon*'s movie *Animal House* came out in 1978, it was like someone had been following us around and writing down what we'd been doing with MOA. The movie takes place in 1962; there is a character named "Otter," which later became my own name; and the actor who plays him is named Tim Matheson. Coincidence, or synchronicity?

(The film was inspired by stories written by Harold Ramis, Douglas Kenney and Chris Miller and published in *National Lampoon*. The stories were based on Ramis's experience in the Zeta Beta Tau fraternity at Washington University in St. Louis, Miller's Alpha Delta Phi experiences at Dartmouth College in New Hampshire, and producer Reitman's at McMaster University in Hamilton, Ontario.)

Between the Atlans and the MOA gang, we had quite a crew of folks to have fun with, and we enjoyed concocting pranks…especially when there were major school functions such as games, dances, and guest speakers. Like, I might stand up at one end of the dining hall and holler across to Lance: "Hey Lance, what time is it?"

And he'd shout back, "I don't know. I left my watch upstairs."

And I'd reply, "Aren't you afraid it'll run down?"

And he'd riposte, "No, we have a winding staircase!" And then we'd sit down and go back to eating.

Grand Lake Lodge, Grand Lake,
Colorado, Summer 1961.
(Tim on stool in back)

Grand Lake Lodge,
Grand Lake, Colorado (June 2008)

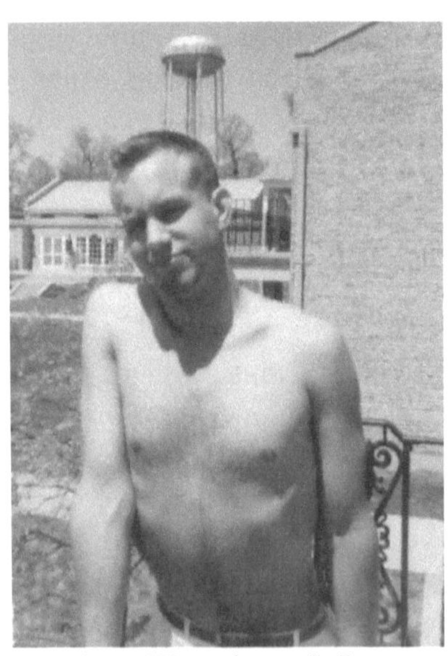

Tim at Westminster College,
Spring 1962.

Tim in his dorm room at
Westminster College, Sept. 1961.

CHAPTER 5:
Family Man
(1962-1965)

Those were the days my friend
We thought they'd never end
We'd sing and dance forever and a day
We'd live the life we choose
We'd fight and never lose
For we were young and sure to have our way.
~ "Those Were the Days" by Mary Hopkins

ARTHA: I BECAME PREGNANT WITH Bryan on December 15th, 1962. It was a Sunday. We had just gone to see a religious epic movie—*King of Kings*. Bryan was born exactly nine months later on September 15th, 1963. We used to have a place in the church that was on the girls' campus. There was a little chapel room upstairs that we used. It was like a tower. Tim had it all rigged up so it looked like it was locked and nobody could come in. Most of the other couples probably had cars they used for doing something like that. But we didn't. This was in the winter when we couldn't go outside.

OZ: Unmarried pregnancy was a very traumatic thing in those days. Of course, we had to talk to our parents about this, which was very difficult. But there was no question in our minds that we wanted to get married. We had been planning on doing that anyway. So we arranged to have a wedding that spring in St. Louis. My parents made all the arrangements and paid for it all, and my fraternity choir came and sang. But just a few nights before the wedding they kidnapped me and shaved my whole body, so I was all bristly for our wedding night. This really put me off against the frat scene, and their so-called sense of "brotherhood." Nobody had a clue that Martha was pregnant. We moved into a little duplex for the remainder of the semester, and I quit the fraternity, as it no longer suited my married or social life. Since no one before me had ever quit that fraternity before, this didn't set well with some of my fellow frat "brothers," especially the President, Greg Sheehan, who declared himself my sworn enemy and made my life miserable for decades—clear into the mid-'70s!

MARTHA: We had planned on getting married eventually. We talked to Dr. Fuller about it. I think Tim's parents were a little disappointed. My college was only a two-year school, so I graduated after the spring semester. Tim and I both went back to live with my parents that summer. My parents loved Tim. He got a job with a moving company (North American Van Lines) delivering furniture and spent the summer making a *Walden Two* baby crib.

OZ: Upon learning of Martha's pregnancy, I had immediately enrolled in a course in developmental psychology, and I read everything I could get my hands on about radical theories and practices of child-rearing and early education. Eventually, these studies led me into a career in teaching and working with children.

One of the books that we'd read in the psychology department was B.F. Skinner's *Walden Two*. It was his vision of a utopian society based on the principles of behavioral psychology. The book had some provocative ideas for communal living that were almost science fiction. And one of these was a crib-type thing that was sort of a habitat environment for infants. So I wrote to Skinner. He had drawn up plans for this thing—which he called an "air crib"—and he sent them to me. It was quite a project—it had to have temperature and humidity controls, and a woven nylon frame that the baby slept on, with a drip pan underneath to catch pee, a Plexiglas window that could be raised and lowered in front, and shades that could be pulled down. I spent the summer of 1963 building it—while working as a moving man. During that time we were living at Martha's parents' farm, staying in her old bedroom with its small four-poster canopy bed. Her father Edward was a banty Irishman, and her mother Ruth was a great Norwegian Valkyrie. They totally accepted me into their family, and we spent a wonderful summer working on the farm and going on Sunday picnic drives in the country.

I was with Martha until Bryan was born. That was a very

traumatic thing for me because the hospital would not let me attend the birth. And I had no idea that would happen. I had been reading about innovations in having fathers participate in the birthing experience, and I just naturally figured that was what we'd be doing. But in those days the doctors just went ahead and made all those decisions and never discussed them with the patients at all. So I was utterly unprepared when she was wheeled away into the delivery room and I was forcibly sent out into the waiting room.

There was another man out there with me who was considerably worried. The nurse came out to talk to him. I couldn't help but overhear the conversation. She told him that his baby had been born dead. The guy fainted right on the spot. I was completely traumatized by this. I demanded to be let in, and they would not do it. I still maintain that was not acceptable. And eventually, of course, all this changed…though too late for us.

MARTHA: I don't remember the delivery. They knocked me out. I knew that there was no way I was going to have natural childbirth. My tolerance for pain is very low. They say that's typical for redheads. It was back in the old days when they gave you ether. Tim was with me the whole time I was having labor pains. But it was a Sunday. It was unusually busy. I remember them giving me something in the delivery room, and it put me right to sleep. When I woke up I was back in my own room.

Back in those days they probably didn't allow fathers in most hospital delivery rooms. It was something he maybe should have planned ahead of time and discussed or set it up with the doctor. Knowing Tim, he waits till the last minute to do stuff. It probably never even occurred to him that you had to do that.

OZ: It had a profound effect on our life. Giving birth is a moment when a woman needs to have her mate with her. And if he is not, the resentment that is created never really goes away. This contributed to the post-partum depression syndrome that she had really badly. After that event Martha completely lost interest in sex and we became alienated from each other. Our relationship was never the same after that.

MARTHA: I guess I was scared of getting pregnant again because it was such a traumatizing experience. My mother kept me naïve about everything so I had no idea what was going to happen or what I was going to go through. It was all a big secret. Now I'm diabetic, so I probably was diabetic during my pregnancy, too. But they never checked those things back in those days.

OZ: Right after Bryan was born, I had to go back to school. Martha stayed with her mom for awhile and eventually came back to live with me in our new upstairs apartment at 601 Jefferson Street. Somehow we got the air crib back there too.

Martha and I became the first students in the history of Westminster and William Woods to get married while in school, and thus to have independent housing. Every other student either lived with their parents, or in a fraternity, sorority, or some kind of school housing. So our place became a hang-out for other students like us. And as we continued using the EPPS test to locate other neat people, we would hand them a copy of *Stranger in a Strange Land* and say: "Here, read this."

In my second year at Westminster, I grew a Beatnik-style goatee, which I retained throughout my years there. Although several other students also grew facial hair, I was the only one to show up at the graduation ceremony with a beard.

Martha and I became the first students in the history of Westminster and William Woods to get married while in school, and thus to have independent housing. Every other student either lived with their parents, or in a fraternity, sorority, or some kind of school housing. So our place became a hang-out for other students like us.

This was in the days of the hootenannies…the beginnings of the folk and protest music that came to define the '60s. On weekend evenings there was usually someone with a guitar, and conversation was interlaced with folksinging. We maintained an open house at all times, encouraging people to drop by at their leisure. And because of the influence of *Stranger in a Strange Land,* it became the custom to be naked in our home. People would come in, take their clothes off, and hang out. Our apartment became an off-campus, clothing-optional haven for our growing Nest of water-siblings—as well as a trysting-place—and we never lacked for baby sitters.

We had a sign posted on the inside of our front door, just like in the book, that said, "Did You Remember to Dress?" We kept that sign for decades—in fact, its successor is on our front door right now. We even had a bowl of money by the door that people could contribute to or take from. We did everything we could to create a Nest environment like in the book. Our pad acquired the reputation among friends as a place they could be themselves, and among our enemies as a den of iniquity. Those were good times.

GALE FULLER: They were living in a house on a corner lot, with a fenced in backyard. They let Bryan go out there *au naturale,* and one of the old neighbor ladies complained about it. The police came by and told the Zells they couldn't do that.

OZ: I commemorated this event in a scathing column for the *Atlan Torch* titled "Obscene Naked Babies."

After that, journalists started coming over to write stories about the Skinner air-crib. I invented and sewed together a baby carrier that was just like the ones you see everyone using now—the backpacks with babies in them. I made it myself because there wasn't anything like that back then. I designed and built a stroller that could also be used as a highchair. We became quite well-known in the community because there was no one else like us.

I got totally into being a father. We slept with Bryan cuddled in our bed at night (the air-crib was mainly for day-use and naps). I designed and sewed cute stuffed animals of "scary" things like bats, spiders and snakes, so he wouldn't grow up with animal phobias. I kept elaborate logs of his feeding schedules, weight, measurements, and developmental milestones. Other than school, we took him everywhere with us, and just doted on him. He was the sweetest, most adorable baby—and was never fussy or crabby in any way.

MARTHA: Tim was a good, loving father. Even though he was in school full time we were equal partners in parenting. As a matter of fact, he was much better at diapering than I was. I never could get the diapers to stay on.

OZ: Martha and I explored possibilities to heal our sexual relationship. One of the ones that seemed reasonable was opening our marriage. We thought that if this thing was damaged between her and me, perhaps she could heal it at her end by getting involved with other people. It was very trial-and-error and experimental. We didn't have any clear-cut guidelines other than *Stranger in a Strange Land,* which laid out a premise that it was okay as long as everyone was open and honest about it. So at least we had a guilt-free context for this. It took me a while to get into it personally, because I was so busy. But we each managed to have a few other lovers during our college years. That worked out quite well, all things considered. Eventually things came back together between us, but there was always a scar across our marriage.

We continued to publish the *Atlan Torch.* The articles that I wrote were not just controversial, but were considered threatening to some. I attacked the draconian security systems set up by the girls' school to keep them from having sex. (Of course since we had an off-campus house anybody who wanted to have a tryst could just come over to our place.) *The Atlan Torch* and our libertine Atlan ways did not set well with the Administration of William Woods, and the *Torch* and I were both banned from the WW campus.

Westminster had all the science, math and history classes, and William Woods had theatre, arts, and stuff like that. So there was a reciprocal program between the two schools for exchange students. I wanted to take art classes—I had the innate talent but not the training. And I was not allowed to do so because I was too controversial a character. But they couldn't keep me out of the drama department. The director got to cast whomever he wanted in the plays, and I always got a major part.

JOHN BRAZELTON: I visited him shortly after his son was born. I was 14 or 15. My stepfather had been born in Fulton, Missouri. His sister Mary was considerably younger than him, and only about four years older than myself. She was dating one of Tim's water brothers, Pete, and he took all of us to the off-campus home of the Zells.

It was rather messy. There were books everywhere. What really caught my eye was the fact that they didn't have the usual crib for their son. Instead, Tim had built this controlled environment to care for and nurture Bryan. It was surrounded by all these play dinosaurs and plastic models of monsters like Frankenstein. His explanation for that was that he wanted his son to grow up without the usual fears that most other children had. There were also play spiders and things hanging over the crib. This suggested to me that Tim was trying to rethink much of what society was into.

We talked for a while, and I soon saw that Tim was extremely well-read. He was going for things far outside the usual learning materials of college students. This was in the early days of psychedelic experimentation. Tim showed me a journal that he had kept of his experience with a mild hallucinogenic seed. He kept very detailed notes. It wasn't a strong thing like LSD. But it was strong enough to make his handwriting change over the course of the evening. It was almost a scrawl by the time he was finished. I was able to make out that "at such and such time I vomited." It showed his dedication to experiencing things and recording it. I think it's funny that they were Morning Glory seeds, because I found out later on that he married a woman named Morning Glory. So she was in his system long before he even met her!

My family and I were all quite impressed with his dedication to learning and thinking things through, and not just accepting what people were telling him. Everything about him seemed to be quite intent on experiencing life. We were sitting around their kitchen table with some drinking glasses and one of us had started to rub his index finger around the rim. It emitted an eerie sort of ring. Then we all did it. Tim really got into the harmonics and group experience of it. It's been over 40 years, and I still remember the look on his face.

I wish there were more people like Tim who wanted the most out of their existence on this planet and were willing to investigate and challenge the usual social/religious norms if necessary to achieve that end.

OZ: Somewhere in that period we got a black-and-white television set, and the earliest shows that we watched were *The Addams Family* and *The Munsters,* both of which ran from 1964-'66. We became great fans—finally, TV sitcom folks we could really relate to. I had such a crush on Morticia—and eventually I married her! 45 years later, Morning Glory and I still remain devoted to the idea of the Addams Family, hosting a big "Addams Family Reunion" party every October. We definitely identify as Gomez and Morticia!

Our other favorite shows of the time were *Bewitched* (1964-'72) and *I Dream of Jeanie* (1965-'70). I enjoyed the magick in them. I was still trying to understand how real magick could work, so I could master it.

Another part of our mythology came from two significant Marvel comic books by Stan Lee that had premiered early in our college years. The first was *Spiderman* (1962) with a hero who had personal problems and angst just like the rest of us. His basic aphorism was "with great power comes great responsibility." The other comic was *The X-Men* (1963), which was based the idea that some people are mutants and not quite the same species as everyone else. That was a good metaphor for us; something we could identify with. The setting also involved a "School for Gifted Youngsters;" an inspiration I actualized fifty years later with the Grey School of Wizardry.

I was on a full academic scholarship, and my folks helped out with rent. But I needed to have more money to support a wife and child, so I started a submarine sandwich business, with deliveries to all the dorms and fraternities at their study break times. Eventually we had quite a business, with a number of students working in it. But of course I really knew nothing about how to run a business, keep books, determine pricing, manage payroll, pay taxes, etc. This was the great gap in my education.

During the summer of 1964 we moved back in with Martha's parents on their farm, and I went back to work for North American Van Lines. Strangely, though we were only a short drive from where my parents lived, they never visited, nor invited us over for dinner or anything. This continued for the rest of my life—with my father being the only member of my natal family to ever visit me at my various homes. Nor have I ever been invited to any family reunions, weddings, funerals, cruises, or other such events. But in later years, I have made a number of trips to visit each of my parents, as well as my brother and sister. However, to this very day, my mother has still never met Bryan, her first grandchild—and she probably never will. This is something I have never understood, and has been very painful to both of us.

That summer we obtained our first car—a red-and-white 1960 Volkswagen Westphalia camper that Lance dubbed the "Super Zell-mobile." We made our first use of it in a trip to Hidden Valley nudist camp in Illinois. We enjoyed our experience at the camp immensely, and I for one felt as if a shadow had been lifted from my world.

Lance and Penny were married in Tulsa, Oklahoma, on Aug. 7, 1964, and Martha and I drove down to serve as Best Man and Matron of Honor. I'll never forget that they went out into the woods that evening for a little tryst, and came back all covered with poison ivy! After the wedding, they moved to Kansas City, where Lance got a job with the health department.

Over Christmas break in 1964, Martha and I decided to go off on a real family road-trip adventure, and we drove to Florida to visit nudist camps. In Mississippi, we had to wait for awhile at a river for the ferry boat to come back for us, and I took advantage of the time to search for fossils along the riverbank. There I discovered one of the greatest treasures in my possession—a lozenge-shaped meteoric rock with an oval hole in one side. It looked like a kayak—or a yoni. Decades later, I learned that it was a *tektite* (molten debris blown out into space and then falling back as meteorites) from the great asteroid impact on the Yucatan Peninsula that had exterminated the dinosaurs 65 million years ago! I still have it in my mojo bag.

In Florida, we had a great time at the nudist camps—especially playing naked volleyball, which I highly recommend! One camp we stayed at was dealing with a lawsuit situation, because a neighbor woman had managed to be able to climb up on a stool in her bathroom, and over the very top of her bathroom window's curtain, could barely peer over the top of the 8-foot fence surrounding the camp, and was therefore complaining that these people were offending her. And the police said, "Well, then, don't get up on the stool."

But an embarrassing moment occurred when my Dad showed up, deciding to surprise us. He had no idea what sort of "camp" we were staying at! Unfortunately, however, our lovely vacation was marred by a bad accident. As I was approaching the sliding glass doors from the pool to the clubhouse, a kid suddenly ran through without realizing the glass door was shut. The door shattered, and a great bladelike piece of glass came down across my right foot, nearly cutting it in half. As I was taken off in the ambulance, I applied my self-hypnosis skills at suppressing the pain, and kept this up throughout the surgical repair, which was done without any anesthetic. But unfortunately, Martha didn't know how to drive, and we soon had to return to school. So I had to drive all the way back to Fulton with my right foot in a cast!

Back at school, we continued to publish the *Atlan Torch*. The editorials I wrote were not just controversial, but were considered threatening to some. I attacked the draconian security systems set up by the girls' school to keep them from having sex. (Of course, since we had an off-campus house anybody who wanted to have a tryst could just come over to our place.) Our libertine Atlan ways did not set well with the Administration of William Woods, and the *Torch* and I were both banned from the WW campus.

Westminster had all the science, math and history classes, and William Woods had theatre, arts, and soft stuff like that. So there was a reciprocal program between the two schools for exchange students. I wanted to take art classes—I had the innate talent but not the training. And I was not allowed to do so because I was too controversial a character. But they couldn't keep me out of the theater department. The director got to cast whomever he wanted in the plays, and I always got a major part. I was in Saroyan's *The Cave Dwellers,* where I played The Duke; I was Polonius in *Hamlet;* and I had the lead role in a play about a retiring Postman. I don't recall the name of that one, but the author was in the audience, and she came up and congratulated me on my performance!

NARRATOR: The Nest continued to meet in the Zell home during the cold Missouri winters. When the weather was better, the party would sometimes move outdoors.

OZ: Exploring the countryside beyond the school and town, we discovered abandoned clay pits that had been mined by the brickworks that had once-upon-a-time been a mainstay of the town. There were hills of rejected materials that had been hauled out of the pits. They had been eroding for years, and were covered with calcite crystals that were just beautiful. The pits had filled with water, and minerals had turned the water different colors—blue, green, and violet. Little marshes, trees and vegetation had come back in and reclaimed the place. It was this incredibly magical oasis that nobody else seemed to know about.

On weekends we would all go out to the clay pits. Lance would make up a big batch of Sangria in a wastebasket. We'd go skinny dipping and roll around in the mud; we'd sing folk songs around a campfire; we'd make love under the stars; and on Monday we'd go back to school. This went on for years. Social nakedness and out-door lovemaking was very liberating, and we carried these ways back indoors during the cold Missouri winters.

OZ's BROTHER, BARRY: His college course load was amazing. He had more credits over four years than any other student his college president could remember, in addition to having a very high grade-point average.

OZ: I wanted to get the very most I could out of the opportunity for education that Westminster offered. I continued taking every single course that I possibly could. Throughout the entire four years I filled up my schedule every semester. By the time I graduated I had the full credits for majors in pre-med, psychology, sociology, and anthropology. I also took every class they had in education, child development, comparative religion and natural history (including astronomy, paleontology, geology, zoology, history...). The senior colloquium assignment was to design a new religion for a newly-emergent intelligent species. I chose sea otters as the subject species, and my thesis, "Freedom Through Existentialism," drew upon our Atlan perspective in trying to live out our visionary ideas experientially, laying the philosophical foundations for the actual Church we would later come to create.

NARRATOR: In an isolated town in rural Missouri Tim Zell had found and created many of the elements that would be the foundation for what would become his Pagan church. And the next step in his spiritual and religious growth would come when he graduated from college and began to make contact with other people around the world who shared similar interests.

HOME WITHIN HOME — Bryan David Zell beams happily from his special crib, patterned after a commercial product by his father, Timothy Zell, 601 Jefferson street. The incubator-like device enabled the parents to rear the infant in controlled surroundings while permitting him maximum freedom. Bryan only uses the crib for sleeping purposes now. Temperature, humidity and air circulation is controlled in the device, which also is virtually soundproof. Bryan is shown at eight months. The 'window' normally is closed when he is sleeping. It is made of unbreakable plastic. His parents say it is virtually impossible for an infant to suffer injury in a crib of this type. (Sun-Gazette photo).

Controlled 'Crib' . . .

'Home Within A Home' Helps Baby's Development, Parents Here Maintain

More bounce to the ounce.

That's one way to describe Bryan David Zell, who will be eight months old on Friday.

His parents, Mr. and Mrs. Timothy Zell, 601 Jefferson street, and Dr. Helen Billings, who teaches education and psychology classes at William Woods College, believe a relatively new technique in infant care is at least partly responsible for Bryan's development.

Bryan has lived much of his early life, when sleep occupied most of his time, in what is known commercially as an Aircrib, a sort of advanced incubator. The system often is referred to as a ...

Daily Sun-Gazette
Wed., May 13, 1964   Fulton, Mo.

Baby Bryan in Skinner Air Crib, Nov. 1963.

Martha, Bryan & Tim with Martha's parents Ed & Ruth McCance at college graduation, July 7, 1965.

CHAPTER 6:
Post-Graduate
(1965-1967)

The Atlan water-brotherhood
Stayed underground and all was good
'Til in '67 we went public in a major way.
~ Oberon Zell, "The Galloping Garrulous Grok-Flock"

ARRATOR: TIM ZELL GRADUATED FROM college in 1965, two years after the assassination of President John F. Kennedy. It was the year when there was rioting in the streets of Watts, California, and when President Lyndon Baines Johnson began to deploy combat troops to fight in Vietnam. The Selective Service system (AKA "the draft") was used to force young men into the military, and by December nearly 200,000 U.S. soldiers were stationed there. Back home the protests began, and as the war continued to escalate the protests got bigger and bigger.

In 1965 folk singer Bob Dylan went electric, and The Beatles and The Rolling Stones toured America. Ken Kesey, author of the popular anti-establishment novel *One Flew Over the Cuckoo's Nest*, and Timothy Leary, a former Harvard psychologist, were working overtime to encourage people to try LSD. The drug was still legal, and anarchist chemists like Augustus Owsley Stanley III began manufacturing mass quantities of it that were eagerly consumed by the more adventurous baby boomers. The psychedelic experience, as Leary called it, often lead to deep reverence for nature and the realization that everything, including the Earth, is alive and is interconnected.

Acid wasn't the only drug being consumed by liberated young adults. They also had access to the new birth control pills, widely available for the first time, which made them the first generation anywhere that could have sex whenever they wanted, and as much as they wanted, without having to worry about creating the next generation. And so began the sexual revolution and the era of sex, drugs and rock and roll.

The British Witch named Gerald Gardner had died the year before, but the news had not made headlines in America. At that point even Tim Zell had not heard of him, and he was not alone. American hippies and college students were not reading Gardner's obscure occult books—science-fiction and fantasy paperbacks were the hip new campus favorites, and no longer just for kids and geeks. *Stranger in a Strange Land* caught on in a big way as the counter-culture book of choice. Tim was joined by millions of others who began to dig the book's spirituality and its philosophy of sexual freedom. Next to *Stranger* on their bookshelves were *Dune*, Frank Herbert's epic saga of the eco-system of an entire planet, and J.R.R. Tolkien's novels about Hobbits, Wizards, Elves and other magical forest dwellers.

And they were reading the underground newspapers that were filled with information about astrology, Tarot, feminism, reincarnation, pantheism, ecology, Mother Nature, and emerging alternative lifestyles. All these things were part of the fertile ground that American neo-Paganism was beginning to grow from.

Tim Zell was ready to join the revolution in whatever way he could, and the most obvious way to that seemed to be by continuing to study psychology.

OZ: After graduation in 1965, I returned to Grand Lake Lodge for the final summer—this time with a family. We loaded our VW camper with all our worldly goods and drove to Colorado. By this time, I had moved up in the ranks to bellhop, and Martha became a cabin maid—with an adorable toddler in tow. We did great in tips, and it was there that Bryan learned his first word after "mama" and "dada:" "horseshit." Very cute. We climbed mountains, canoed on the lake, and made side trips to touristy Estes Park.

On the drive back from Colorado to Missouri, we stopped for gas and were boarded by a beautiful and vocal seal-point Siamese cat, who'd evidently been abandoned (no one at the gas station knew anything about her). We named her Mai Su, and she became our devoted family companion for the next five years, until she died in October of 1970.

I had received a full scholarship in Clinical Psychology from the U.S. Public Health Service, to attend graduate school at Washington University in St. Louis. So after a lovely summer of "Rocky Mountain High, Colorado," we drove to St. Louis and rented a house on Park Avenue downtown where we could watch the St. Louis Arch being built way down the street.

And in Sept. of 1965, I started graduate school. At the same time, Lance went on to the University of Oklahoma in Norman. For awhile we each continued publishing separate editions of *The Atlan Torch*. I also developed a short column in the *Torch* into its own independent publication, *Atlan Annals*. This consisted of letters written among Atlans, which I would retype and collate into a single newsletter, run off copies on a mimeograph machine, and then mail to everyone. In sci-fi fandom, this sort of thing is called an "apazine" (from APA—the acronym for "Amateur Press Association").

Martha, Bryan, and I settled down into our new life in St Louis and were soon able to buy a nice house at 1539 Annandale in the suburb of University City. My dad gave us the money for the down payment, and the mortgage payments were only $127/month. I designed and constructed a great big play set for Bryan in the backyard that he could climb on. It had ladders, decks, sliding poles and stuff like that. I was very devoted to Bryan when he was little and spent as much time with him as I could. The neat thing about having a kid is they don't know anything, and you get to show them all this stuff. It was a constant adventure. We took him everywhere we went.

After graduate school, one of the ways Martha and I earned money part time was by nude modeling at the school art department. In those days male models had to wear a jock strap. Female models didn't have to wear anything. Being naked was no problem for me. I was totally cool with that, as I'd been into nudism for years. But I found it very weird to be standing up in front of a bunch of people wearing a jock strap. There was something sort of obscene about it. If it had been a Speedo it would have been okay. But a jock strap didn't really work for me. At one point I took my jock strap, dyed it flesh colored, and sewed a little patch of bunny fur on it.

Through the art school I met Rodney Winfield, who may very well be the best artist I have ever known in my life. The man was brilliant. He did all kinds of stuff—paintings, etchings, sculpture, leatherwork, bronze, stone, architectural designs, and more. At that time he was doing a series of stained glass windows for a church. They were images of Jesus and the 12 apostles. And he had me model for all of them—as well as for the Virgin Mary!

During that time I kept in touch with the other Atlans I had known at Westminster. They would come by and visit and stay at our house, which became the center of our Nest activities.

While I was in graduate school, Martha pursued her calling to become a Montessori teacher. The nearest place to get her training was in Kansas City, so while I was attending Washington University in St Louis, she was on the opposite side of the state, about 200 miles away. I would drive across on weekends to visit with her and Bryan, but being away from my family for so much time was a real hardship on all of us. We hung out a lot at Sycamore Hollow nudist camp near Lawrence, Kansas, which we later learned had once been frequented by Robert Heinlein. One amusing episode during one of my visits was when Bryan picked a big bouquet of brightly-colored leaves and lovingly dumped them in Martha's lap—they were poison ivy!

As I soon learned, the psych department at Washington University had a very different agenda than Westminster. Instead of the Transpersonal Psychology of Maslow and Fromm that had so inspired me, the Wash U. psych professors were all into B.F. Skinner and his Behavioral Psychology. This wasn't about understanding and helping people, but more about doing horrible experiments on animals—such as cutting open cats' heads and sticking electrodes into their brains. And the other grad students didn't seem to give a damn about making a difference in the world, and in people's lives; all they seemed to be interested in was making money, and in playing manipulative political games. I rescued a white lab rat as a pet for Bryan (he took one look and delightedly squealed "Hupu!" which became the rat's name), and I managed somehow to get through one year. But I really hated it.

Regrettably, Wash U was so huge, and the different Departments were so isolated from one another, that I had no idea that William Masters and Virginia Johnson were conducting their ground-breaking work in human sexuality at that time (their *Human Sexual Response* was published in 1966); or that Buckminster Fuller—one of the greatest minds of the 20th century—was also teaching there. Had I known, and made connection with these brilliant pioneers, my subsequent life and work might have been considerably different. But I missed it.

Somewhere in there, I came to realize that the "Liberal Arts" college system had not been designed for students whose sole criterion was academic aptitude. These schools had all been set up for the scions of the wealthy, to prepare them to take their places in the ruling aristocracy, where servants and underlings would handle all the mundane details of life. So there were significant gaps in what non-business colleges were offering. There was absolutely no mention anywhere of how to earn a living. There was great stuff in literature, languages, philosophy, history, mathematics, social studies, comparative religion, and science—but absolutely nothing about how to survive in the material world outside of Academia. The very concept was disdained. A whole generation of us were dumped on the street in the mid-'60s with absolutely no clue of what do with our vaunted education after we graduated.

In 1966-'67, we rented a big old Victorian house in downtown St Louis, which we shared for awhile with a Boston debutante and Atlan named Pam Lawry and a big Black radical from San Francisco named Bill Taylor. We identified strongly with "The Addams Family," and painted much of the interior black, with red and gold trim. We got a lovely big bird cage and some finches, but our cat, Mai-Su, managed to kill them all.

In the summer of 1966, my father came for a visit. We sat out in the back yard, and he confided in me that with his kids all off to college and on their own, he was planning to divorce my mother. This decision, he said, had first taken hold in his mind back in 1959, when he had been hospitalized with a nearly-fatal attack of kidney stones, and my mother just left him in the hospital and continued on our vacation to the Black Hills of South Dakota, without ever even phoning to see how he was. I hadn't given the matter much thought as a 16-year-old kid, as we all just cheerily went along our way. But seven years later, as a family man myself, I found the episode unimaginable, and I totally sympathized with my dad. So later that year, my parents divorced. I didn't see much of my mother for many years, as she has never visited me to this very day. But my dad continued to visit me every few years, in nearly all my different homes.

My father's mother, Mary (Gramma Zell) whom I dearly loved,

had disappeared from my life back in high school, when (as I much later found out) my mother had banned her from visiting us. She died on March 28, 1966, but I never got a funeral notice or invitation. I never knew what had become of her until 50 years later, when my father finally told me. This still seems incomprehensible to me. What kind of family does that? And how could my father have acquiesced to the banishment of his own mother? I think there are things about my family that I will never understand.

NARRATOR: Instead of returning to graduate school in the fall of 1966 Tim began looking for a full-time job. After trying different things, including teaching grade school, he was hired by the Human Development Corporation as a social psychologist and did that for the rest of his years in St Louis. His work there encompassed family counseling, working with abused women and kids, job training and placement, educational programs and scholarships, halfway houses, rent control, emergency food, clothes and shelter—it was a huge array of programs under President Johnson's "War on Poverty."

OZ: After school let out, and Martha and Bryan were back from Kansas City with me, I was walking down the street one day wondering what I was gonna do about my college career, when I came upon a building with a large sign saying: "Human Development Corporation." They had just opened. I walked in and said, "I'm interested in developing humans. Whatcha got for me?"

Well, they put me to work as a Head Start recruiter in the Pruitt-Igoe public housing projects. And at the end of the summer of '66, I didn't return to school at Wash U, but continued to work for HDC off and on for the next decade. The Projects—which were almost entirely Black—were armed citadels of crime and drugs, so dangerous that the Mafia wouldn't go in there for a short-order pizza! Lower-story windows were all broken out, the elevators didn't work, the halls and stairways were filled with garbage and graffiti, and the grounds outside were covered in broken glass. But I—a young white Hippie—knocked on every door, and went into every apartment to try and recruit kids for Head Start. I have never been a fearful or insecure sort of person, and I am not easily scared or intimidated. I saw a lotta stuff...but no one ever threatened or even bothered me. I guess I just had a Teflon attitude of invincibility which protected me. One kid even asked if I was Jesus!

Taking a break from HDC, in the spring semester of 1967, I applied to the Wellston Unified School District for a job as a substitute teacher and got hired for a 4th grade class. One of my great desires was to be a teacher—I had been inspired by *Summerhill,* Montessori, A.S. Neil, and *The X-Men.* Eventually I was hired full time, and I was told that if I wanted to continue doing it I had to get my teacher's credentials. So at the end of the school year I enrolled in Harris Teachers College in St Louis, and I signed up for the program to teach "exceptional children."

This was a miscommunication of a monumental level. I had always thought that *exceptional* meant "better than average." But in the school system then it was a euphemism for below average. Early in the program I realized that I was not being taught to teach brilliant kids. Just like going to graduate school, it was not what I expected. But I went through the program and got my certificate. I continued to work part-time for the Human Development Corporation while I was going to school to be a teacher.

I taught grade school for two more years. The '67-'68 school year was the first one. In the summer of 1968 I worked as a door-to-door encyclopedia salesman for *World Book* (the same encyclopedia I'd known and loved as a child), which I was not very good at. In the '68-'69 school year I taught 5th grade, then I went back to the Human Development Corporation, where I remained until I eventually left St Louis in 1975. My work there encompassed family counseling, job training and placement, arranging educational programs and scholarships, working with abused women and kids, halfway houses, rent control, emergency food, clothes and shelter—it was a huge array of programs under Johnson's "War on Poverty."

There was a functional hierarchical system at HDC that worked well. I had six or eight people working directly under me. There was only one person above me, and that was the Director of the entire office. There was a high turnover in that position, and for awhile the Director was Ron Gregory, brother of the famous Black comedian, Dick Gregory. Ron and I hit it off splendidly, and when he finally quit, in April of 1971, we stayed after closing and got royally drunk together on a case of Cold Duck, telling stories back and forth. Martha and Julie both had to come get me (to drive my car back), and take me to the Nest meeting that evening at Tom Williams', where I thoroughly embarrassed myself by throwing up and passing out. I've never done that again!

My position in the Human Development Corporation solidified at the Chouteau-Russell Gateway Center, and I became the Director of Social Services for the entire south side of St Louis. For most of the time I was the only white person there. It gave me a complete emersion into urban black society. In fact, I often think of the high point of my experience there as the time I overheard some black guy asking our receptionist who the white guy was back there (at that time, I was the only one). She said, "Ain't no white guys here. We're all just niggers here." I have been tickled by that ever since.

Eventually, in the early '70s, all 33 of those 11-story buildings were infamously dynamited into oblivion, and photos and film clips of their demolition appeared widely in the media.

NARRATOR: Tim's dad gave him the money for a down payment on a house, and Martha got a job teaching at a Montessori school. With a home and a steady job in place he was then able to continue expanding on the visionary pursuits that he had begun in college. After moving to St Louis he had maintained his connections with the other Atlans. In fact there was almost never a time when one or more members of the Atlan waterbrotherhood weren't staying with Tim, Martha and Bryan, and living the social experiment 24/7. For the rest of them he continued to publish *The Atlan Torch*.

OZ: Lance and I had both moved to different cities, and we continued our conversation regarding our mission of changing the world. We wanted to create a world that would be safe for people like us. One that we could live in comfortably—where it would be safe to go outside and say (and be) who we were without being lynched or burned at the stake.

So, we started talking about how we might best go about that. And two different directions emerged. One of them was to continue to be a secret underground society and work in various revolutionary causes, and inject these ideas into them—just sort of shaping things subtly from behind the scenes. And the other was to go public, with a church that would be right out there. In typical fashion, we decided to do it all. And so we formed two branches—the Atlans and the

Church of All Worlds.

LANCE CHRISTIE: What's important to realize here, and it's kind of difficult to grasp, because ordinarily when you have people that have been involved in starting something, and they're not working together on it, it's because there has been some sort of a falling out. That's the normal pattern in our culture. But that was never the case with Oberon and me. It was rather that obviously his talent lay in a different form of expression than mine. I did what I could all the way through to help him be clear on what he was doing and be a sounding board. But I viewed us as being collaborators who were walking different paths that were related. Both of us were experimenting. We knew what it was that we wanted to get to, but we didn't know how to get there, because what we were trying to do was not something for which there was a standard cultural template.

Basically we were cultural architects in a world which did not have any explicit instructions for how to do that. We have both been doing our thing in respect to that, but it has been a matter of bumbling along and trying to discover how to do what it was that we were intuitively drawn to do.

I realized that where OZ had flare for the dramatic and getting out there and showing off and blowing minds, that I was, and am, a social engineer, in the sense that I have a propensity for solving problems and figuring out how to make things work—in both a technical and a social sense.

I realized that where OZ had flare for the dramatic and getting out there and showing off and blowing minds, that I was, and am, a social engineer, in the sense that I have a propensity for solving problems and figuring out how to make things work—in both a technical and a social sense.

OZ: One group we formed was sort of a secret society, which we called the Atlan Foundation. Lance headed it up and became its main Director. I can only speak of it now because it went public just a few decades ago, after 20 years of secrecy. And it was involved in some very interesting stuff. They took lessons from things like *Cats Cradle,* by Kurt Vonnegut, and especially the final chapter of *The Harrad Experiment* that talks about having this secret group move to some under-populated state in the western US and infiltrate the governmental arena. Well, this is what they did. Lance became the Director of Public Health Services for New Mexico, and was responsible for some of the earliest reform laws for medical marijuana in that state. And a lot of other things they did even I don't know about, because they were somewhat secret about a lot of stuff.

LANCE: There is a body of Atlans who are still affiliated with me. We are still a functioning entity. We incorporated in 1986 as the Association for The Tree of Life (ATL). The original crew is the Board of Directors today. The body of work that I'm working on within the context of ATL is called the "Renewable Deal." It essentially deals with the questions of renewable and sustainable energy production, renewable and sustainable agriculture, water efficiency, ecological restoration, implementation of the precautionary principle, the use of ecological economic analysis to make policy decisions, how to run the educational and health care systems and so on. So it has all these planks that deal with all these various aspects, and they're all interlocking from the point of each one reinforcing the other and being compatible with each other. It describes an ecological system of human culture—one that is suited to restoring and then working in harmony with ecological integrity. The Neo-Pagan religion is the natural spiritual adjunct for that, and not by accident.

OZ: And I was chosen to head up the Church of All Worlds, because I seemed to have that kind of a personality. With my theatrical background and experience, I was able to go out in front of crowds of people and do public speaking, rituals and other charismatic stuff. For the rest of our lives—until Lance's death at Samhain of 2010— he and I were like Kirk and Spock to each other (Lance being Spock, of course).

LANCE: Oberon had, and has, a real desire and talent for theater. There is a certain element of the Zen master in it, and a certain element of the little boy showing off. So he was really enjoying creating this Neo-Pagan church, with all the theater and ritual that went with it, and seeing what he could do by way of using that as a vehicle for changing people's consciousness. And also having a helluva good time. Lest all this sound too serious, one of the things that we intuited very early on was, as we put it, "What good is a religion if it doesn't have a good belly laugh now and then?" And of course OZ, very early on, adopted the self-mocking title of "Primate." A lot of the stuff that we put together and did had self-mocking or pun-based connotations. The whole idea was to keep people from getting locked into a rigid seriousness, which gets in the way of examining ideas and learning about yourself, working things out and having a fruitful life.

Oberon was inspired with a vision of a better way of running a world, along with other people, like me, who came upon the same vision. And as a consequence of this, OZ has always lived outside the box trying to find the path to this alternative future. (Much less so in my case. I went through a normal career path trying to support myself and my family.) And his leadership has been more by example than by authority. He rejects the idea of leading by authority. That's a very important thing. Our society is so locked into the concept of the authoritarian leader, as opposed to the authoritative idea leader, who inspires people to change themselves and change the culture in which they live.

What Oberon was doing, when he was doing his theater and expressing his ideas, was and is experimenting. Instead of having this revelation of, "Okay, this is the way to do it! Come and I shall lead you to the promised land," it was rather a case of "I know there is a promised land. I have a general sense of the direction in which we need to go to find it, but I'm exploring. And I'd like you to join me and explore too."

Both Oberon and I, when we have compared notes in recent times, have mutually agreed that our fundamental take on everything—religious philosophy, human social affairs, etc.—has not changed one whit. The only thing that has changed is that we have acquired language and concepts that permit us to put it into focus. That is a lifelong process of learning, and a continuing process. Neither one of us are anywhere close to ossifying. Both of us are still going full-tilt boogie, learning new things, and evolving as it were.

OZ: My basic philosophy has always been pretty *laissez-faire,* live-and-let-live, "you-do-your-thing-and-I'll-do-my-thing." I codified this during those years in my most famous personal aphorism:

"If you don't like it, you can't have any!" (The corollary, of course, is "more for me!"). I've even had bumper stickers made up with this saying. I've applied it to everything from religion to food, and I expect it will probably be engraved on my tombstone! I consider it my contribution to principles that, if generally applied, would contribute to making the world a better place—such as "Do as you would be done by" and "Be excellent to each other!"

Demolition of Pruitt-Igoe housing project.
On July 15, 1972, the city of St. Louis admitted defeat and demolished three of the project's 33 towers. By 1976, the razing of Pruitt-Igoe was complete.
(Photo courtesy of the U.S. Department of Housing and Urban Development Office of Policy Development and Research)

CHAPTER 7: The Church of All Worlds (1967-1969)

The Church of All Worlds was incorporated
And some people asked just how we rated
Our trad—were we Christian, Hindu or what?

And we said "We're Pagans," which raised a fuss
'Cause no one had ever said "Pagans are us*"*
And many people showed up and said "Me too!"

So we published a zine we called Green Egg
For all the Pagans of every peg
And we made a sandbox big enough for all to play
~ Oberon Zell, "The Galloping Garrulous Grok-Flock"

ARRATOR: TIM AND LANCE DECIDED TO take the Church of All Worlds public in 1967. It was the year that the Summer of Love and the Human Be-In took place in San Francisco. On the radio Jim Morrison was living the myth of Dionysus and the Jefferson Airplane were telling everyone about eating mushrooms, smoking hookahs and having fun hallucinations. And on Broadway it was declared that it was the dawning on the Age of Aquarius. People were beginning to explore, and exploit, what a few years later would be called the New Age. African Americans, Latin Americans, women and gays were learning about liberation. And anyone who had an idea for creating a new social or spiritual movement had the opportunity to bring a like-minded group of people together for just that purpose in parks, communes, collectives and churches and anywhere else that the spirit moved them. In September of 1967 Tim jumped right in by arranging for a garage sale at a local coffeehouse to raise money to buy a ditto machine to start a CAW newsletter. (A ditto machine is also known as a "spirit duplicator!")

OZ: In September of 1967, when it was decided that we would take the Church of All Worlds public, I arranged for a garage sale at a local Beatnik coffee house, to raise money to buy our own ditto machine so that we could start a CAW newsletter. Well, if you're a church you can have free advertising. We did well and sold all of our stuff. After that people asked, "Just what *is* this Church of All Worlds?" So the guy who was running the place asked me if I would come back the next Thursday and talk to people about the CAW.

At that time there was a fellow in California known as Omar K. Ravenhurst, whose actual name was Kerry Thornley, and who later became one of the founders of the Discordian Society. He was involved in a San Francisco group called Kerista, a utopian visionary cult that had been founded in New York City clear back in 1956 by John Peltz "Bro Jud" Presmont. Kerista was premised on the creation of intentional "utopian" communities of group marriages. Kerry had written a little article called "Functional Religion," which came to my attention. In the article, he proposed the use of the word *Pagan* as an identifying term for the kind of religious expression that he felt Kerista embodied.

Before that I had never seen the word *pagan* used in the context of a positive identification, let alone a religious one. The "pagans" had always been the people who were not religious and needed to be converted to Christianity. But Kerry applied the term to a particular type of religious thinking and perspective that embraced pantheism, polytheism, classical mythology, ancient cultures, and all that cool stuff I was really into. Jud rejected the term for Kerista, considering himself, as he much later told me, "an authentic Hebrew prophet." But I thought it was perfect for us. Previously, the word had been used to refer to *others* in a derogatory fashion, as "*those* pagans." I seem to have been the first to claim it as a religious self-identification—as "*us* Pagans"—with a capital "P."

I showed up at the coffeehouse and I got up there on the little stage with a stool and a microphone where guys wearing goatees and black turtlenecks would usually read poetry or sing folk songs.

I introduced myself as "Your friendly neighborhood Pagan" and I proceeded to talk about the Atlan vision in terms of the "First Pagan Church of All Worlds." Afterwards the manager invited me to come back and talk again.

Adoption of the term "Pagan" as an identification of our religious identity precipitated some very profound discussions in the *Atlan Annals,* around the whole aspect of identifying with people who have been misunderstood, feared, marginalized, and intensely persecuted throughout Christian history. In creating a new church, did we really want to take on all that baggage? The other Atlans mostly thought not, and chose not to become involved, remaining below the public radar. But those of us who gravitated to the vision of a public CAW had read Frank Herbert's *Dune* novels, and considered that a certain amount of persecution may be a necessary ingredient to consolidate a group identity. Certainly this had been the case in *Stranger in a Strange Land.* As long, of course, as the persecution isn't powerful enough to destroy the group utterly—as the Catholic Church did with the Cathars, Adamites and Albigensians! But since America guaranteed freedom of religion, and the Christian Churches no longer had the legal right to burn heretics at the stake, we felt we could pull it off with nobody getting killed.

Similar questions and issues were being raised elsewhere among the new generation of Witches. But there has always been the lingering concern that we were making potentially life-or-death decisions for future generations of Neo-Pagans who may have no idea what they would be getting into. Happily, our worst fears of a lethal backlash never materialized; but at that time, who could know?

That fall I came back every Thursday and pretty much talked off the top of my head. I read excerpts from *Stranger in a Strange Land* and Carlton Berenda's *The New Genesis,* and shared the ideas, philosophies and thinking that we had been doing in the Atlan waterbrotherhood for years. And people really responded. They would come back the next week with their professors, and then the professors would come back and bring their whole classes with them. Soon people wanted to join this cool new church; the first one to actually do so was a very fat fellow named John "Tiny" McClimans.

Somewhere in the middle of that scene a guy by the name of Ravi Kristen, who was the local Boo-Hoo of the Native American

Church, came up to me and said, "I've got this money in our treasury, but there isn't much interest in doing anything with it. So I'll use it to hire a lawyer to legally incorporate the Church of All Worlds."

Heinlein had pointed out that "religion is a null area of the law"—the first amendment of the US Constitution precludes any governmental regulation of a church. If you set up a church, and get all the paperwork straight, you can pretty much do anything you want to. You can have schools, you can own property, and do all kinds of things that other agencies have to have all kinds of elaborate licensing to do. So this looked like a good idea.

We approached Richard Rabbit, the attorney for the local Archdiocese of the Roman Catholic Church. I told him that I wanted a Pagan church that was legally structured so that anything the Catholic Church could do, we could do. I especially wanted us to be able to establish subsidiary Orders that would be covered under our Group Exemption. And any challenge to our legality would impact the legality of the Catholic Church, and therefore we would have to be defended.

He created for us Articles of Incorporation and Bylaws that were absolutely amazing. Martha, I, and Atlans Frank and Corinne signed the Articles of Incorporation. On March 4, 1968, we received our legal certificate of incorporation in the state of Missouri. And then began the struggles. The state initially wanted to deny us tax exemption, as they didn't consider us a "real religion." After all, we had no dogma regarding the nature of God, salvation, and the Afterlife! That resistance to our legitimization was just what we had been hoping for. We took the matter to the ACLU and they got involved. We got big write-ups in the paper. And we won! It took several years, but we won. And we got great publicity, which then put us on the map. And we also had to apply to the Feds for a 501(c)(3) religious exemption, which we finally received on June 18, 1970.

NARRATOR: In the decades that would follow many other Pagan groups would benefit from the legal precedent that was set in St. Louis. The CAW's successful efforts were a major building block for every Pagan group that came afterwards that wanted legal recognition and non-profit status.

OZ: I also enrolled in a correspondence course in theology with Life Science College in Rolling Meadows, Illinois. They were a small-scale Christian Seminary supported by the Life Science Church. I followed the prescription that Heinlein gave in *Stranger in a Strange Land,* where he had Michael Valentine Smith enroll in a small divinity school. I completed the program for a Doctor of Divinity (DD), and become ordained as the first Priest of the Church of All worlds at Yule of 1967.

Interest in the CAW continued to grow over the winter of 1967-'68. I hung out at the local underground radio station, KDNA and was a regular guest on Elizabeth Gips' show. Our activities centered around Gaslight Square, which was kind of the Greenwich Village or the Haight-Ashbury of St Louis. There was a lot of counter-culture stuff going on there.

Some friends of ours, led by an older Beatnik and Irish poet named Jim Igoe, opened up a coffeehouse they called "The Agora." Named for the forum in Athens, Greece, where philosophers used to meet and talk, it was sort of a co-op. It was very laid-back and comfy, and I hung out there quite a bit.

As an outgrowth of that scene I came upon another coffeehouse on Gaslight Square that was called "The Exit" (in reference to Sartre's play, *No Exit).* It was run by a collective of Christian Churches, and it wasn't accomplishing what they wanted it to (i.e. bringing Hippies to Jesus). Since I had been a guest speaker there, one of the people involved asked me if my church wanted to take over the lease, and we decided to do it.

As of the first of March, 1968, we took over the coffeehouse and renamed it the "Instead." On the 4th the incorporation of the Church of All Worlds was officially approved by the state of Missouri. For Spring Equinox we put out the first issue of a little one-page newsletter called *Green Egg.* Run off in green ink on the ditto machine we'd bought with the money from the garage sale, it had a calendar of events and an essay on what we were all about.

The coffeehouse was in the basement of a huge old five-story Victorian House, which became our first Temple. We called it "Lothlorien Center," after the home of the Elves in J.R.R. Tolkien's *Lord of the Rings.* The rent for the whole building was a whopping $175 a month! We painted the interior of the coffeehouse black, with black lights directed at the walls. We put out day-glo colored chalks, and invited patrons to draw and write on the walls. We got little round tables and covered them with checkered tablecloths. On each table we put a straw-wrapped chianti bottle with a candle in it, all covered with dripping wax.

People would gather around the tables and have great conversations. We had a stage where people could get up and perform. We had poetry readings. People who played regular gigs in the clubs on the strip would come in late at night and jam. One of our most committed regulars was an outrageous folksinger named Frank Batton. Another important person was a sweet young runaway named Debbie Dietz, who sort of became our Temple "house mother."

DEBORAH DIETZ: I left home when I was 15. I was your basic honor student forced to live on the street. My dad attacked me in my sleep in some kind of violent rage. I could have stayed at home and been battered, but fortunately there was a hippie sub-culture in place to receive me.

I was attracted to the Church of All Worlds because it was outrageous. I lived in the coffeehouse. They tried to do decent things there. There were no drugs to speak of that I can recall. Everyone talked about drugs a tremendous amount of the time, but none ever materialized. There was a tremendous amount of sex. But maybe that's in the eye of the beholder. I hadn't left home so that I could have sexual adventures. I was kind of a bookish person. So when I looked around and saw everyone constantly running to the clap clinic and getting pregnant, I just decided to steer clear of the whole sexual issue.

So I became sort of a mascot for everyone. Me being such a youngster, there were a lot of people who took care of me. From the best of them I got encouragement to be just as smart as I wanted to be. Women did not get that kind of encouragement back then. And that continues today.

OZ: We didn't pay anybody—mostly people volunteered to help. People basically lived there, and they did things in exchange for that. So we had quite an assortment of people coming through. As we were all very much involved in the anti-war and civil rights movements, the Instead also became a stop-off point for draft-dodgers on their way up to Canada—such as one real go-getter who went by the name of "Jefferson Davis." An older businessman named Howard Rothman also took an interest and became our Business Manager, helping us with things like bookkeeping, fund-raising, and organizing and maintaining the place as a business. Every Wednesday we would take everyone out to Howard Johnson's for their special $1.19 "all-you-can-eat" clam or fish dinner.

BARRY ZELL (BROTHER): He enjoys eating more than anyone I've ever known. Nearly any type of food, nearly any amount. I once challenged him to a pancake-eating contest—I threw in the napkin after 20! And good luck to anyone trying to out-eat him with lobsters! He savors the preparation as well as the actual consumption of every meal, so don't try to hurry him.

OZ: I am a man of prodigious appetites!

NARRATOR: The Instead was like many other gathering places that were opening at that time, most of which weren't considered to be "temples." According to musician and social critic Frank Zappa, all across the nation there were "psychedelic dungeons popping up on every street." They were part of the ongoing cultural changes that were setting the stage for the Pagan revival.

The Instead became a stop-off point for draft dodgers on their way up to Canada. And there were people that, basically, were living there, and they did things in exchange for having a place to crash. Every Wednesday the CAW would take them all out to the Howard Johnson's restaurant for the special $1.19 "all-you-can-eat" clam or fish dinner.

DEBORAH DIETZ: Tim would organize these trips where we would all arrive for "all you can eat" clams at Howard Johnson's. It was a real popular thing for the general public to do. It was like Grand Central Station in there for business, and then we would descend on this place *en masse,* painted and bizarrely dressed. This was the kind of idea that I recall him coming up with. He so enjoyed outraging convention, and providing food for thought for onlookers. Materialism wasn't exactly embraced freely.

The other people in the restaurant would be pale with loathing. At that period of time there was much antagonism between conventional people and unconventional people. You'd be walking down the street and people would just scream stuff at you out the windows of their cars. It was so polarized. It wasn't uncommon for guys that had long hair to have bottles thrown at them out of passing cars.

OZ: Once we got the Temple on Gaslight Square, then my life split into three aspects that had very little to do with each other. There was my life at home with Martha and Bryan; there was my life at work; and there was my life at the Temple with the crowd there. It was a juggling act to keep my three worlds in balance.

I would go to work in the morning. Then I'd come home and have dinner with my family. Then, most evenings I would go to the Instead. Often I would take Bryan there with me. When he got tired he would just go to sleep in the corner, and I'd bring him home with me. We enrolled him in an alternative school. The first week he was there I got called into the principle's office. It seemed that the class was expected to stand and recite the Pledge of Allegiance every morning. And Bryan had refused. The teacher had grabbed him by the shoulders and tried to force him to stand, but he just kept his legs in a seated position. While *I* didn't ever tell him not to say the Pledge, I myself had ceased to do so since 1954, when the phrase "under God" had been inserted. So I was proud of Bryan for sticking to his principles. Since the school refused to back down, I called a meeting of the other parents, who were mostly alternative folks like us. We agreed that the school's policy was unacceptable, and we made them change it. Bryan became a hero.

In early 1968, I came across the most remarkable vehicle I have ever seen. It was a grey and silver Mercedes Benz bus, all fitted out as a luxurious "land yacht." It had fancy yacht-style wood paneling, red velvet upholstery, a kitchen, and a toilet (a "Destroilet" that used intense heat to convert all organic material into CO_2 and water vapor!). There were couches that converted into beds, a dining table, and many other features we now find in RVs—only much, much fancier. But this was long before the RV, with its only predecessor being the Volkswagen Westphalia camper—the first car I owned. This was a one-of-a-kind vehicle, created as a demonstration model for car shows, and never sold. It had practically no mileage on it. I converted the life insurance policy my father had taken out for me into cash, traded in my VW camper, and bought the "Ultramobile."

I'd take the whole Exit crew out to Forest Park in it, with folks climbing out the roof hatch to ride on top. At night, we'd take over a lovely waterfall and pool in the middle of the park, which few people seemed to know about, and no one visited at night.

Forest Park was a beautiful place. It was established in 1876 and developed for the Louisiana Purchase Exposition of 1904 (better known as "The World's Fair," which my grandfather had attended when he was 29. Much of the Victorian architecture from that exposition was still extant—including the St Louis Zoo, where I spent a lot of time during the years I lived there. Its coolest feature was the giant walk-through aviary, which put you right in there among the birds. A guy I knew had raised a turkey vulture and eventually gave it to the Zoo. The big bird really liked people, and would often come over to visitors and untie their shoelaces.

One of the other neatest things about the zoo was all the animal shows—often with elaborate costumes and props. Performances featured chimps, big cats, elephants, parrots, and sea lions.

A favorite hangout in Forest Park was the World's Fair Pavilion atop Government Hill. Every weekend in the summer, all the local Hippies would congregate there in an ongoing weekly "Love-In."

I planned on having the Ultramobile for many years, and traveling all over the country in it. But this was not to be. When I took it to the local dealership for a minor check-up, they told me it needed a special part that they would have to order from Germany. They rendered it inoperable, and it sat in their yard for months supposedly awaiting the part, which never came. What I didn't realize was that it had come to the attention of a wealthy vehicle collector, who wanted it for his own. He'd made a deal with the dealership to get it away from me. After months without a car—while I rode my bicycle everywhere—the collector finally offered me a trade of one of his cars: a silver Cadillac. I saw little choice, and accepted. The Caddie was not something I ever wanted, or had much use for, but it was wheels, which I desperately needed. And so I lost my dream vehicle, along with all of my savings. A bitter lesson!

In the summer of '68, Gaslight Square got really weird. The whole hippie scene in general underwent some rapid changes everywhere. The same thing happened in the Haight-Ashbury in San Francisco—bad drugs and violence got into the scene. A biker gang called the Boneshakers started hanging out at our coffee house. Their president was an artistic Atlan water-brother of mine named Virgil Elliott who had gotten beaten up by the cops one too many times and became a biker to protect himself. Unfortunately the Boneshakers weren't very stable folks, and their presence became a real problem. One night I had to throw them out because they were getting too rowdy, and smashing up the place. Probably no one but me could have gotten away with that!

DEBORAH DIETZ: Tim was always very kindly. I remember times when people would take advantage of him. I always thought it was because he was a decent person. He would say something, and he would mean it, and he would expect that from others. I guess I'd have to use the "g"-word a little bit. Maybe he was gullible. There a number of times when people would come in, and they were supposed to deliver services, or provide things, or trade things, and they would completely fail to hold up their end, or they would just rip-off. I recall that quite a bit, and getting the impression that Tim was too trusting and good-hearted. He drew some really nice people into his sphere, and some really terrible people into his sphere. And I think that the ones who wanted to take advantage of the situation tended to fare a little better than the ones with the good intentions.

OZ: In the fall of '68, with all the escalating violence, places started shutting down. Gaslight Square became a dangerous, gloomy wasteland haunted by bikers and drug-crazed derelicts. The economy of the place just plummeted, so we had to give it up. We closed down our temple and coffeehouse in September, and had to start looking for other places to meet.

NARRATOR: The Vietnam War continued to escalate and the presence of over 500,000 American troops there couldn't stop a brutal defeat in the Tet Offensive. In the spring of 1968 Martin Luther King Jr. and Senator Robert F. Kennedy were both assassinated. At the end of the summer protests at the Democratic Convention in Chicago turned into riots as the police tear-gassed and beat the protestors in the streets. And in the fall Richard Millhouse Nixon was elected President of the United States.

Any city that had Hippie hangouts soon had problems with police harassment, homelessness and crime. The psychedelic drugs that had been so popular were over-taken by hard drugs like heroin and amphetamines. The result was a lot of pushers, junkies, speed-freaks, bikers and crime. The Gaslight Square neighborhood had the same problems with drugs and violence that places like the Haight Ashbury in San Francisco and the East Village in NYC did. As a result, in the fall of '68 the Instead was closed. Tim had to start looking for another place for the CAW to meet and, as he often did, got what he wanted as the result of a love affair.

OZ: Fundamentally I was still pretty much a shy, geeky kid, in spite of all this outrageous stuff that was going on. I really didn't know quite how to approach someone cold, and do the courtship and art of seduction stuff.

Then in October of 1968 I met a woman named Patrice. She was a journalist who was doing a feature story on Halloween for a local newsmagazine, and she approached me for an interview. She took me out to an ancient, abandoned graveyard somewhere in South St Louis, hidden behind high walls. It was completely overgrown with vines and flowers, and nobody came there. She took me there initially to do photographs for the article. But when we became lovers that became our private Garden of Eden and trysting place.

Patrice was in her early 40s and I was 27. She took me on as a protégé or a project, and she took my raw, untapped potential and turned me into a sexual phenomenon. She taught me about flirting, courtship, seduction, and exactly how to please a woman. I was determined to be a good student and learn everything I could! The movie *The Graduate* had just come out, and she readily identified with the character of Mrs. Robinson. I highly recommend this kind of relationship to younger men!

So then Patrice wanted to introduce me to her friends. She took me to the Unitarian Church and I got to be good friends with the minister, Webster Kitchell. I got involved in his church and even taught a course of evolution in Sunday school for a year. We went on canoe trips and campouts together, and talked around the fire long into the night. I reprinted some of Webster's sermons in another

Pagan magazine I created, called *The Pagan!* I got some exposure to their liturgy and incorporated elements and style from that, which was very helpful. That gave us something to work with when we were developing things like marriage ceremonies in CAW. Since we were a legal Pagan Church, we got a lot of young Hippie couples wanting me to perform their weddings—held in Forest Park.

One Sunday Webster asked me to skip teaching Sunday school and attend his sermon. The title was "Is it possible to be a Christian and live the good life?" He said: "No, I don't think so. I've come to realize that I'm really a Pagan at heart." Then he took off his robe, stepped down from the podium, and left for a year-long sabbatical. He returned with a beard; the first Unitarian Pagan!

Another very supportive Unitarian friend we made at that time was Paul Wesley, who invited us several times to come and do guest services for his church in Rolla, Missouri. These also helped us to develop a functional liturgy.

After the coffee house closed, Patrice invited us over to her house on Friday nights. That was a big deal and a social occasion, and became the foundation of our Nest meetings. She invited her other friends and we got to meet a different class of people. Then other people began to offer to host Nest meetings at their houses, so we started to rotate, and did it every Friday for the next year.

NARRATOR: The meetings continued to happen on every Friday. Eventually they were moved over to Tim Zell's house as the full-time location and the "Did You Remember to Dress?" was once again posted on the wall. During this time he visited his old college campus to recruit more Pagans.

TOM WILLIAMS: In September, 1968, I was a graduate student at Washington University. I was walking across the campus when I spotted a sign that said, "Have You Discovered Paganism? You may be a Pagan and not know it." The sign announced a meeting of something called the Church of All Worlds the next evening. I went down to the Student Union and sat down in the meeting. It was there I first saw a well-groomed young man with a goatee wearing white slacks, a white turtleneck and a white sport coat. The young man's name was Tim Zell and he was talking about a book called *Stranger in a Strange Land.* I listened to his pitch and I found it very intriguing.

So I went up and talked to him afterwards. He loaned me a copy of the book, which I took home and read.

That book changed my life. What was especially interesting and synergistic about it was that all around me the sixties were happening and people were proposing, talking about, and actually *living* the very things Heinlein talked about in his book. The hypocrisy of the "normal" society couldn't have been more blatant due to the racism, the war, the lies about drugs, and hollow rewards of material success. Mind you, the sixties were a time of relative prosperity, so while there was certainly poverty, a lot of young folks could exist and even thrive on no work and little money—or so it appeared. So I went to some meetings.

Now you have to picture the house. On the outside it was a normal-looking suburban bungalow with a lawn and some bushes and a little walk up to the door. But once you went through that door...

You found yourself in a large L-shaped room with cushions on the floor and low tables. There were shelves with models of dinosaurs and space ships (come to think of it, OZ's surroundings aren't much different today). The walls were painted black and there were day-glow posters on the wall, some plants, a stereo and over the years a menagerie of strange animals ranging from cats to boa constrictors and pythons to a six-foot iguana, a parakeet that somehow managed not to be devoured, a muscle-bound tegu lizard, a possum, rats rescued from the psychology lab, caymans in the bathtub, an owl perched on the shower head, geckos roaming about at night, and various species of Hippies and other bizarre life-forms.

OZ: As a kid I'd collected as many wild critters as my mother would let me keep in my room. Now that I finally had my own house, I got back into this. Our first family pets were Mai-Su (the cat) and Hupu (the rat). They got along well together—so much that when Mai-Su had kittens, Hupu would snuggle together with the litter. Later, Mai-Su taught them all (including Hupu) to use the litter box, and Hupu taught the kittens to sit on their haunches in a circle around the bowl of kitty crunchies, take a piece out with their front paws, and gnaw it politely. But no, Mai-Su did not teach Hupu to catch mice!

But the most special critter in my life during this period was Histah—a lovely boa constrictor I bought as a baby from a pet store in 1968. I named her after the ape word for "snake" in the *Tarzan* books by Edgar Rice Burroughs (Tarzan was one of my greatest childhood heroes—along with Captain Nemo from Jules Verne's *20,000 Leagues Under the Sea*).

Histah soon became much more than a pet. She was my constant companion and a true Familiar. Although I built a really spectacular habitat for her—using a curved truck windshield for a front—most of the time she had free run of the house. At night, I could "dream-fast" with her, and in my dreams I would see through her eyes as she roamed around the house and finally settled on a new place to sleep. Then in the morning I would go straight to her hiding place and take her out, where she spent most of the day wrapped around my shoulders. As she grew, I often took her to children's schools and other places, where she would win everyone over—even confirmed ophidiphobes. Whenever there were people around, she was as social with them as any cat.

DON WILDGRUBE: My wife Alene seemed to enjoy herself at her first Nest meeting—until she had to use the bathroom. Now at that time, Alene was deathly afraid of Snakes. She went into the bathroom and when she was getting up, Histah, who was coiled around the shower curtain rod, stuck her head down to meet Alene's stare head-on. It was quite a shock but she eventually got over it. In fact she became on friendly terms with Histah and when Histah was injured she held her while Tim was sewing up an injury.

Also running around was a rat (Fred) who was to be a meal for Histah but they became friends instead of food. Fred was asthmatic and while we were sitting around, we would hear snorting, Fred would appear and take nuts, chips and other munchies off of the table and then stockpile them in various corners around the room. The kitchen was just a galley where Tim always made the popcorn for the *Green Egg* collating parties. In the refrigerator you would find a large water bottle with a ceramic cube in it. This was Eco-Pure, the magickal cube that was supposed to purify water.

TOM WILLIAMS: The focus of CAW in the early days was a very secular one. If humans were perfectible or at least improvable—then it could be done by embracing *human* values, that is values that arise from our intrinsic nature as human beings rather than values imposed by some abstract creed or philosophy. Why, these folks didn't even mention the word "spirituality."

> *Long past, in the Days of Legend,*
> *When Star Trek newly had its birth,*
> *Our ancestors met to honor*
> *Sacred Fridays with sweet mirth!*
>
> *And the precious snackraments were passed around the Circle:*
> *Strange popcorn and the tasty yellow squares;*
> *What a friend we have in Cheez-Its;*
> *Pass on what the Ancients started there!*
> ~ "What a Friend We Have in Cheez-Its," by Maerian Morris

TOM WILLIAMS: In the midst of deep philosophical discussions, there would be a break while everyone went into the room where the TV was to watch *Star Trek*, which was then in its final season. It was at this juncture that the CAW came by its tradition of eating Cheez-Its, which were ultimately to become our church "snackrament." Now *Star Trek* had a special appeal for this crowd. Not only was it the best science fiction series that had ever—to that date—appeared on television; it had a unique message.

Among other things, "Star Trek" celebrated the urge to go out, to explore—not only new worlds but also other ways of being. It affirmed that it was possible to improve society and appreciate and honor diversity among peoples.

In the middle of the Cold War, here was an exploratory starship with a Russian ensign in the same crew with a Japanese navigator, a black African woman officer, and a green-blooded Vulcan—all part of a grand United Federation of Planets. In all the situations that arose, violence was always the last resort and practically never solved anything. *Star Trek* appealed to that desire to improve the human condition by improving humans. And "human" took on a much broader meaning in light of the other races encountered in *Star Trek*—it was more a quality held in common by sentient life forms, a thing that all living intelligent beings shared. It was exhilarating!

First CAW altar, St Louis, 1967.

Bryan David Zell, 1968.

Tim Zell with Histah, the boa constrictor. 1968

PART Three:

An Old Religion For a New Age

CHAPTER 9:
An Old Religion
for a New Age
(1969)

Thou art God and Thou art Goddess—Immanent Divinity
Sharing Water, sharing Life; Priestesses along with Priests
Worshipping Nature through the turning Wheel
With naked rites and sacred sex, our mission is a world to heal.
~ Oberon Zell, "The Galloping Garrulous Grok Flock"

NARRATOR: 1969 WAS THE YEAR THAT hippie Paganism seemed to take over the world, or at least it seemed like that for one weekend when 400,000 people gathered on a farm in upstate New York for the Woodstock festival. According to Arlo Guthrie it was "a lotta freaks, man." Author Ayn Rand would later describe it as being Dionysian. Although she didn't mean it as a compliment, many people agreed and thought it was a great idea.

People were inspired by books like Henry David Thoreau's *Walden*, and there was a lot of talk about getting away from it all and moving to the country. The *Whole Earth Catalog* was published (and regularly updated) to give them access to the tools needed to make the transition. Joni Mitchell told the flower children that "we've got to get ourselves back to the garden," and the new comic book hero was a rustic, bearded sage named Mr. Natural (who looked a lot like OZ does now.)

OZ: Of course, the most significant event in 1969 was the first moon landing on July 20—which I had been looking forward to all my life. Tom Williams and I watched the whole thing together on TV from start to finish. It was incredibly emotional for us—as I'm sure it was for nearly everyone on Earth. Finally, the world was catching up to science fiction!

FATHER: While other kids were interested in sports and social activity, Tim was interested in nature, in space, in the new sciences that were coming along in the '50s. He was very interested in the new movement toward space exploration. He told me we were gonna get to the moon, and I didn't believe him. I was gonna call the men in the wagon with the white coats. He not only told me that we would fly to the moon, he told me that we would fly there and get back! I could imagine rocketry getting something to the moon, but not landing and coming back again. And he said, "You wait and see, Dad." He was reading books about space travel, and he believed it. And he understood how it could be done, which I didn't.

OZ: So just over a month later, when the World Science Fiction Convention was held in St Louis, we just had to go! After all, we were a science-fiction-based religion!

NARRATOR: I first crossed paths with Tim Zell on Labor Day Weekend, 1969. It was at the St Louis World Science Fiction Convention, and I was 16 years old. Science fiction books were, at that time, not generally recognized as serious literature by academics or book reviewers in mainstream newspapers and magazines. But science fiction fans were a loyal and intelligent bunch. Starting in the 1930's they connected with each other through the letter columns in the back of magazines, formed clubs, held conventions and published their own fanzines—and, in fact, coined the word "fanzine." (Curiously, this all began right around the same time that Gerald Gardner was starting his involvement with Witchcraft.)

Science fiction fandom in the sixties was still pretty much an underground subculture. The Worldcon moved to a different city every year, and there were smaller regional conventions, but the general public didn't know they existed. The fans were not a bunch of hippie freaks, but since they were outsiders themselves, and were used to reading about alien species and alternate realities, they accepted people like Tim and myself at their gatherings.

When I arrived at the Worldcon I was fresh with excitement about two recent popular culture events: the movie *2001: A Space Odyssey*, which I had seen in its original Cinerama presentation in Chicago, and news about the Woodstock rock festival, which had happened less than two weeks earlier. Both the movie and the festival seemed to me, insane heartland adolescent that I was, to be important—maybe even "cosmic." It felt like there was some big change happening, or about to happen, and I wanted to be part of it. "2001" and Woodstock immediately became modern mythology.

I went to St Louis with some older friends who had arranged transportation and booked a hotel room. (We all stayed in the same room, with most of us crashing on the floor.) It was a weekend of book-swapping, getting autographs, panel discussions, awards ceremonies, a masquerade and more. I spent a lot of time watching the movies that were shown all night in the hotel ballroom. (This was in the days before cable TV, DVDs, etc.)

But the real action was at the parties that people had in their hotel rooms into the early hours of the morning. There was a bulletin board in the hotel lobby where fans posted notices of when and where they were hosting a party. One of those little cards had the number of the room where people from the Church of All Worlds were staying. As a result of that, when I went back home to start my junior year of high school, I was a subscriber to *Green Egg*. And was on my way to learning much more about modern mythology.

OZ: Another person we met at the St Louis Worldcon was a 17-year-old kid from Winnipeg, Canada, named Bill Morris (later Orion). He'd hitchhiked down to the con, and we put him up in our room. Over the following years he became very much like a younger brother to me, and along with Tom Williams, we became quite a trio—sometimes like the Three Musketeers, and other times more like the Three Stooges!

NARRATOR: As a result of going to the '69 St. Louis Worldcon I became a *Green Egg* subscriber. At first I thought it was a science fiction fanzine, and in a way it was—there were book reviews, amateur fantasy art, and lots of letters. At that time Pagans and people in science-fiction fandom had one big thing in common: they often didn't know anyone else with similar interests in the towns where they lived. Writing letters to zines enabled them to express themselves and not feel so isolated—they could be part of a community, even if it was only through the mail. It might be difficult for anyone who has grown up with the internet to understand what it was like to live in a small town, not have any close friends, and to go to the mailbox and find a friendly fanzine waiting there for you.

Publishing *Green Egg*, long before home computers, desktop publishing or even copy shops, was in itself something of a magical act. In the years that would follow *Green Egg* grew in size and in circulation, and it went nationwide and global. Tim Zell was able to discover other people, both individuals and groups, who were walking down similar paths, and they were all able to find out about and learn from each other. Tim printed all the letters he got unedited, so there was an ongoing discussion of what was going on and what could happen next. *Green Egg* and its fabulous forum became an important part of the formation and early growth of modern Earth-based spirituality—in all of its many variations.

This was also way prior to the internet, search engines and social networks. But in a way it provided the same services—just at a much slower speed. The basic idea for it came from, once again, science fiction geeks. For decades sci-fi fans, who typically didn't know too many people with similar interests in their local communities, had been using self-published "fanzines" to communicate with like-minded individuals in other towns. These 'zines frequently featured prominent letter sections – it cost a lot of money to make long distance phone calls back then. Tim Zell used the same tools and format that they did, and helped create a different kind of "fandom."

One of the first people Tim Zell connected with was an artist and visionary named Fred Adams, who had founded a group he called *Feraferia* ("wild festival") and published a newsletter called *Korethalia* in California.

OZ: What I read in *Korethalia* seemed very much along the lines of what we were looking for. At that time we hadn't developed much liturgical and theological stuff. We had just decided that what we really were was Pagans, but all we had was a rough philosophy. We didn't know how to put it into a coherent form, or what to do with it. Feraferian literature was filled with liturgy, ritual, theology, mythology, sacred art and poetry. It was all about the seasonal cycles of celebration, and that was the first time I came across that idea.

TOM WILLIAMS: In *Green Egg* number 12, dated Dec. 12, 1968, there are the first mentions of Pagan holidays—the periods of Repose and Yule. These came from a little pamphlet called *The Nine Royal Passions of the Year* that Tim got from a group called Feraferia in southern California. I remember in 1968 when Tim first showed me the pamphlet, which was printed in four colors. I felt a twinge go through me like some half-remembered longing, like some affinity with long-forgotten rituals and connections.

I've still got a copy of that pamphlet. It was a brief description of the old Celtic Pagan cycle of the year, the celebrations and their significance. It had come to Tim from Feraferia earlier that year in about April. Somewhat naively, we started to date our *Green Eggs* according to Robert Graves' tree calendar, which Feraferia followed. These were the first seeds of what was to eventually lead to the transformation of the Church of All Worlds. Or better put—the expansion of our purpose and consciousness to embrace the living planet. The influence of Feraferia and our contact with other Pagan groups around the country was to have a profound influence on all of us—an influence that is continuing to this day.

OZ: As soon as we got the information about the Wheel of the Year, we started aligning ourselves with it. There were marvelous revelations around finding out that the annual holidays and celebrations that I grew up with were linked to a greater and more ancient cycle. There was a sense of deepening and of feeling the roots of all these things and weaving them all together. It was very exciting to have a larger context for that stuff. Most of us have always loved the holidays, but now we were finding out what they were really all about. I started researching worldwide holiday customs, and the more I learned the more I started to appreciate them.

Our central format for rituals, that allowed a lot of this stuff to be woven around it, was that there always a circle where things were passed around. Of course, the first time was with a glass of water. Later it would be food, or stories. We didn't have a "doing" ritual as much as a "sharing" ritual. We would read little passages and poetry that were relevant to the season. It was very simple and unstructured back in those days. Over time these things evolved and we got better and better at it. We would find out what other folks were doing and take bits and pieces of it and integrate them into our rituals.

These things were foundational to what happened in the '70s. The '60s were all about finding the pieces, bringing them all together, putting them in the same place and taking a look at them. We started putting out notices and inviting people to join us. People started showing up, and the idea spread. The only form of printing we had access to was ditto machines, and they could only print in four colors: green, red, purple, and a washed-out grey. I decided to designate the different colors for different newsletters. Green looked the best, so we used that for the most public one. Green is the starting color in a lot of magical systems. For the next levels inward it would be red and then purple. The name seemed appropriate in that an egg symbolizes potential and new beginnings and something that was about to hatch. (It was purely coincidental that there was a Dr. Seuss book with that name.) We called the red newsletter *The Scarlet Flame,* because that had to do with the powers of inspiration. We called the purple one *The Violet Void* at first but many years later we changed it to *The Violet Vision,* which was much better.

NARRATOR: Early on in this process Tim Zell contacted Fred Adams and discussed the possibility of forming a Pagan ecumenical organization.

OZ:　　I decided to get hold of Fred Adams. I wrote him a letter, sent him a *Green Egg,* and said, "You sound like a fellow Pagan."

And he wrote back and said, "Yeah, that's great! Pagans! That's the perfect word for what we are." You have to understand that up to that point nobody had called them*selves* "Pagan." It had been used for centuries as a derogatory slur to refer to other people, but it had always been *"those* pagans," not *"us* Pagans." That's what made the difference. Fred was aware of a few similar groups in California, and he turned us all on to each other.

Our contact was the first ecumenical connection between Pagan groups. There were groups that knew of each other's existence, but they never did anything together. So Fred and I discussed the possibility of forming an organization. The way my thinking has often gone in my life has been "let's throw a party and invite all our friends." Virtually everything I've done has been a version of that. Fundamentally I'm a host (which would explain the parasites...).

Fred came up with the name "The Council of Themis." Themis was the Goddess of harmony in Greek mythology (in Rome she was called Harmonia), and is depicted in our modern iconography as the blindfolded figure of Justice holding balance scales in one hand and a sword in the other. The Council rapidly expanded as word got out. In the process of discussing this we coined the term "Neo-Pagan," which were the modern groups, to be distinguished from the primordial pagans. Most of the groups that got involved were from California. There were maybe a dozen groups total.

NARRATOR: As time passed the CAW purchased bigger and better printing technology and *Green Egg* continued to grow in page count. Circulation increased, they began to take advertising, and new people were reached not just by word of mouth, subscription, and trade but by retail sales in bookstores.

REV. DR. J. GORDON MELTON: In March of 1968, the *Green Egg* appeared. From its inauspicious beginnings as a one-page ditto sheet, it grew over 80 issues into a 60-page journal, becoming the most significant periodical in the Pagan movement during the 1970s and made Tim [Oberon] Zell, its editor, a major force in Neo-Paganism (a term which Zell coined).

NARRATOR: The magazine continued to be published, in what was to be the first phase of its existence, for the entire time Tim was in St Louis. During those seminal years it helped to both create and unify a community and the use of the word "Pagan" to describe it. *Green Egg* had a direct influence on many, including a young journalist named Margot Adler.

MARGOT ADLER: My book (*Drawing Down the Moon*) would not exist if it hadn't been for the *Green Egg,* and its letters column. When I was coming into the Pagan movement there were no festivals, there was no internet. There were little newsletters. And most of those you found out about by complete chance, or by knowing someone who knew someone. *Green Egg* devoted some 20-30 pages of each issue to letters, and those letters were from the real theorists and theologians and thealogians of the Pagan movement. It and

Nemeton were the first intellectual Pagan publications. I started doing research for my book in fall of 1975. I took the *Green Egg,* and I looked at every single interesting letter over 20 issues, and I wrote those people letters and said, "Hi! I'm thinking of doing this book on Paganism. Can I come visit you?" And that's how I constructed *Drawing Down the Moon.* Once I had a bunch of people who I went to see, they would introduce me to other people, and one thing led to another. But the *Green Egg* was my best source for guidance.

It is popular today to talk about 'synergy'—a combination that has a greater effect than the simple addition of its components—and that perhaps best describes the effect of *Green Egg.* It connected all the evolving and emerging Goddess and Nature religions into one phenomenon: the Neo-Pagan movement.

NARRATOR: I finally understood what *Green Egg* was about when I read an article in it that explained how Christmas and its traditions (including Jesus' birthday!) were actually taken from other cultures and religions that had been around before Christianity. I was quite surprised. And I think it's safe to say that I wasn't the only one who picked up a copy of GE and had that kind of experience. Like the mimeograph machine that Tim used to print the magazine with, that kind of information wasn't easy to get your hands on.

OZ: I was intensely focused on my Work, and I disciplined myself to get by on six hours sleep a night. My life was a constant training program. I didn't give myself any time to just veg out. From 1970 on, I used to bicycle to work every day, unless it was raining or snowing. It was 11 miles each way. When I was at work I would use my break periods to work on the *Green Egg.* I'd take a bag lunch and sit there at my desk eating and typing at the same time.

I didn't go out and hang out in bars or go to football games. It's amazing what you can do with your life if you make room for it by not doing things that are not productive. Even now I have to make an effort to un-discipline myself, to pry loose and hang out. If I'm left on my own my default mechanism is this focused behavior. If somebody says, "hey, let's go for a walk" or "let's go to a party," then I may break loose and join them. But if I'm left alone I'll just keep on working by sheer momentum. I was kept going by a utopian vision of creating a new world and a new society.

My whole life I have been trying to make the world a better place, and to have an impact and change things for the better. Lance used to refer to me as a "tame fanatic." I had that fanaticism, but it was in the service of the community

NARRATOR: But Tim's efforts to make the world a better place were causing stress in his family life, as was their open relationship.

MARTHA TURLEY: I was always the jealous type. Deep down I was probably not happy with our open relationship. Tim was my first sexual experience, so I made up for lost time. I enjoyed being with the other guys, but I was still jealous of Tim. I never really accepted it too much emotionally. That was there from the beginning. I'm a very passive person. I go along with things and don't cause trouble. I think it comes from hearing my parents argue constantly. I said, "When I get married, I am not going to fight." I don't remember Tim and I ever having any arguments. I always did everything Tim ever wanted to do. I'm not saying that he was a domineering, pushy person. I'm kind of a sheep, you could say.

Tim became more Pagan and I didn't. At our house they used to get together on weekends. If I was there I stayed by myself in the bedroom. Or else I went out with whatever gentleman I was dating then. I don't even know what they did at those rituals. Bryan was at them, but not me.

DEBORAH DIETZ: There was a period of time when I lived at Tim's house. My function was to take care of his son. I think that Martha was more conventional in many respects. The impression I always had of her was that she was being swept along like in a tidal wave. I remember thinking that she was married to someone who was completely different from her—she was a nice woman in a difficult situation.

NARRATOR: The CAW expanded their meetings from Fridays to weekends, for a program of comparative religions…

BRYAN ZELL: Dad wanted to expose me to different churches and religions. He didn't want me to be influenced by just one perspective. So on Sundays we went to different services, everything from a Catholic mass to a Jewish Synagogue to the Hare Krishna Temple. We went to Christian bible schools once or twice. I would ask them questions like, "If there is a God who created us, who created God?"

And they would say, "God just *is*."

And I'd say, "Well, then why can't *we* just be?" We weren't invited back.

DON WILDGRUBE: We would have people from various church denominations come in and talk to our Nest meetings, and we would go to their church services the following week. We had a couple of members that were Quakers that would come by every so often. They told us about their religion, and we would go to their meetings.

I asked Alene (my wife at the time) if she wanted to visit and she came and brought our youngest son, Tom. That was the meeting that Barry and Fu were talking about the Quakers. The only thing that Alene commented about when we got home, she asked if she joined did she had to screw everyone there. She did say that Barry and Fu seemed like good people that she could trust. I just laughed and told her that no there were no things like that and that the two people she trusted were swingers! We went to the Quaker meeting the next week and found it very spiritual with silent meditation until "the Spirit moves you," then say something. It was great.

We also had someone from the Baha'is. He told about his group and when Tim mentioned that we didn't follow the Ten Commandments or other Biblical edicts, he got a strange, horrified look on his face. "If you don't believe in the 10 Commandments, what would keep you from killing me right now?"

Although I like a lot of things about the Baha'is, we didn't pursue it further. Next we had someone from the Christian Science talk to us. The next Sunday Tim, Julie, Tim's son Bryan, and I attended the First Church of Christian Science in St. Louis. It was almost like coming into a Funeral Parlor. There were about three sets of Ushers, each with a pasted-on smile and a white carnation. We went in and got our seats. I found the meeting very boring. They had no trained speakers. The service consisted of someone reading from the Bible, then someone reading a parallel from "Science and Health," and both did a poor job. Even the "sermon" was a text directly from Boston headquarters and was read, poorly.

Finally, one of the readers called for a prayer. He read, "Oh most Holy God, most omnipresent God, most impotent God" (instead of omnipotent). I looked at Tim, Julie looked at me and we strained to keep from laughing. It was after this that we stopped the Comparative Religions group.

OZ: Our comparative religion experiences were very enlightening. It became clear from the outset that none of our guest presenters were the least bit interested in learning anything about us; they were there solely to attempt to convert us to their faiths. I remember one guy who was telling us that social morality was absolutely dependent upon a belief in divine rewards and punishments. He said, "If people didn't believe in heaven and hell, there would be nothing to stop them from killing each other." And we replied that we didn't believe in heaven and hell, but we had no interest in killing anybody. And you could see the wheels turning in this guy's mind, as he realized that there were a lot of people between him and the door who, as far as he could comprehend, would have no reason not to murder him on the spot!

At one point, we were having a weekly book-study group at our house which we called the "Human Values Course," based on an idea in one of Robert Rimmer's books. Eventually, this became the foundation of our CAW Bibliography and study courses. We had a couple of nuns join our meetings, who provided a very interesting perspective!

TOM WILLIAMS: We began to have small (by today's standards) festivals timed at the seasonal points described in Feraferia's *Nine Royal Passions of the Year*. The Royal Passions, by the way, describe the eternal round of the God and the Goddess, called the Royal Pair. Here's a sample: "BELTANE—The festival of full flowering. Sex crowns the holy nakedness of blossoming flesh. By sex the Two are divided only to be molded closer in bliss. All glistening, dewy and hot, the Holy Pair announce their engagement."

OZ: At our 1969 Yule festival, over a hundred people showed up at the house. It was pretty crowded, so we decided we needed a bigger place to gather. We passed the hat around and collected a fair chunk of change.

NARRATOR: At the end of the '60s Tim Zell, the changeling child who hadn't fit in, found himself in the center of a very busy circle of friends and activity. This didn't slow down in 1970, a year of sex, drugs, the first Earth Day, and some major spiritual activity for Tim Zell and his tribe. The circle would soon be expanded to include a great many people and places far beyond what was happening in his St. Louis living room. And it would include not just living beings all over the Earth, but the living Mother Earth herself.

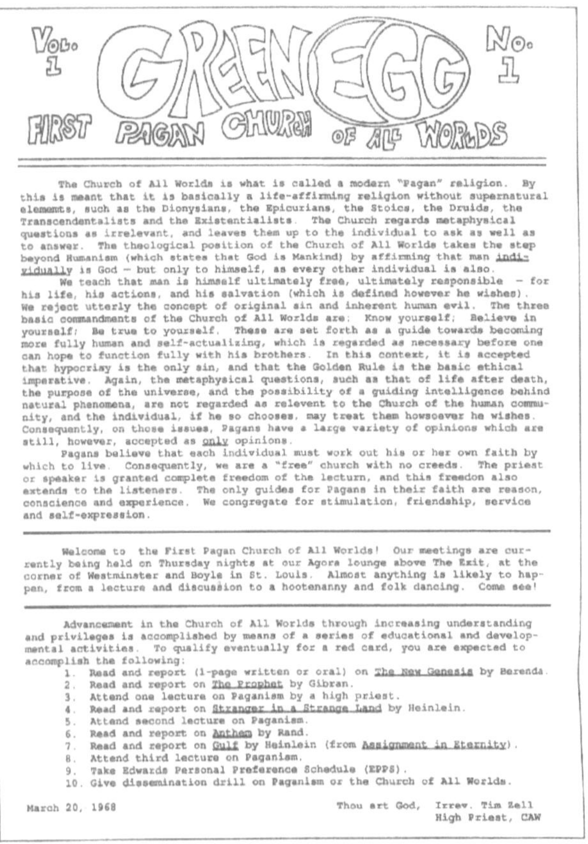

Vol. 1   GREEN EGG   No. 1
FIRST PAGAN CHURCH OF ALL WORLDS

The Church of All Worlds is what is called a modern "Pagan" religion. By this is meant that it is basically a life-affirming religion without supernatural elememts, such as the Dionysians, the Epicurians, the Stoics, the Druids, the Transcendentalists and the Existentialists. The Church regards metaphysical questions as irrelevant, and leaves them up to the individual to ask as well as to answer. The theological position of the Church of All Worlds takes the step beyond Humanism (which states that God is Mankind) by affirming that man _individually_ is God — but only to himself, as every other individual is also.

We teach that man is himself ultimately free, ultimately responsible — for his life, his actions, and his salvation (which is defined however he wishes). We reject utterly the concept of original sin and inherent human evil. The three basic commandments of the Church of All Worlds are: Know yourself; Believe in yourself; Be true to yourself. These are set forth as a guide towards becoming more fully human and self-actualizing, which is regarded as necessary before one can hope to function fully with his brothers. In this context, it is accepted that hypocrisy is the only sin, and that the Golden Rule is the basic ethical imperative. Again, the metaphysical questions, such as that of life after death, the purpose of the universe, and the possibility of a guiding intelligence behind natural phenomena, are not regarded as relevent to the Church of the human community, and the individual, if he so chooses, may treat them howsoever he wishes. Consequently, on those issues, Pagans have a large variety of opinions which are still, however, accepted as _only_ opinions.

Pagans believe that each individual must work out his or her own faith by which to live. Consequently, we are a "free" church with no creeds. The priest or speaker is granted complete freedom of the lecturn, and this freedon also extends to the listeners. The only guides for Pagans in their faith are reason, conscience and experience. We congregate for stimulation, friendship, service and self-expression.

Welcome to the First Pagan Church of All Worlds! Our meetings are currently being held on Thursday nights at our Agora lounge above The Exit, at the corner of Westminster and Boyle in St. Louis. Almost anything is likely to happen, from a lecture and discussion to a hootenanny and folk dancing. Come see!

Advancement in the Church of All Worlds through increasing understanding and privileges is accomplished by means of a series of educational and developmental activities. To qualify eventually for a red card, you are expected to accomplish the following:
1. Read and report (1-page written or oral) on The New Genesis by Berenda.
2. Read and report on The Prophet by Gibran.
3. Attend one lecture on Paganism by a high priest.
4. Read and report on Stranger in a Strange Land by Heinlein.
5. Attend second lecture on Paganism.
6. Read and report on Anthem by Rand.
7. Read and report on Gulf by Heinlein (from Assignment in Eternity).
8. Attend third lecture on Paganism.
9. Take Edwards Personal Preference Schedule (EPPS).
10. Give dissemination drill on Paganism or the Church of All Worlds.

March 20, 1968   Thou art God,   Irrev. Tim Zell
                                                         High Priest, CAW

First issue of *Green Egg.* March 20, 1968.

CHAPTER 9:
"TheaGenesis"
(1970)

So Yes! Yes! to the beating heart,
That echoes the surge of the sea,
And sends blood's course with primal force,
Urged on by the will to be.
And Yes! Yes! to the pulse that flows,
The stream of life's rebirth,
The sacred flame intones your name,
Oh Gaia, soul of the Earth!
~ "Hymn to Gaia" by Tom Williams

ARRATOR: 1970 WAS THE SECOND YEAR OF Richard M. Nixon's presidency. With Nixon as Commander-in-Chief the war in Vietnam continued, and even expanded into the neighboring countries of Cambodia and Laos. In America anti-war activists bombed government buildings and banks, and on the campus of Kent State in Ohio four students were killed by the National Guard. *Rolling Stone Magazine* did a cover story that declaring America to be "a pitiful, helpless, giant." In the midst of all this the CAW decided to try to reach more people by moving from meeting in Tim Zell's house to establishing an actual Church center.

TOM WILLIAMS: We set out to find a suitable center and eventually located a vacant storefront. Interestingly, the place we found was adjacent to another storefront church that was home to a predominantly black congregation called "Mother Martin's Temple of God in Christ." The building, which housed both churches, was long and narrow. Our side had three large rooms arranged in line front-to-back. We decided to allow access according to the Ring system.

The front room (painted green) was open to the public and

contained our printed materials and comfy chairs where we could discuss our philosophy with people who wanted to come by and learn about us. The middle room (painted red) contained desks, records and files, and had a stairway to the basement where we kept the newly-purchased mimeograph machine that was now used to publish *Green Egg*. The back room—its walls painted black with dayglow posters, etc.—was used for rituals and for the inner circle membership. We called it, naturally, "The Inner Sanctum."

I was in charge of making arrangements with the city of St Louis for occupancy permits, rental agreements with the landlord, etc. I encountered a lot of bureaucratic resistance from the city, such as impossible requirements for parking space, load-bearing specifications for the floor, and such. The fact that there was already a church next door in the same building ("Mother Martin's Church of God in Christ") eventually made it impossible for the city to deny us permits.

OZ: We rented it on the first of March, 1970. We spent much of that month getting it all fixed up and ready to go. There was no real grand opening. We had stuff going on in the temple almost every evening. We had study groups, our human values reading program, and a comparative religions program. It was a center of activity. We boarded up the windows in the back room, put up a big metal door and completely sealed it off. We made it a place where we could have weekend retreats, which we did eventually.

I paid most of the expenses for the temple myself. Back in those days it didn't cost much to do something like that. I took a vow of poverty, which meant that my paychecks from the Human Development Corporation were written to the Church, and taxes weren't taken out of them. I used the money that would have gone to taxes to pay for things like the temple and *Green Egg,* and supported my family with the rest. We put the hat out whenever we did anything.

When we put up the big sign out front saying "Church of All Worlds" Mother Martin and her husband came over to meet us and brought coffee and doughnuts. They invited us to their services. But the services that we held in our inner temple were basically done naked, so we couldn't really invite them to join us. It kind of put us in an awkward position, but it never became an issue. What we didn't understand at the time was that Fundamentalist Christians just don't go to other people's services.

TOM WILLIAMS: We actually formed a good relationship with the church next door. Reverend Martin was a 6-foot four strapping black preacher with a booming basso profundo voice and a heart of gold. His wife, Mother Martin, was a solid, good-hearted woman who wore a cloth coat, pill-box hat and purse, and thought it was just wonderful that another church was moving in next door.

OZ: The most amusing episode of that spring was when Mother Martin invited Tom and me to attend their Easter Services. We could hardly refuse, but we were quite taken aback when she and her husband not only welcomed us effusively, but brought us up to the front of the church and seated us up on the stage across from them. It was a long way to the door. And then, after the usual set-up songs and announcements, Mother Martin turned to me and asked if I would lead them all in prayer! I was totally unprepared for this, but somehow I managed to stumble through with appropriately Easterly platitudes about divine rebirth and mortal regeneration—accompanied by many "Amens" from the congregation. Tom was enjoying my discomfort, until I sat down and Mother Martin invited him to do the guest sermon! But really, he amazed not only me but himself as well with a really good one, and everyone was happy.

OZ: We also used the inner sanctum of our Temple for rituals and retreats. It was painted all black, floor, walls and ceiling—including the windows. There was a heavy metal insulated door separating it from the 2nd room (which was painted in red, with little cafe tables). In addition to a huge altar, psychedelic posters and countless dayglow cutouts of stars and planets adorned the walls and ceiling. When only the black lights were on, the background disappeared entirely, as if you were in outer space. There was a full kitchen and bathroom, and many mattresses and cushions, so the room was entirely self-sufficient for the weekend-long Esalen-style encounter groups I conducted there. We were totally isolated, with no clocks or contact with the outside world. We did several of those, and they were quite transformative.

NARRATOR: The activities in the Temple were unique in St. Louis, but not unusual for the times. In other places feminists were holding consciousness raising sessions, humanistic psychologists were experimenting with encounter groups, the repressed were working towards liberation, libertines were having orgies and, oh yes, Pagans, along with countless other seekers of wisdom and truth, were trying to find new spiritualities that were relevant to their lives. And some of this was even happening in rented storefronts.

But the CAW was trying to do all this and more all at once, and in a politically and socially conservative city. If the Temple had been in Cambridge, Berkeley or some other liberal locale, things might have turned out differently. But St. Louis, birthplace of Budweiser beer, is not only in the Bible Belt, it is the buckle of the Bible Belt.

OZ: There was a total eclipse of the sun on March 7, 1970, which passed over just outside of St Louis. And some of the folks who lived there threw an eclipse party that featured a big bowl of electric orange juice (that is, spiked with LSD). At that point I decided that the occasion I had waited years for had arrived. I was waiting for the perfect moment to try LSD, having been given all the big build-up by Tim Leary's writings about having the perfect set and setting.

It was an amazing, totally transformative experience. I had such a great trip—including an incredible sexual encounter with two lovely women in a bathtub full of balloons—that I never actually went out and looked at the eclipse itself! I have regretted this ever since—especially after I finally witnessed such a spectacular celestial event in 1979.

TOM WILLIAMS: In early 1970, some of us decided to get involved with a St Louis group called The Coalition for the Environment. We attended meetings with some well-intentioned liberal types who were trying to work within the system to address some of the pressing issues of urban and automobile pollution, clean air and water issues and local environmental concerns. These were the beginnings of what would eventually blossom into the environmental movement.

Earth Day was a world event even though we didn't realize it at the time. We did notice that we were the only group at the event that called itself a Church. Where were the other churches? It wasn't hard to figure that out. The admonition in the book of *Genesis* that humans shall "have dominion over the Earth and over every creeping thing, etc." suddenly stood out in sharp relief. Why should Christian churches care about Earth Day when their real goal was Heaven and when their Bible admonished them to exploit the Earth? We began to see ever more clearly why people who called themselves Pagans were basically different.

OZ: We decided that we were going to do the Earth Day thing in a big way, with a booth, presentation and display. We designed and worked on them for weeks. One of the things we wanted to do was create a big poster based on Robert Grave's 13-month calendar of the year. While I was going through *National Geographics* and selecting pictures to put on the calendar, a young woman came in to help out.

She was just 18 at the time, and one of those beautiful, Witchy, vegetarian kind of girls that you ran into in those days. Her name was Julie. In the process of working on the calendar, as we got to know each other and talk about what we were doing, we fell in love. Our relationship became quite a romance, and a major focus of my life for the next few years.

So on April 22, we toted all of our stuff to Forest Park and set it up. The idea that Earth Day topics could be of a religious concern was unheard-of at the time. So we made our theme all about what would eventually come to be called "Deep Ecology"—or "Green Religion." In addition to our "Eco-Psychic Calendar," we created a pile of trash with a large globe and a human skeleton (from my days in Pre-Med) tossed akimbo into the heap to convey the idea that trashing the Earth was also destroying humanity, as we were all interconnected. This was the first inkling of the expression—originally stated by Cicero: *Omnia vivunt; omnia inter se conexa* ("Everything is alive; everything is interconnected"). 34 years later, this would become the motto of my Grey School of Wizardry.

I brought Histah, who was then six feet long, and she spent the day wrapped around my shoulders as I talked to people. At one point I sat in the grass with her, and soon a large circle of people gathered around. Some guy on the other side of the circle asked if she'd come to him and curl into his lap the way she was doing with me. I said,

"Close your eyes and visualize her. Tell her in your mind how beautiful she is, and how much you'd like to meet her and befriend her. Invite her to come to you."

The guy did that, and while everyone else watched (the guy couldn't see this because his eyes were closed), Histah uncoiled herself from my lap, crawled across the open space, and right into the guy's lap. Needless to say, everyone was quite impressed!

TOM WILLIAMS: That May 4th, for daring to protest a brutal and senseless war that was destroying the soul of America, four students were shot dead by the National Guard at Kent State University in Ohio. Just in case anybody had trouble remembering what his or her ethical priorities were.

OZ: I first heard about the Kent State Massacre that evening, in Forest Park. At the World's Fair Pavilion atop Government Hill a bunch of young people were standing around a trash barrel fire and talking about it. Some were throwing their draft cards into the fire. I pulled mine out of my wallet and charred it all around the edges, so I could still keep the burned remains to display.

Julie and I became passionate lovers. The summer of 1970 involved a lot of sex and acid. Some of us went into it hammer and tongs. We discovered an abandoned gravel quarry along the Mississippi that became our swimming hole for skinny dipping. We would go out and party all weekend.

DON WILDGRUBE: Our festivals lasted way into the night, and most people stayed all night and crashed in various spots around the house. In the morning, Julie would fix pancakes for all of us. One Sunday morning, we were sitting on the floor around a very low table, and since the festival the night before, none of us had any clothes on. We were hidden by the low table. There was a knock on the door. Julie answered it wearing an apron (and nothing else). The Jehovah Witnesses came in and started preaching to us. Soon Julie came in with more pancakes and bent over to serve them. Her bare butt was facing them, and just about that time Tim got up to discuss things more. They looked at Tim's naked body, looked back at Julie and then the rest of us, and decided that good Christians should not be there and beat a hasty retreat!

OZ: We had lots of adventures as a group, often in caravans of several cars. One of the most memorable was a road trip in August of 1970 to Normal, Illinois, to visit Michael Hurley, who was teaching at the college there. We drove up in my Cadillac and had a barbeque picnic at a park which was adjacent to a cornfield. Julie and I got it into our heads to go out into the cornfield and make love. We left our clothes just inside the cornfield, and went deeper into it naked. While we were off having our little tryst, the cops came into the park and told everyone they had to leave. Hearing the sirens and commotion, we snuck back to discover that someone had taken our clothes, but left us a couple of beach towels. We wrapped these around ourselves like togas, and rejoined our Nestmates as they were all packing up to leave.

That evening, at Michael's house, we covered the floor with plastic, got naked, and sprayed whipped cream and oil all over ourselves for a rollicking frolic. But afterwards, we realized that Michael had no shower, so we all bundled up in sheets and towels, and drove over to a friend of his, where we trooped in and out of the shower—a procession of gooped-up naked people that must have provided some amusement to the host!

My old Beatnik friend, Jim Igoe, was a gifted Irish poet with the traditional alcohol problem. I read about LSD being used as a cure for alcoholism, so I took Jim into the sanctum and gave him a suitable dose, for which I served as his guide. At one point in his trip, I walked over to a wall and grabbed two water pipes that ran from floor to ceiling about two feet apart, and a foot out from the wall. Since they, like the wall, were painted black, they were completely invisible under black light. By gripping the pipes firmly, and not missing a stride, I was able to walk right up the wall to stand upside-down on the ceiling, looking Jim eyeball-to-eyeball and completely disorienting him as to which way was up! The experiment was successful, and Jim never went back to alcohol—though he did become a serious tripper!

In August, upon Jim's recommendation, I read Robert Grave's *The White Goddess.* Until that time CAW didn't have a coherent theology, per se. We vaguely embraced mythology, in general, and used science fiction as a mythic framework. But there was no coherent theological basis of how it all worked. Grave's book moved us in that direction, at least from the point of view of the impact of the Divine Feminine in culture and literature. It gave me something to think about.

TOM WILLIAMS: It was about then that we began hearing from a number of Witchcraft groups around the country and became increasingly aware that there was a great deal in common between what we were starting to grok as Pagan in terms of the writings of Fred Adams and a lot of what these Wiccan groups were saying and doing. So Tim and I signed up for a 16-week course in Witchcraft taught by a local St Louis Witch named Deborah Letter. I still have the course material from that class and was impressed to see that the definitions and orientation of the class does not adhere to any one Wiccan tradition but are general enough to appeal to more general Pagan sensitivities. For example, the definition of a Witch in the first lesson is as follows: "A Witch is a person, either male or female, who has learned to use the powers of the body and mind (as well as those of nature) to either help or hinder."

That's a definition that could apply to shamans and magicians in general. After we took the class, Tim and I both eventually received initiations in different Wiccan traditions. However, the generalist nature of the background we received in our first encounters with shamanism and magick (in addition to the "eco-psychic" awareness we had begun to cultivate) made it difficult for us to commit to any single, strictly defined tradition. We were on our way to becoming Pagan generalists—a trait that has marked the Church of All Worlds ever since.

NARRATOR: As editor of *Green Egg,* Tim was probably the best-informed person on the planet about the Pagan population, and at that point he had still not heard anything about the existence of real Witches or a Witchcraft movement. The prevailing mythology then in popular culture was that Witches were different from regular humans, who were referred to as "mortals." One had to be born a Witch—Witchcraft wasn't presented as a religion or something that someone could join or get trained in. And in fact this fictional idea of Witches continues today in the Harry Potter books, where anyone who doesn't come from a magical family is a "muggle."

OZ: I had first become aware of modern Witchcraft in the late '60s. When Sybil Leek's *Diary of a Witch* was published in 1968, she came over to the US on a promotional tour, and appeared at Washington University, where I went to see her. I sat in the front row, where I kept trying to contact her telepathically. I was quite disappointed (and disillusioned) when she didn't respond! But I didn't give up on my quest to find real Witches, and read everything I could find on the subject, by people like Louise Heubner, Valerie Worth, and Gerald Gardner.

In the late summer of 1970 Tom Williams and I began formal training in magick and Witchcraft under Deborah Letter, a classic Hippie Witch who had opened an archetypical occult shop called "The Cauldron" in 1968, and just started offering classes. She taught a mixture of Strega, Ceremonial Magick, Leland, Crowley, and Paul Huson, and we had really amazing rituals in her temple room—where I was introduced to The Fugs and The Mothers of Invention.

I received my first formal Wiccan initiation in a Great Rite with her in the spring of 1971. I gave her in trade the articulated human skeleton that I had kept from my days at Westminster, and at the same time I acquired from one of her other students a full deerskin shaman's robe—antlers, hooves, and all. She is now Deborah Bourbon, with the store "Pathways" in St Louis, and she mentions me on her website as her student. She still has the skeleton, whom she calls "Roach," and brings him out at every party.

My lifetime of interest and pursuit of studies of biology, natural history, evolution, and paleontology all came together over Labor Day weekend of 1970. At that point Julie was getting ready to go away to college. We decided that we needed to do something really spectacular before she left. Jim Igoe, the guy who'd turned me on to *The White Goddess,* had a brother named Vince who was a prominent attorney with a very nice house. Vince had gone away for the weekend, and left Jim in charge of the house. And he invited us to come over on the evening of Sept. 6.

Jim had a few doses of what he had been told was organic mescaline (though I later found out from Lance that there was no such thing). It was probably acid laced with something else. We went into the back yard in the night where there was a big trampoline. We lay stark naked on it on our backs looking up at the sky. It was easy to imagine just floating off into space. I know the constellations—it's one of those things I picked up as a kid. Julie, like most city people, didn't. But this was a clear night, and you could see the stars well. I started tracing the constellations to show her what some of the more prominent ones were. I discovered that if I stuck my finger up into the sky and drew a line with my aura, the line would stay there (in acid-speak this is called "trails"). So it was easy for me to connect the dots.

I made the Vulcan "live long and prosper" sign (from *Star Trek*), and got absorbed in watching the auras of my fingers as they moved back and forth. And in the pattern of the auras, I had a vision of a cell dividing. As the concept of the cell formed in my mind, I linked myself with what I was seeing. I went diving down through the continuity of cellular division, of mitosis. It was like running a film backwards as the cells divided, until I was back to the first cell that I was, a zygote fertilized in my mother's womb. I felt how my life began, when I was conceived as a single cell that multiplied and became all of me.

And then I went further down, through all the cells that coalesced to form my parents. I kept going through this reverse coalescence all the way back through geological time, experiencing all these cells congealing, all the way back for half a billion years, 'til I reached that first original primal cell that began all complex life on Earth, and from which we are all descended (what scientists now call LUCA—"Last Universal Common Ancestor). And it was like all of us were condensed in that single cell. It was sort of like the Big Bang of biological evolution.

And then I ran the film back the other way—forward. And that cell divided and all the living things came out of it. And the different species emerged, and I saw the whole tree of life open up, down through the different lineages. I traced the protoplasm through all these different divisions, which was like tracing the entire history of the DNA molecule. As that life from the first cell spread out across the planet, my consciousness rose from the surface and looked down on the whole Earth below me.

Just that previous year the first photographs of the Earth from space had been taken by the Apollo astronauts returning from the moon. So I rose above the Earth and I saw the life spreading across the planet. And I saw all this connection, I saw all this as one, vast, single organism. Because it was absolutely identical to the way my own body had grown from the first fertilized cell. I realized that evolution was nothing but embryology on a planetary scale.

I looked down, and at that point, the mythology of Gaea overlaid itself upon this entire organism. I suddenly saw the Earth in a whole new light, through this perspective. I saw this single vast living being instead of just a planet full of unrelated creatures. And at that point, it was like She opened her eyes and smiled at me, and said "Now you know me."

And I did know Her. I was overwhelmed with this incredible sense of love, kinship, and recognition. It was an astonishing epiphany. And with tears streaming from my eyes, my immediate response was, "I shall ever serve You!" And I have, from that moment forward.

It wasn't just a vision; it was a Revelation. I felt this in the deepest part of my soul. It is still hard to speak of this without choking up with tears, because it was the most profound experience of my life.

I have no idea how much time passed. When we came down Julie and I went into the house and I told Jim about the whole experience. And if I hadn't done that the whole thing might have simply gone. It's like a dream—if you don't tell it to someone you can lose it. At the end of all that, Jim said, "Well, I knew that if I hung around with you long enough you would get some great revelation. That's the kind of guy you are." He encouraged me to write it all down, which I did over the next few days.

A week later was our weekly Nest meeting, at Tiny's, and I came in with it all written up, and delivered my first actual sermon in the history of the Church of All Worlds. Interestingly enough, I got a considerable amount of argument. There were people who were deeply offended, fearing that this church that they had joined specifically because it didn't have any official dogma was now going to be saddled with such. They thought I was going to establish some orthodox set of doctrines that everybody was going to be required to believe in. So there was opposition. But the seeds were planted.

I kept coming back to it over the next few months. Though I contributed the gist of it to a couple of books by Leo Louis Martello

(*Black Magic, Satanism & Witchcraft;* and *Witchcraft: The Old Religion*), I didn't officially publish it in *Green Egg* 'til the next year. It was so far out there, so radical, that I really wanted to be on solid ground before I tried to bring it out to the world. I sought more information, background and details on the biology involved. I did research into genetics and DNA and cosmology and nucleotides and the nature of amino acids found in meteorites.

Forty years later, we know a whole lot more. But this was three years before James Lovelock first published his famous "Gaia Hypothesis." He was an atmospheric biochemist on assignment from NASA to help them design sensors for some of their probes they were developing to detect life on other planets. And that led to a lot of additional research, which essentially confirmed the premise that all life on Earth is a single organism. Lovelock said he initially got the idea from seeing that famous photograph of the Earth. But he saw it from the outside looking in. I saw it from the inside out, equating evolution with embryology.

TOM WILLIAMS: Tim had articulated what came to be known as "TheaGenesis." Basically what that means is that the Earth is a living being; the various biomes and ecosystems, plant and animal communities, and their interaction are analogs to the organs and systems of a living body. In addition, this Being has a spirit, a consciousness. That spirit has been instinctively revered and worshipped through the ages by native peoples as a Goddess whose names are as numerous as the cultures and peoples who honor Her. Eventually, we settled on calling her Gaea for the Greek Earth Mother. Still, we worship Her in her many names according to the appropriate festivals and energies that were at hand.

The Church of All Worlds transformed that year of 1970 into a new dimension, not abandoning the values on which it had been founded, but adding the ecstatic identity of ourselves and all living things with this Grand and Nurturing Being, this Divine Mother, and realizing that we were both Her and Her children. The Church of all Worlds had finally become Pagan in the truest sense of the word.

RALPH METZNER: Oberon Zell was the first person to conceive and publish the biological and metaphysical foundations of what has become known as the "Gaia Theory"—the unified body and emergent soul of the living Earth. Oberon's profound reconciliation of science, mythology and spirituality inspired and infused a world-wide neo-Pagan, panentheistic movement.

MARGOT ADLER: In 1970 Tim Zell began writing about the planet Earth as deity, as a single living organism, and this became the Church of All Worlds' central myth. Since 1971, the myth has been revised constantly and has become a unique eco-religious perception…

Tim took the reader on a long tour through biology, cell division, reproduction, and evolutionary theory. The central idea of his tour was that all life had seemingly developed from a single original cell that divided and subdivided, passing its cellular material on and on. All life was interconnected, part of a single living organism.

The publication of "TheaGenesis" was followed by a number of other articles which had a strong influence on the development of the Church of All Worlds. CAW Co-founder Lance Christie wrote of them:

> "You've begun the creation of a myth, and a most livable one at that. It is a myth which defines a role for man and answers a lot of mystic questions. It seems to fit very will within the total tradition of man's symbols and myths, expressing in clearer and expanded form a theme as old as consciousness can remember….the worldview you are creating is compatible with objective consciousness and science in a way no other religious myth is…"

Several years after the TheaGenesis articles were written, *Newsweek* magazine, as well as a number of less popular journals, mentioned the work of British scientist James Lovelock, who had posited the "Gaia Hypothesis:" that the living matter on Earth—air, oceans, and land—was all part of a system that Lovelock called after the Earth-Mother Goddess, Gaia… Zell entered into a brief correspondence with Lovelock, comparing their world views.

The effect of 'TheaGenesis; the Gaea Thesis' on CAW's history and on the thoughts and goals of church priests, priestesses, and members has been extraordinary.

"Gaea" by Daniel Blair Stewart & OZ, 1989

CHAPTER 10:
Cross-Pollinating
(1970-1971)

Z: AROUND ELECTION TIME, 1970, OUR Kingsbury Temple was set up for a bust, along with other counter-culture groups in town like the underground radio station, KDNA.

TOM WILLIAMS: One night there was a raid by officers looking for drugs and underage girls allegedly staying there. The cops found no drugs but confiscated some switches and wires we had gotten to set up a burglar alarm system. The next day the *St. Louis Post Dispatch* ran an article on the raid, saying the police had entered the temple where "Charles Manson-like activities were going on," and had seized material used for making bombs.

OZ: The newspapers printed my picture, with my long dark hair and beard, practically side by side with Manson's. Apparently he also was some kind of fan of *Stranger in a Strange Land,* so that also got mentioned. But Mother Martin next store stuck up for us, which helped us turn this around.

TOM WILLIAMS: Fortunately, we had a lawyer who called in the TV people to counter the charges and threatened the paper with a lawsuit. There was a correction printed in the next edition that was followed by an interview with Tim that actually cast the CAW in a positive light. The incident was a net gain for our image in the community. We were also able to go on the local alternative radio station, KDNA, and present our case and our philosophy.

NARRATOR: The Temple was closed after six months. After that a lot of the Church activity moved back to the Zell's house, which put additional strain on a marriage that was already having difficulties.

DEBORAH DIETZ: There was a period of time when I lived at Tim's house. My function was to take care of his son. I think that Martha was more conventional in many respects. The impression I always had of her was that she was being swept along like in a tidal wave. I remember thinking that she was married to someone who was completely different from her—she was a nice woman in a difficult situation.

OZ: Martha wasn't opposed to the Church stuff, but she wasn't interested at all in any of it. Both of us during that period were dating other people. I still spent my nights at home—Julie and I didn't sleep over together, except on the weekends when the CAW was having seasonal festivals at the quarry along the Mississippi.

During this period of time my life began to shift in a different direction, away from the urban life and work that I had been doing and towards the rural community life that had always been a dream of mine. We started planning to buy some land. My attention, thoughts, magick, and correspondences with people all became about that move.

This shifted the dynamic at home. Martha really did not want to do that. She had grown up in the country on a farm, and the last thing in the world she wanted to do was move back to one. At that point we had been together almost ten years. If anything, what she wanted to do with her life was to be more of an urban person. So we started talking about that, and agreed that at some point we would have to go in different directions. In early 1971 Martha started dating a guy named John who was a lot more like what she had been looking for. She was looking for a father figure, and I just didn't fit that role.

Around spring break Julie decided she had had enough of college. It wasn't working out for her, and she wanted to move in with me. Around that time Martha was spending more time with John and feeling that this was what she was really looking for. So, starting around March 1971 Martha moved out and Julie moved in—there was a brief overlap period when both of them were there but we worked it out okay. It was very amicable at that time. Our lives were clearly going in different directions. What we wanted out of life was completely different.

MARTHA TURLEY: As I got older then I became not so much into the Hippie life. I had multiple partners to begin with and then I met an older man. He was married and had children. Eventually I met my second husband, John, and married him. He was married at the time, too. When that girl Julie moved in it became a choice of living with the two of them or moving out. John left his wife and we got an apartment together. I didn't want to take Bryan out of the school that he was in. So he would stay with Tim and go to school during the week, and I would have him on weekends. Bryan didn't want to eat at their house because Julie was always making everything out of tofu. He wasn't crazy about that.

BRYAN ZELL: Julie was a strict vegetarian and I was a fussy eater. I couldn't stand her food. I called it Hippie goulash. She made her own yogurt too, but it never had any flavor to it.

OZ: Julie would make up little signs and post them around the house. One on the bathroom mirror reminded: "Things to do today: Brush your teeth; Wash your face; Smash the State!" Another, over the toilet, said: "Flush twice, it's a long way to Washington!"
Several of the people that we had been discussing the community adventure with said that they were ready to make the move. These included Erinna Northwind, with her husband and their kids, Tad and Sarah; and Craig Daniels from Minnesota. Between us all, if we sold our homes and cashed in all of our resources, we would have enough money to buy the land. We were looking at a 100-acre farm property down in the Ozarks with a river bordering it on three sides. It had a farmhouse, barns and old orchards—as well as a marvelous cave underneath!

NARRATOR: At the end of April, 1971, Erinna Northwind and her family moved from Florida to St. Louis to be a part of the intentional community to be called Lothlorien. They lived in the Annandale house with Tim, Julie and Bryan while waiting for that to happen. During this time the CAW activities continued to be held there. Tim Zell, in addition to all this, was still working full time and trying to set up the deal for the rural land. After about two months Erinna's family found a place of their own and moved out, and her husband started working in the city.

OZ: We kept making trips to the land and negotiating with the owner, but it never came together. He wouldn't return our calls. We had the money and were all living in what we considered to be a temporary situation. Our lives were on hold. What we eventually learned was that after we began talking to him he also began negotiating with a real estate speculator who was trying to essentially buy the property out from underneath us. So eventually the whole thing fell through. That really screwed us up. We had changed our lives to move to that property.

At the end of August, Judy O'Rourke and her kids, Laura, Chip, and Sandy moved in with us for awhile, along with Craig Daniels, so we always had a full house. And Erinna and her kids continued to spend a lot of time there. I have fond memories of reading aloud chapters from *The Weirdstone of Brisingamon* every evening to all the kids. Laura, Chip, and Bryan bonded instantly, and became great friends, having many adventures together.

OZ: Here's what Judy's daughter Laura wrote about her family's arrival at the end of August, 1971:

LAURA O'ROURKE DAVIS: Somehow, my mother had guided three sleepy children off the bus and into a cab at the Greyhound station during an ungodly hour in the morning. Dropping the biggest suitcase by the front door, my mother pauses to find the light switch. I push inside behind my sister and brother, and stop too. The walls and the ceiling are painted totally black. "I didn't know you could use black to paint a house," I say.

"Well, you can," says my brother, "See, even the ceiling is black." My mother shuts the door as we step hesitantly inside, huddled together. The large cabinet in front of us is covered with papers on the top, and there is a long table about two feet off the floor in the middle of the room.

"Where are the people, Mommy?" my sister asks.

"They are on vacation, and we will be taking care of their house and pets for them until they return at the end of the month." Oh. Where were we supposed to sleep? In their bedrooms? No, my mother instructs. We will all sleep out here, in the living room.

This won't be hard to do, since there are four mattresses and box springs along the walls of the L-shaped room, rather than a traditional couch and chairs. They are covered with Indian printed cotton bedspreads that match my mothers' paisley peasant blouses. It is late, and we wash up to fall quickly asleep in this new place.

The next morning, I wake to find my mother mopping the kitchen floor. My mother had starred in a television commercial for Windex once few years earlier. We would proudly scream "It's YOU!" to her whenever we saw her beautiful smiling face appear on the screen as she said, "I like the ammonia!"

Kitchen sterilized, she begins to vacuum the living room. Pulling up a mattress to get close to the wall, she shrieks, non-stop, as we run to her side. Still shrieking, she points to the floor. "WHAT is THAT?!" she manages to gasp.

"That" turns out to be a very large South American tegu lizard. We run to find the letter on the table addressed to us, with instructions in case this happened... The lizard has been roaming around for awhile, and when it comes out, would we please kind enough to feed it? "We're supposed to feed it," my brother says.

The letter provides details on the raw egg and cat food recipe we should put on the floor in a bowl for That. My mother is sitting across the living room, head in her hands, as we take over the management of this creature. He seems to be happy, creeping towards the bowl on his four short legs. "This is a pretty cool place," my brother announces.

Soon we discover the other resident pets. Fred, the white rat, lives under the laundry pile in the basement. When Fred is hungry, or when he smells our dinner, he hops up the stairs and comes to stand near the dinner table. Table scraps are all he needs, the directions told us. Okay, no problem for us to share our vegetables! Even

Judy leans over to offer it bread. "Hey, at least it doesn't have a litter box!" I observe. My mother puts down her fork, silently.

As we attempt to tidy the entry hall table and slide some papers to one side, we realize that this is a cage. Histah, the seven-foot boa constrictor, is securely in her cage made by taking a car's windshield and attaching it to an opened cabinet. We can see the snake coiled and resting in the back corner. Reviewing the instructions, I am grateful to learn Histah will not need any food until they return, but "it would be nice if we changed her water dish." It is something none of us wants to attempt, but finally my mother leans over the top of the cage and pours in some clean water. Histah sticks out her tongue, but remains curled up in the corner. We secure the latch on the top in case she decides to move around.

From the outside, this house looks like the other suburban ranches on the block. The neighborhood is completely middle-class, but the streets are unusual. Instead of being paved with asphalt, the streets are covered with gravel, and a tar truck drives by spraying fresh black liquid tar on top to keep the dust down. This is something we had never seen in New York, and it seems rather odd. "We're not in Kansas anymore," my brother jokes. Ever since the Greyhound bus had traveled through Kansas from Minnesota, this reference to the Wizard of Oz is particularly funny to us.

After three weeks of playing in this house and in their backyard, we sense that something is changing. My mother is re-washing everything. "They will be home soon!" she tells us, putting down the telephone. "I am getting the house ready!"

Later that evening, Tim, Julie, and Bryan walk thorough their front door; they do not ring the doorbell. They hug us, introducing themselves, and thank us for taking care of their pets, and admire the way my mother has cleaned up the house without changing anything. "It smells soooo much better than it did!" Bryan smiles. His age is right between my brother and me. I had just turned 12, Chip is 10.5, and it turns out Bryan is eleven.

We all sit down cross-legged around the low table; Tim explains he had cut the legs down to make it so there was no need to use chairs. This was a more natural position for people to sit in, he explains, and the beds were off their frames so that people could be closer to the Earth.

Tim is about my mother's age, in his early 30s, I guess. He has a full mane of black hair, and a thick, full beard that reaches down to touch his chest hair. When he smiles, his eyes crinkle and his teeth look so shiny framed by his black beard. I have not ever met a person like him before, certainly not in the Mormon Church. He is gentle, and when he speaks to us, the children, it is with full attention and respect. When I speak to him, I feel like he is paying attention and cares, and I like him. Even though the house belongs to him, I feel like we all belong here equally.

(*~From Scratching the Surface–Polishing my Soul,*
an Autobiography by Laura O'Rourke Davis)

NARRATOR: During all this time Tim was a steady worker at the Human Development Corporation and using his salary to fund the Church and *Green Egg,* which were both growing in popularity. There wasn't much time or money left over for his personal life.

Julie did some nude photo modeling work to bring in some money to help with their financial situation. One night she brought Tim down to the studio with her to have some professional photographs taken that could be used for PR work.

OZ: I wore my white robes and brought along Histah. We got some really great photos, and then headed home. On the way, we were pulled over by the cops. It seemed they still had a warrant out for me over some case which I had already gone to court over years ago and had all charges ("suspicion of trespassing") dismissed. But they arrested me anyway, and threw me in jail in my robes, which was all I was wearing. So there I was, this white guy in a white robe with a pointy hood, tossed into a cell with a bunch of very tough-looking black guys. Awkward, to say the least. Thinking quickly, I tucked the hood into the back of the robe and came on as a nutty cartoon-style end-of-the-world street preacher; the beard and long hair reinforced that image. That got me left alone until Julie could show up the next morning and bail me out.

NARRATOR: A few years later one of the photos from that shoot turned out to be quite significant. But the money earned wasn't enough to make much of a difference for their household...

OZ: Julie had thrown herself completely into all this, and yet she and I never really got a chance to build a life together. I wasn't paying enough attention to my family. She was far too young to be a mother and got into a competitive thing for my attention. One time she was playing chess with Bryan, and he was beating her, so she flew into a rage and knocked over the chessboard. The pieces went flying across the room. She yelled, "No nine-year-old kid has a right to beat me at chess!" Whoah!

My larger vision of the community, and all the activities with CAW and GE, took precedence, and I neglected the closer stuff that was really important—especially my wonderful son, Bryan. This is one of the saddest aspects of that period—and one I have deeply regretted ever since. One time we were sitting together at dinner, and Bryan asked each of us, "What is the most important thing in the world to you?"

We all gave our answers, and mine, uttered with great pomposity, was, "Why, the whole world itself!"

But Bryan's answer, from his open heart, shamed me: "The most important thing in the world to me," he said, "is my family."

In my fanatic obsession with saving the world, I never could get into just looking out for my own best interest—or that of my family. Most religious people are only interested in personal salvation, not in making the world a better place for present and future generations. But in my whole life I have never given a thought to personal salvation, and I've been disdainful of people who have that obsession. It always seemed narrow-minded, provincial, and selfish to me. Decades later, I finally came to appreciate the importance of family, and have tried to make up for my early failings as a son, husband, and father.

BRYAN ZELL: Dad spent all of his spare time working on the *Green Egg,* and I was a little bit jealous of that. We never played sports together.

OZ: So in late '71, after everyone else had moved out, Julie, Bryan and I really tried to make it work as a family. The biggest difficulty during that period was having to cope with extreme poverty. In my entire life, I've never achieved financial prosperity. I have not focused my life on making a fortune or really even earning a good living. That can be a real draw-back if you have a family. I'm trying to get better at that, but it's always been kind of an after-thought to me.

Of course, what I didn't realize at the time, but found out years later, was that Martha had been secreting a good portion of our income into her own private bank account, as a Nest-egg for when we inevitably divorced! But I have never held this against her—it was a perfectly prudent thing to do. Perhaps I should have done the same.

And then Martha got re-married. She and her new husband, John Kirby, went off somewhere for a secret wedding and didn't invite anyone. Then John pushed to file for custody of Bryan. Essentially, he had always wanted a kid. So it suddenly became an issue. They didn't even have a room for him, but they filed for custody and we went to court. Martha made the case that we were Pagans and that we had nudity in our home and stuff like that. The Christian judge decided that the kid should go with his mother. There wasn't a whole lot that we could do about it.

BRYAN ZELL: They had snuck into my dad's house and taken a bunch of photographs that they used in court against him. The judge asked me who I wanted to live with. At the time I thought I should stick with my mom. I think that kind of hurt my father's feelings. I sometimes wonder where I would be today if I had stayed in his custody.

OZ: I was devastated by the ruling. As far as I know it was the first such child custody case in the Pagan community, involving the religion and lifestyle of a Pagan parent as a justification for having their kid taken away. Over the years this became an issue throughout the community in more and more situations. There is a basis for those concerns. But it wasn't what we were about.

John really resented me on many levels. One evening, as we were having a Nest meeting at our house, he showed up drunk and actually challenged me to a fight! We all got dressed and trooped out to the front lawn, where everyone gathered in a circle around John and me. He took a swing at me, which I blocked with the same reflexes I'd honed to ward off my mother's slaps. Then I knocked his feet out from under him, pushed him to the ground, and pinned him. It was over in moments, and I didn't even break a sweat. But of course, he never forgave me for the humiliation.

Somewhere during that time a bunch of local Hippies got some land on which they decided to create a summer camp experience for kids. They called it "Camp Tribe," and I sent Bryan there for two summers. They built tree houses, rope swings, fire circles, and even a miniature golf course using bent sticks for putters and black walnuts for balls! Everyone had to find their role in the Tribe; the counselors, of course, being the Elders. Bryan achieved the position of Shaman. It happened this way:

Bryan had early discovered a gift for magick, which he developed in his own fashion. Much of it revolved around finding particularly interesting stones, to which he would attribute associations—usually regarding weather-working. For instance, one time when we were out walking he picked up a dark stone with white specks that looked like snowflakes. He promptly decreed this to be a "snowstone." The following April, he came home from school complaining that it hadn't really snowed all winter. So he got out his snowstone, placed it on his altar, did his juju, and the next day there was a blizzard and the schools had to be closed. Since he'd previously told the kids at school what he was going to do, he acquired quite a reputation!

Well, this time at Camp Tribe, the campers were told to take their sleeping bags and make their own campsites away from each other. Bryan got his all set up, and turned off his flashlight, when he noticed a strange glow in the dark nearby. Flicking on the light, he could see nothing unusual. But with the light off, he could see an arch of rooted wood glowing with phosphorescence. Of course, I know this phenomenon as "foxfire," a bioluminescence created under rare conditions by a few species of fungi that decay wood. But neither Bryan, the counselors, nor any of the campers knew this.

Bryan called everyone over to see, and they were all suitably amazed. So one of the counselors asked Bryan what they should do regarding this miracle. Bryan said, "We should build an altar." And right nearby he discovered a pile of stones from a long-gone building foundation. They all worked together to build the altar, then someone asked if there was some magick they could do with it. Since there was a drought going on at the time, Bryan suggested they should make it rain. He found a suitable rainstone, placed it on the altar, and got everyone to visualize rain. The next day it poured, and all the kids tore off their clothes and frolicked in the rain. After that, Bryan's position as the tribe's shaman was secure! When I came out the next weekend, I got the whole story from the counselors.

I deeply regret that during all those years in St Louis, I only visited my grandmother Gogi—whom I had adored all my life—a couple of times. The last time I saw her, she was afflicted with Alzheimer's, and had no idea who I was. I would tell her I was her grandson, Tim, and she would immediately ask again, "Who are you?" I was so emotionally traumatized seeing her like that—and the specter that I might someday become so myself—that I never went back to see her again. Eventually she died of pneumonia on Jan. 16, 1987, at the age of 95, when I was out in California. I was never notified of her death, nor invited to the funeral. I only learned of these particulars in early 2009, as I was gathering information for this autobiography.

We continued to have Church Nest meetings, festivals, and to put out the *Green Egg*. The circulation of *Green Egg* continued to increase. I did all the typing, layout and design for each issue. (I did most of that at my office job on my lunch breaks.) I didn't do much of the actual writing because there was so much stuff coming in from other people. My main job was to be an editor. I would deal with all the letters than came in. I really enjoyed it—I had ink in my blood. I learned how to do every single aspect of it.

When the issue was all ready and printed up we would have collating parties. People really looked forward to this—it was like a quilting bee. We'd lay all the pages out on a long table and sit around it on pillows on the floor. People would collate the pages, and we'd straighten them out and staple them. We'd bundle them and put on the mailing labels. Most of it would be done in one day, in one big push. We were all naked when we did this—we kept the temperature at around 80° for Histah, so it was uncomfortable to keep clothes on, which was part of the plan. After all, there was a sign inside the front door which asked, "Did you remember to dress?"

MARGOT ADLER: Eight or nine people sat around a long table that was covered with stacks of freshly-printed pages. Th sound of friendly chatter mingled with the rustling of pages, the steady firing of a stapling machine, and the occasional crunching of popcorn, which was being passed around in a large bowl... Only one person in the room was wearing any clothes, a fact that didn't seem particularly noticeable after a few minutes... Everyone—dressed or undressed—was engaged in the business of the day, which was sorting, collating, stapling and mailing the 74th issue of *Green Egg*. This peculiar journal had become one of the most important sources of information on Neo-Paganism, and played a key role in facilitating communication among Neo-Pagan groups.

(~Margot Adler, Drawing Down the Moon, pp. 265-6)

We had somebody named Calvin back in New York who was doing mailing labels for us back in the days when computers used punch cards. We were certainly the first Pagan publication to use a computerized database mailing list. And this guy just did it as a service. I never met him face-to-face. Every issue we'd send him all of our corrections and updates, and he'd send us back printed labels and a directory. That kept us going for years.

NARRATOR: When I began to get *Green Egg* it was mimeographed. Mimeograph machines were not created for personal use—they were mostly used by businesses and schools. And there were no places like Kinkos then where you could just drop an order off and have them quickly print it for you. The only way to make a copy of something at home was with carbon paper! So for Tim Zell to buy a mimeograph machine, set it up in his house, and use it to connect people, share ideas and communicate was certainly a magical act.

OZ: Eventually we got a little Rex Rotary desktop printing press that we put in our basement, then we got a bigger one, and finally we bought a big Multilith which was in our basement briefly till we moved it out and put it in Don Wildgrube's basement.

NARRATOR: Tim, Julie and Zell were able to take a road trip together at the end of the summer of 1971. This was affordable, even for them, since gas was so cheap, and everywhere they went they stayed at people's houses and apartments. In fact, that was the whole point of the trip. Their goal was to attend Noreascon, the 29th World Science Fiction Convention, which was held in Boston that year.

But it was the journey, not the destination, that was most important. And Tim Zell was a man on a Mission from the Goddess.

OZ:	In a sense, without being conscious of it at the time, the pilgrimages I was making from one end of the country to the other were seeding and pollinating events that had never been done before. This was many years before there were festivals where people got to meet each other. So what you would have would be a small number of groups in a particular area, who may have been vaguely aware of each other, but they didn't have much interaction. There were no big public gatherings on Beltane, Midsummer or Samhain. But we would show up, and because I was publishing *Green Egg,* and it was the only publication that was interdenominational—it wasn't just one group's own little newsletter—it would be an excuse for people to all come together and meet.

BRYAN ZELL: Dad has always been a great networker. He would do his research in advance. When we went on these road trips he knew where we were going and who we were going to stay with. Wherever he went he had a circle of people who were just fascinated by every word that came out of his mouth. As a child I was awestruck by this. I was a little shy.

OZ:	That was our first personal contact with the better-known figures in the Pagan community. We had lunch with Robert Rimmer, author of *The Harrad Experiment.* We really hit it off, and he gave me several cases of his latest book, *The Rebellion of Yale Marrat,* to circulate among CAW folk. Susan Roberts had just published *Witches USA.* In New York City we stayed with her. She took us on a tour to introduce us to many of the Witches that she had written about, such as Ray Buckland. We visited several occult stores and spent memorable evenings sitting around telling stories and singing songs and chants. At that time the New York Witchcraft scene was pretty much straight out of the movie *Bell, Book and Candle.*

NARRATOR: Raymond Buckland was the first UK Witch that Tim Zell met in person. And it was also his first meeting with someone who had been initiated in the Gardnerian tradition. By then Tim knew who Gerald Gardner was and had read his books, but he was still surprised by what he found in New York. The American Pagan groups that Tim Zell had interacted with up till that point had typically been started by college students, and their Paganism had been born from the ecstatic discoveries of the Psychedelic sixties. One of the first of these eclectic groups, NROOGD (New Reformed Orthodox Order of the Golden Dawn), had been formed just a few years previous as a result of a homework assignment to create a ritual that several students had been given in a class at San Francisco State College (now SFSU.)

But Gerald Gardner claimed to have been initiated by a coven in England in 1939, and he was not a college student or any kind of early beatnik or hippie at the time. He was a retired British civil servant who had just moved back to the UK after having spent most of his adult life in southern and south-eastern Asia. When the English Witchcraft Act, which had been the law for centuries, was repealed in 1951, he went public about being a Witch. He wrote about it, gave interviews about it, and operated the Museum of Magic and Witchcraft. The story Gardner told was that his lineage went all the way back to an ancient, pre-Christian Witch-cult that he called "The Old Religion," that it had been underground since then, and that he was trying to keep it alive.

Buckland became friends with Gardner in the early '60s, and was initiated in his presence shortly before Gardner died at the age of 79. After that he brought Gardnerian Wicca to the US, and settled down here. Gardner's historical claims were dubious even in 1971, and in the years since there has been abundant debate and research about where his tradition really came from. But at that time the details were still being kept secret, and there was intentional mystery surrounding what actually went on in a Gardnerian coven. No *Book of Shadows* had been published and there were no public rituals.

Raymond Buckland was the only Gardnerian in New York City who even had a coven, and it wasn't a part of the Council of Themis. The other Gardnerians who lived there all worked as individuals. Today they would be called "solitaries." And, like the characters in *Bell, Book and Candle*, they were urban Witches, and weren't interested in a rural lifestyle. It was a completely different scene from the one Tim Zell was used to.

After that Tim went up to Boston to attend the science fiction convention, where he hoped to get a glimpse of the future. Little did he know that he had just gotten one in Manhattan.

OZ: On our return trip home we stopped off in Philadelphia where we met Mike and Penny Novak, who had just started up a Pagan Way group, based on liturgy created by Ed Fitch. They wanted to create a Wiccan tradition that would be publicly accessible. It would be sort of like an "outer court" for Witchcraft. But it was an unfortunate choice of name. People who joined the Pagan Way thought of themselves as generic Pagans, but what they really were being considered by the organization was proto-Witches. If they continued on they would eventually get initiated into Witchcraft. So the idea became embedded in the community that Pagans were proto-Witches who hadn't gotten initiated yet. The notion that was promoted was that Witches were the clergy, and the Pagans were the laity. Which was really annoying to non-Wiccan Pagan groups who had their own distinct traditions! We still run into this unfortunate attitude among some Witches.

We were really surprised to learn that these lovely folks didn't include their kids in their religious practice. It wasn't a family thing for them, as it was for us in CAW. They were sending their children to Christian Sunday Schools. And when they would have their full moon Esbat circles they would have their kids taken care of by a babysitter, and the kids would never know what they were doing. We thought that was weird. For us, Paganism was a *religion* that included everybody. They were thinking of it more as an esoteric lodge or a secret society like the Masons. We hadn't assimilated that that's where a lot of people were coming from until that trip, because we had developed all this stuff on our own over the years, with practically no real connection with Witches.

Today many folks think that Witches founded the Pagan community, but it wasn't that way at all—at least not in the US. Here the Witches came into a Pagan community that was already in existence. What a lot of my work was engaged in at that time was weaving together some of these different threads by publishing *Green Egg,* which went out to all these different groups. The Pagan community has roots in what were then very separate communities.

Tim Zell—famous publicity photo, 1971.

Strider (Mark Whitroth), Goldberry (Julie), Frodo (Bryan), Tom Bombadil (Tim) at Noreascon, 1971; "Best Group."

Tim 'n' Julie as "Cernunnos & Cerridwen" at LAcon, 1972; "Best of Show!"

Carolyn Clark & Tim Zell, Beltaine 1973.

CHAPTER 11:
California Dreamin'
(1972-1973)

All the leaves are brown and the sky is gray
I've been for a walk on a winter's day
I'd be safe and warm if I was in L.A.
California dreamin' on such a winter's day.
~ "California Dreamin'" by the Mamas and the Papas, 1966

 Z: AT LITHA (MIDSUMMER) OF 1972, BOBBIE (Roberta) Kennedy came from Ohio to study for her ordination, which she received at Litha of '73.

BOBBIE KENNEDY: It was my first trip to St Louis and to the home of Tim and Julie Zell. I had come for the Midsummer Festival, for a Magical Celebration of Life, Earth and World Family; and that is exactly what I experienced.

I walked through the front door and into another world. Black walls acting like picture frames to set off the contents of the room. Mattresses and books everywhere. One boa constrictor wandering freely in the house, one lizard in a cage, two alligators in the bathtub. And no chairs.

Affection flowed freely in the Zell household. Julie gave me such an exuberant hug that I felt immediately at home. She was lovely: alabaster skin set off by long silken dark hair and an effervescent spirit. And Tim was likewise stunning. He had the typical sparkling bright eyes of a Sagittarian set in a long face framed by long flowing locks of hair and a luxuriant beard—giving a strange impression of regal dignity and jovial merriment combined.

There were some things there that I expected to see: A sign by the outside door reminding "Did you remember to dress?" Another proclaiming "Thou Art God" and one asking "Have you thanked a green plant today?"

There was color everywhere: a tie-dyed sheet for the kitchen doorway, Indian print covers for the mattresses, softly striped curtains closed with gigantic snowflakes, and Tim's artwork accented by bright colorful stars. The bookshelves that weren't crammed with books had skulls and candles and incense, complete sets of models of cave-men scenes, Frankenstein, and even Pogo dolls.

The basement was likewise fascinating with its additional books, Pagan Altar, and printing equipment.

Friday night we had a party. Everybody was hugging and kissing hello and goodbye just as if they were all members of one large family. No need for them to preach about brotherly love when they were so actively living it! The high point of the evening was body painting. Have you ever seen psychedelic paint on live bodies under black light? There were frequent comments of "Wow, far out!"

DON WILDGRUBE: Bobbie immediately fell in love with Michael Hurley. She was at the same time a good punster. When confronted with the idea that she was so into Michael that she was giving up her Goddesshood, she replied, "I worship the very Earth that Michael walks upon." We were taken by surprise and it took us a week to see the pun she was making.

OZ: In the summer of 1972, Michael Hurley was living with us—we always had people staying with us. There has been virtually no time in my entire life when I have not had somebody living with me. In late July, Julie and I went away for a few days, leaving Michael to take care of our animals. At this time Histah was seven feet long, and she lived in the house and wandered around where she wanted to. When we came back home Histah was missing. Michael had taken her out for a slither in our peach tree, which I used to do with her often, and had forgotten to bring her back in. I couldn't find her any-where. I slept in the back yard at night and tried to dream-fast with her, but it didn't work. After several weeks I gave up.

CAROLYN CLARK: I had met Tim at the first Earth Day in April of 1970. It was his snake, Histah, that first got my attention. Tim was in a long white robe, and he had the most magnificent snake I had ever seen. So I walked over and started talking to him. Later there was a little article in the newspaper when the snake was missing. So I called Tim and said I hoped that Histah returned safely. He invited me over to his house to hang out. We talked and then he invited to their next festival—which in Wicca would have been called a Sabbat. I found out later that that was their way of screening people. They would first talk to them for a couple of hours, and then if that went well, invite them to a festival. And if that went well, they were invited to the weekly Nest meetings.

At the time I joined the Church had never ordained a priestess. So I studied, and after a year I became the first—ordained at Beltane of 1973. I took on the duties of priestess—eventually High Priestess—and found a real purpose in life.

OZ: The 1972 World Science Fiction Convention was to be held in Los Angeles, and we spent months getting ready to go there. Since my previous VW camper had been wrecked the year before, on the way back from Noreascon, I bought a 1968 Volkswagen van and spent the few weeks before the trip building camper components into it. I was in the front yard one day, cutting wood for the project, and I suddenly felt Histah in my mind. I dropped my tools, ran around to the side of the house, pulled away the big sheets of plywood that were leaning against it and there she was. I picked her up, wrapped her around my shoulders and I must have been floating a foot above the ground as I carried her into the house.

But as I uncoiled her I saw that she had a serious wound in her side. I took her to the vet, and he cleansed out the wound and sewed it up, and gave her antibiotics, but it he couldn't do anything more. She wouldn't eat, and she got thinner and thinner. She sustained for some time, but she never got better.

I finished converting the camper, and we hit the road, arriving in Los Angeles on Tuesday, August 29, where we settled in at Lance Christie's house. Harold Moss and Donald Harrison of the Church of the Eternal Source came by, along with Michael Kinghorn of the Delphic Fellowship. We spent a long evening discussing the Council of Themis and the various problems therein.

A year or two after the Council had been started, Poke Runyon from the Order of the Temple of Astarte got the notion of appointing himself and Fred Adams as Directors. I was not part of that deliberation at all, and as co-founder of the Council I thought I should have some say. But Poke did not feel that the Church of All Worlds was a legitimate Pagan religion because we were based on science fiction instead of something ancient. He dismissed CAW as a "science-fiction grok-flock," a term we delightedly took to heart, henceforth often referring to ourselves as "the Galloping Garrulous Grok-Flock."

I was trying to build an inclusive coalition, but their idea was that only people they approved of should be a part of it. This was one of my first experiences of being cut out of something that I had founded. I couldn't understand why Fred would go along with all this stuff. I later came to understand that Fred was a very sweet guy, but psychologically he was not a strong person. And someone who was had no trouble telling him what to do.

The next evening Julie and I went over to Donald Harrison's house for a truly splendid Egyptian ritual to Ma'at, goddess of Truth and Justice. Donald is an artisan of the first order, and his home was resplendent with authentic reconstructions of ancient Egyptian furniture and ceremonial objects he had made. Ed Fitch of The Pagan Way came over for the ritual, and afterwards Ed, Harold, Julie and I adjourned to Harold's house where we discussed plans for a new Council of Earth Religions.

Thursday evening, Aug. 31, we went up to Pasadena to visit with Fred Adams and Svetlana Butyrin. Their house was an artistic vision, both inside and out, replete with Fred's beautiful paintings of the Magic Maiden. They showed us their woodhenge in the orchard in back, and led us through a purification ritual in their hidden ritual chamber. Nelson White of the OTA and his new bride were the first guests to arrive after us, and before long there was quite a crowd.

Later, when Poke Runyon arrived, we all got into some heavy discussions on the future of the Council. We explained our intention to withdraw and form a new Council in conjunction with CES, Pagan Way, Dancers of the Sacred Circle, Rainbow Coven, and such other groups as would join us. We all agreed that the present Council should be dissolved and two new groups formed: one—the Council of Earth Religions, with Harold Moss acting as Coordinator—to be a broad-based affiliation of Neo-Pagan religious communities administered democratically; the other an alliance of Magickal orders, Mystery cults, and other closed initiatory societies—to be administered autocratically by Fred and Poke serving as "Directorate."

Saturday we finally made it over to LAcon '72—the 30th World Science Fiction Convention. Bryan spent most of the day in the pool and kept asking when he could go skinny-dipping. That evening we went to the masquerade. When Julie and I stepped onto the stage, painted blue and garbed in the Priestly vestments of an authentic portrayal of Cerridwen and Cernunnos, the Goddess and Horned God of Celtic lore, we were greeted with a thunderous applause. Histah, who was draped around the forked stang I carried, really got off on the good vibes, and scanned the audience. Julie carried a dry-ice smoking cauldron, out of which she lifted a real human skull. At that moment, you could have heard a pin drop.

We had several hours of suspenseful waiting for the judging, during which we were photographed constantly, until one by one the names of the winners were announced.

Finally the stage was full, all the best costumes had been awarded prizes, and we had not been mentioned. Just as we were consoling ourselves that our costumes were probably too esoteric, came the final announcement: "…and for Best of Show—Tim and Julie Zell as Cernunnos and Cerridwen!"

NARRATOR: I was in the audience that night. The Zells weren't just modeling costumes when they walked out in front of the audience of science fiction fans. They had already worn them before as Priest and Priestess, and they had played the God and Goddess in CAW rituals. And what sometimes happens when playing the role of a God is that the person manifests the God, even if only on a psychological level. So, I think that maybe one reason why they were so impressive at the Worldcon was that, in a certain sense, they actually *became* Cernunnos and Cerridwen when they were on stage! The costumes at Worldcons were getting more elaborate every year, but there had never been anything like that before.

(The experience of embodying a deity in a ritual setting is called "aspecting." As I understand it, the word was first used in that context by Roger Zelazny in his book *Lord of Light,* when characters would take on an aspect of one of the pantheon of Hindu deities. *Lord of Light* won the Hugo award for best novel at the 1968 World Science Fiction Convention.)

OZ: One of the judges was Alison Harlow. Afterwards she came up to us and introduced herself and lots of other people. Some of them we had already corresponded with, like Isaac Bonewits, and many others whom we didn't know. It really brought us into connection, in a major way, with many of the people who movers and shakers in the California Pagan community.

After washing off the blue make-up and changing, Bryan, Julie, and I joined the crowd in the pool in a skinny-dipping party—the hotel management was cooperative and kept the pool open all night. Then we visited several parties and finally crashed in our camper around 4:00 am.

Tuesday we took Bryan to Disneyland. In spite of it all being plastic, it was a thoroughly delightful experience. Thursday we set off on a leisurely drive up the Coast Highway, digging the beautiful scenery of cliffs and ocean. Around dusk we stopped in Big Basin Redwood Forest and had dinner among the Big Trees. We had many thoughts on these ancient giants and their fate at the hands of man.

Alison and Isaac had invited us to come up north to the Bay Area. When we got there, Allison threw a big party for us at her place, where we met Gwydion Pendderwen. She and Gwydion were living together in this big house in Oakland, called *Caedderwen*. They were both involved in the Society for Creative Anachronism and the Renaissance Faire crowd that eventually grew out of it.

NARRATOR: The Society for Creative Anachronism had been started just four years earlier as a medieval sword and shield tournament in the Berkeley backyard of Heathen writer Diana Paxson (then a UC graduate student). It currently has 19 Kingdoms, where people work together to recreate the Middle Ages "as they should have been, not as they were." Their biggest yearly gathering, the Pennnsic Wars, attracts over 10,000 to a site in Western Pennsylvania. The SCA has always been a safe haven for Pagans—everyone gets to be someone other than who they are. They create a character, wear historical clothes, and interact with other people who are doing the same thing. Gwydion was the Bard of his SCA Kingdom, and it gave him a place to write and sing his songs before there were any regular Pagan gatherings.

OZ: So that was another community we were weaving into the mix. We became fast friends and lovers with various people in that group. We deeply shared the same vision of Paganism being a community, tribal kind of a thing, and living on the land.

Continuing north, we stopped off in Sausalito to visit Jack and Rae Hurley, whom we had come to know through *Green Egg* correspondence. They were living on a houseboat, and they had the first hot tub I'd ever experienced. I loved it, and decided right then and there that our eventual home would have to include a hot tub!

Alison and Gwydion took us up to Greenfield Ranch in Mendocino County, which was just in the process of being acquired at that time. Tim Baker, a successful Hippie entrepreneur, had inherited some money and bought up an old, bankrupt 5,600 acre cattle ranch and subdivided it up into parcels for people who wanted to move to the country. Alison showed us the parcel she was buying. She and Gwydion had decided to go in on it together. Gwydion owned his own house in Oakland, called Caedderwen, and Alison was living there with him. She had recently come into a nice inheritance, and she put down the money to buy 220 acres, with the idea that when Gwydion sold his house then he would buy half of it.

ALISON HARLOW: In the mid-70's I was looking for a secluded place in the country to have Pagan gatherings and so forth, where we could be skyclad in the woods and celebrate close to nature. I wasn't looking for a place to live.

I heard about Greenfield Ranch—5,600 acres of beautiful land in Mendocino County that was once a working cattle ranch. We knew Tim Baker, the man that was putting the real estate deal together—he had done something similar before. Basically he would take out an option for some land, then he would create communities by finding ecologically-minded people to buy parcels of it.

At the time I was living in Oakland with Gwydion Pendderwen and his wife. Gwydion and I went up to look at Greenfield Ranch and we both just fell in love with it. I wound up buying a 220-acre parcel. We went there on weekends, but we wouldn't go there at all in the winter.

OZ: We spent the day hiking, exploring the magnificent terrain, and working on the road to the place. At night we sat under the stars listening to and learning some of Gwydion's Pagan folk songs. Gwydion was telling stories about raccoons sneaking up on the campers and stealing their food, so Bryan was determined to watch out for raccoons. We pitched our sleeping bags beneath a great and ancient oak, and he stayed up at night while the rest of us were asleep. At one point I was awakened by Bryan who was yelling at some raccoons and chasing them away as they tried to get into the coolers: "You get out of here, you damn raccoons!"

We left the next morning with the idea that in a couple of years we would sell our house in St Louis and move to California.

NARRATOR: The Zells had other reasons to leave the Midwest. Tim was being regularly stopped and harassed by the St Louis police. The previous year he had been arrested and held overnight in jail for a $25 occupancy permit fine from the Temple that, it turned out, he had already paid. The officers on duty at the station knew his name and history, and were convinced that the CAW was some kind of "drug cult." The Bay Area was at that time, and still is, the home to many diverse spiritualities, subcultures, and alternative lifestyle. In San Francisco, Berkeley or Oakland he would have had much more freedom to be who he was and express his ideas.

OZ: We drove back down to the Bay Area and visited Alta and Aidan Kelly, founders of the New Reformed Orthodox Order of the Golden Dawn. Without previous training or initiation, Aidan, a brilliant poet and scholar, had engaged in monumental research to reconstruct on his own a very solid interpretation of the Old Religion. He said that whatever you can do today to put yourself in the same place as your ancestors is thereby authentic.

Before we left we went over to Victor and Cora Anderson's, where we talked about magick and the Craft. Victor, a legendary shaman who was blind but gifted with "The Sight," showed us his ritual chamber and performed a short, intense ritual that combined traditional elements with Huna and Voudun.

After we got back from that trip we were still trying to get full legal recognition for the Church of All Worlds. We were incorporated, but we were still trying to get our tax exemption from the state of Missouri, and were still dealing with the IRS to get our 501(c)(3) exemption. Those were ongoing legal battles. The state of Missouri wouldn't recognize us as a religion because of our "lack of primary concern about the hereafter, God, the destiny of souls, heaven, hell, sin and punishment and other supernatural matters." So we put out a call to people to write letters saying that we were not only *a* religion, but that we were *their* religion. We got statements from quite a few people. When we presented this as part of our case we had something solid. We also got the ACLU involved. There were articles in the newspaper and it became quite an issue.

I continued trying to get Histah healed. I tried to stay in constant contact with her. We were psychically bonded—she was the most intense familiar relationship I have ever had. On October 17, at 2:30 pm, I was sitting at work and suddenly I just felt her presence. It was like we were connected, and then suddenly she dropped the other end of the connection. She dropped her body and was snapped into just being in me. I completely felt this. I called home and told Julie, "Histah just died."

And she said, "No, she's fine. I just saw her in the bathroom." I told her to go take another look. I waited. She came back and she said, "You're right. How did you know?"

And I replied, "Because she's now in me." That was a powerful experience. Ever since then I have felt that inside me is the soul of a serpent. And in the language of J.K. Rowling's *Harry Potter* novels, I became a *"parseltongue,"* able to communicate with snakes ever since.

Right after that a cat showed up at our door looking for a home. It was a beautiful male Burmese I named Oberon. That was the first time I had used that name for a creature. I was open to a new Familiar connection, and this cat just totally took that. When I would come into the house he would jump up onto my shoulders. He would look right into my eyes and talk to me and expect me to understand what he was saying—which I could. After about a month of that I was getting ready to go to work one morning and I pulled out of the driveway and saw Oberon on the road. He had been run over and killed. So I didn't go to work that day; I just stayed home and buried my cat. I was really shattered. I felt like I was under psychic attack— all these devastating things were happening to me.

A couple of weeks later I was at work at the Human Development Corporation when the receptionist called me. I went out to her and there standing on her desk, in the middle of this office building, was this cat. And it was indistinguishable from Oberon. I said, "Oberon?" And the cat leaped up on my shoulder in the way Oberon used to. Then he settled down and started purring.

I was blown away. I had buried that cat, and there he was back again! I went back to my desk and sat down, and he remained on my shoulder for the rest of the day. I took him home and he was exactly the same cat in every way. He talked to me the same way, looked at me the same way, and curled up in the same favorite spot.

The next morning when I went to work I left him there with Julie. When I came home in the evening Julie told me that after I left Oberon went out the window and didn't come back. And I never saw him again. It was like somehow he came by to say good-bye. Subsequently, I have come across whole books of stories like that about cats, but this one I can vouch for from personal experience!

In late '72 we had our first confrontation with the Fundamentalists. At the Los Angeles Worldcon we had participated in a "Pagan summit conference" arranged by Allison. We talked about Pagan public relations and the importance of communicating Neo-Pagan ideas to the public before Earth is utterly destroyed by the ravages of Western "Civilization." Groups that were mounting anti-Witchcraft campaigns were mentioned, and the necessity of all of us being willing to stand up for our religion. Well, this guy named Rev. Herschel Smith, of the Morris Cerrulo Ministries, showed up in St. Louis on an anti-occult crusade with his big bus he called the "Witchmobile." Inside he had a museum of occult paraphernalia. It was all spooky and Halloweeny-looking. It was a very impressive display, actually, but it was pretty much your Hollywood scary movie kind of thing. He claimed to have once been a member of a Satanic group that he had done terrible, bloody things with that should have landed him in jail for life. We saw him on the news issuing a challenge to any Witch or Warlock to a debate.

So of course we rose to the challenge. We arranged a press conference ahead of time—we knew all the local journalists. Then we showed up at one of his revival meetings, at the New Life Evangelistic Center, run by a Rev. Larry Rice.

DON WILDGRUBE: The first speaker was "Rauel," who spoke of his girlfriend who grew fangs and wanted to drink his blood. Finally Hershel went to the small stage. He preached for awhile before he saw us. He then got a strange look in his eyes and exhorted the audience to "Pray like you've never prayed before, there are Witches and Warlocks amongst us!" He gave an altar call and walked off the stage. Tim stood up and accepted his challenge to a debate. That's when all "hell" broke out. Tim was shoved against a wall and dragged to a back room by a couple of burly guys. The rest of us had to put up with the rantings of others about "This is not fighting, it's righteous Christian Wrath!"

I had Larry Rice (a popular public evangelist) nose to nose to me shouting, "I love you, but I hate the devil inside of you."

We waited around and finally Tim came out. He had talked to Hershel Smith and they agreed to meet down the street in the Public Library for the debate. We showed up at the appointed time. There was to be a panel of Tim, Carolyn and Tom. Hershel was to debate with them. Gavin was there carrying his *Etymological Dictionary*. The press was there, the cameras from the three major networks were there, but no Hershel Smith. So we got great coverage. The next day we delivered a certificate to Hershel's wife, stating that he received an award for the advancement of Paganism.

OZ: In February of 1973, Julie turned 21. She wanted to get some independence because she had moved into my house straight from her parent's home, with only a brief stint at college. So she moved out. That was quite a big thing for me. This was the first time in my entire life that I had lived alone. I felt strongly that she was my soulmate. She was completing her work for ordination and getting right to the edge of becoming a priestess. But we also had a fairly tumultuous relationship.

I didn't quite know what to do. I wasn't used to not having someone to share my life, bed, meals, conversations, and everything. There were a few people in the community that I had lover/friend relationships with. That was all very nice, and it helped me get through it. But having someone you can spend the night with isn't the same as having a companion.

One day I went down to the co-op to buy some groceries and this woman, Sue B, came up to me. I'd never met her before. We got into a conversation that somehow revealed that I was alone at the moment, so she invited me over for dinner. I ended up spending the night. At that time I was extremely susceptible and vulnerable. Within a week or so of our meeting she moved into my house. It wasn't like we planned it exactly. She took the initiative and I didn't say no.

But then it got kind of weird. She borrowed my credit card, which seemed reasonable at the time. I didn't realized until a month later when I got the bill that she was racking up quite a lot of expenses. It got to be pretty intense. After a month or so she moved out again; but we still continued to date.

Julie then told me that she had had enough time on her own and would like to move back in. I said I wasn't quite ready for that yet, which was really stupid of me. I don't know if it was my wounded pride or what. I should have said, "Boy, am I glad to have you back! I really missed you." But I didn't. Idiot.

All this led up to Beltane of 1973, when we had probably the most amazingly intense erotic celebration that we had ever had. It was instigated by a Yemanese belly dancer named Solwa Rajah who was astonishingly gorgeous. So she did a topless dance for us at the Beltane ritual. Somehow the intensity of the evening precipitated an amazing sexual experience all the way around. It wasn't specifically with her. There were people all over the place feeling aroused and getting it on. This was the evening that went way out there.

DON WILDGRUBE: Two people at the Beltane festival had a contest to see how many people they could screw. The next thing you know, about 10 or 12 of us came down with trichomoniasis. At that time, there was a lady from Dayton, Ohio, named Bobby Kennedy. She was a nurse, and she went to the free clinic, and when the doctor told her what it was, he asked, "How many people were infected?"

CAROLYN CLARK: When she said 23, he said, "That must have been one helluva party."

DON WILDGRUBE: He wrote prescriptions for all of us. So everyone was on Flagyl tablets. It eats up all the yeast. Girls had to take two pills a day, and the guys one pill a day for ten days.

OZ: However, we didn't get the rap about the side effects: an incredible increase in irritability, anxiety, paranoia and general bad attitudes. Within a fairly short time of everybody taking this stuff, this very tight, intense community, people started to go nuts. They were going off the wall with accusations, hostilities, jealousies and weird stuff like that.

In late May we had a Nest meeting that went all awry. It started reasonably enough. Someone suggested that we had to tighten up our boundaries about who we were having sex with and maybe stick with our own Nest mates. Someone said, "I wouldn't want to sleep with anyone who wasn't a water brother."

And then Julie, who was at this meeting, said, "Well, I wouldn't want to sleep with anyone who was sleeping with Sue B!"

I was sitting over in the opposite corner across from her with Sue sitting next to me. In one single movement I rose up from the couch, swept across the room and backhanded Julie across the face. It seems utterly unconceivable that I would have ever done such a thing. But I did. It was devastating. We rushed her to the hospital, where it was determined that I had broken her nose.

DON: Well, weeks later I happened to be doing some floor work in a hospital, and at lunchtime I was behind the nurse's station, and I got out the *Physician's Desk Reference,* a big thick book that gives you the breakdown of various medications. And I looked up Flagyl. And there is a long list of side effects. And that's when I realized what had happened to Tim. He's a pacifist. When we were all taking Flagyl we were always at each other's throats, always arguing, always fighting.

CAROLYN CLARK: That was why he hit her. He was angry with her, and under ordinary circumstances it would have stopped with raised voices. Immediately afterwards he was horrified, ashamed and broken up that he had actually become violent towards anyone, especially Julie.

OZ: So, there I was. It was the summer of 1973, and I'd lost the woman whom I'd expected to be with forever. I'd blown any chance of getting her back, and I had no one to blame but myself. I'd heard about the Rainbow Family gathering which that year was being held in Wyoming on the Fourth of July. And I decided that what I needed to do was go Walkabout and find myself.

I hitchhiked across the country and got as far as the outskirts of Boulder, Colorado. When I got let out of the car on the highway a cop car pulled up and they took me to prison. I'm not talking about the local county jail—this was the state prison. I'd hitchhiked all around the country before. And right around that time the John Denver song, "Rocky Mountain High," was really popular. Colorado was thought of as being a Hippie paradise. And there I was in prison for hitchhiking! They took away my clothes and my pack of camping supplies, put me in an orange uniform and locked me up in a cellblock with serious felons. That was pretty scary.

I tried to make friends as fast as I could. I found the biggest, meanest, nastiest-looking guy in the place and learned that he was into comic books and chess. So I started playing chess with him, and talking comics, and after that nobody was gonna mess with me.

I had to spend the whole weekend there. The bail was $20, which I didn't have on me. I wasn't able to use my credit card to get cash till Monday morning. This was the first time that I fully realized how people like me could be treated by the authorities at any time.

Monday evening they let me out and put me on the side of the road, where I wasn't allowed to stick my thumb out. It was getting darker and darker, and there was a cop car waiting for me to try it again. Finally somebody pulled over and picked me up.

I got up to Lander, Wyoming, and spent some time with Bonnie Sherlock, whose coven tradition fused Gardnerian and Lakota Native American practices. She gave me a 2nd degree initiation into her Tradition—I'd already had enough background to qualify. Then I went on up to the Rainbow Gathering. I'd never been to one of those before. I didn't connect with anyone because I wasn't in the mood for that. I just camped in my little tent and wandered around. It gave me time to think about things, and that was the most important part.

I realized that up 'til that point in my life I had taken everyone around me for granted and focused on my own mission and desires.

I really got a chance to see that a bit more objectively, and I felt like an ass. If I had just paid a little more attention to what it was that other people needed or wanted, things could have been very different. The fact that they went along with it was all I needed. I just automatically made all the decisions and presumed that it was all up to me. I got perspective on this and felt terrible.

I realized that one of the things that Julie had hated the whole time she had been living with me was that the living room had been painted black and that I had day-glo cut-outs of stars and planets all over the walls. So the first thing I did when I got back from the trip was re-paint the whole place white. I threw away all of my black clothes, which is mostly what I'd been wearing since the Beatnik days. I started wearing more white and light colors. I looked at the images I surrounded myself with, the music I listened to—I spent the rest of the summer going through my life and tried to turn around everything that I could.

I had to accept that there was no way that anything I did was going to get Julie to come back to me. But I still fantasized and hoped that it might happen—it was too little, too late, but it did change me. There had been something built into me from the time I was a kid and had to deal with bullies. I didn't want that to be there at all. So I totally shifted myself over to the sweetness and light side of the equation. I had to abandon the whole concept of being a powerful, alpha male dominant figure. It was a big, major overhaul.

CAROLYN CLARK: I became very close to Tim. I was over at his house an awful lot. We were intimate, but we were not in love. Although at one point he did ask me if I would leave my husband and move in with him. I thought about it for a couple of minutes but then I realized that it would cause so much trouble that it could have really bad repercussions on CAW. So I declined. Plus I also had this feeling that the period we were in was a waiting period, and that someone else was going to come along and be Tim's—I hate to use the word soulmate, because it's so hackneyed—but that's what I felt, that he was going to meet the person with whom he could become one—two distinct personalities complementing each other.

PART FOUR:

Enter Morning Glory

CHAPTER 12:
Dianasaur
(1948-1961)

NARRATOR: WHEN TIM AND MORNING GLORY met it was like something out of one of the many myths or stories that they both knew so well, but it was real. And as they got to know each other they found out that though their family histories were very different, they had many things in common with each other. And so we will now go back in time and look at what Morning Glory's life had been like before her fateful meeting with Tim Zell.

MG: I was born on May 27, 1948, in Long Beach, Southern California; and I grew up there in the '50s. My parents had emigrated there from Mississippi during WWII, and they would go back to see their folks there every year or so, and so I ended up spending quite a bit of time in rural Mississippi as well. My Mother's name was Polly Browning and she came from a large family; she was the youngest of thirteen. Her Mother was a fourth-generation Irish dairywoman named Anniebelle Ramsey. Her Father, Hester Browning, was a planter with an English father and a mother with Choctaw Indian ancestry.

My Mom's parents died before I was born, but Polly always kept their memories alive and most of her brothers and sisters were still around while I was growing up. My Father, James Moore, was the youngest son of a Methodist Minister. He had an older brother and sister, but he was a pretty typical PK (preacher's kid) being quite a hell-raiser when he was young. His parents were still alive and I spent a fair amount of time with them off and on as a child and as a teenager and I heard all these stories from them and the other Old Folks on the Hill.

Granddaddy Moore was the terror of the local folks, always domineering and prone to doing or saying unpredictable things seemingly unbecoming in a Minister. But he was a brilliant scholar and always had a witty point to the unusual things he said that were meant to shake people up. He always said he tried to get people to think, but I know he also liked making people uncomfortable and keeping them off-balance. He was typical in that way as a Southern white male control-freak.

My Grandmother, born Ellen Jane Ritchey, was every inch the respectable Minister's wife—a double Virgo with all those special powers of detail and organization as well as a wealth of wifely skills like good cooking and fine stitchery which she tried her best to teach me with mixed results.

Granddaddy Moore's Mother, Violinda Gainey was a Natchez Indian woman who had been found as a baby on the banks of the Pearl River after an Indian massacre by the local Minister's wife and was raised as her daughter. No one wanted to talk about Great Grandpa Moore. I finally learned that he was an alcoholic and that is why my Grandpa went into the ministry.

I never got to meet Grandma Ellen Jane's Papa, but everyone always said that he was the wisest and kindest man in four counties. Local people would come to him and ask him to help settle disputes. He married a Choctaw woman around the time of the Removal when the Choctaw people were mostly sent off to reservations in Oklahoma along with the Cherokee.

I learned all these stories and was especially interested in the ones about my three Indian Great Grandmothers. I used to beg them to take me up to the Reservation in Carthage, but they never would do it and always shushed me when I asked.

My parents were a traditional couple with the father who worked and the mother who stayed home with the child, at least for the first eight years of my life. I was an only child; my mother wanted to have thirteen children but instead she had six miscarriages and almost died in 54 hours of labor with me. I was born by caesarian section. So I was her sun and moon and stars; she decided that all my friends (and later my lovers) would be the adopted other children she never could have.

She was the best mom and also the best friend anyone could ever have wanted and remained so until the day she died. She was very sweet and childlike with a thick Southern accent that she never lost, and she loved everything and everybody indiscriminately like a puppydog. I was often frustrated as a teenager and young woman by her emotional immaturity, but she had a great wisdom born of Love that could pierce through the thorniest problems and touch the heart of Truth. She also delighted in being silly and dressing in bright colors and the only thing she loved more than me was Jesus, who she loved with all her soul. She was a true Christian.

My Father was a serious fisherman who loved to fish like Mama loved Jesus. Mostly he was a pretty taciturn guy except when he was cussing a blue streak. He was always busy working on projects and could fix anything you broke, and he always helped me build kites and make my Halloween costumes. He was a senior mechanic at Long Beach Oil Development and he worked very hard, sometimes moonlighting as an auto mechanic. He invested in property so that by 1956 he owned a house, a duplex next door, and a vacant lot with an apricot orchard on the other side of us that became my jungle gym, fort, imaginary horse corral, and the playground for all the kids in the neighborhood.

I was not an easy kid to raise. I was pretty fearless and had a little too much of an independent spirit coupled with a stubborn streak, so I was always getting myself into trouble. When I was a baby I managed to crawl under the heater and fall asleep. My folks found me and I was bright red and wouldn't wake up, so they rushed me to the hospital and found I had carbon monoxide poisoning.

Then when I was about three years old, I was playing in the green house area of our backyard and I saw this cool little door just about my size about ten feet up on the side of the house. I was just certain that little door had to lead to somewhere wonderful, so I climbed up the trellis and edged myself along some molding on the side of the house until I could get to the door. I found a butter knife that my Dad had left there to help open the door when it got stuck. When I opened the door it didn't go anywhere but it was full of strange round glass knobs and a row of bright copper switches. It was the main electrical fuse box for the whole house. I guess I thought that I needed to do something to make the door open up to the wonderful place, so I stuck the butter knife into one of the slots inside the box and that's all I remember.

Meanwhile my mom and dad were having a little afternoon snuggle and just before it started to progress into something more intense, the lights in the house went out and they both stopped. Then with that radar-like sixth sense common to parents said: "Hmm, we haven't heard anything from the kid for a while; we better go check up on her." My dad found me lying on the ground beneath the fuse box where I had fallen after being knocked backwards by the force of the shock. I was blue and my hair was all frizzy and I wasn't breathing. Next my dad did this crazy sort of counter-intuitive thing. He picked me up by my heels and whirled me around over his head, then pulled me to his chest and squeezed me hard. I started to breath. He didn't even bother to get the car, he just ran four blocks to where the hospital was. I recovered fine and my dad always said that it was a good thing that our house was only wired for 110 volts of electricity instead of the 220 volts that he had out in his shop.

My next adventure of this nature came when I was about four and my dad took me fishing with him off the jetty in Long Beach. My mom always worried when I went places with my dad and so she dressed me in my little bright red overalls that had a yellow rooster patch on the front. Dad carried me for a ways and I hip-hopped from rock to rock along with him. But we finally got to a rock that was too far for me to jump, and it connected to the wilder ocean side of the jetty instead of the calmer one inside the breakwater. He parked me on the big rock and stuck his finger in my face: "Stay here, Stinky, and don't try to follow me; it's dangerous. I'm just going over there and see if I can catch us some rock cod."

My dad always thought that you trained a kid like you trained a dog: sit, stay, come, speak. But kids, unlike dogs, aren't naturally obedient and have the attention span of a gnat. I pottered around the big rock and poked around in the crevices hunting for crabs and sea urchins. I looked across the big crevice that my dad had jumped over with his long legs and I could see an orange starfish down there. I saw my dad on the other side and decided to go ask him to help me get the big starfish. I had forgotten anything he had said to me and

just stood back and made a running jump to get across the crevice…and missed.

I wasn't actually afraid even when I went into the water and got
sucked out to sea. The thing I remember from being underwater was
how everything around me was all green and swayed back and forth
in a soothing rhythm. But I did have a peculiar thought that just
popped into my head: "Gosh, I guess I haven't lived very long this
time."

The next thing I saw was two huge fizzy silver things coming at
me. I thought they might be fish but they were my dad's arms pulling
me out of the water. For years I always thought this had been just a
dream, but before my dad died I had a conversation with him and I
told him this memory and asked him if it really had happened. His
face went chalk white and he said: "I never told your mom 'cause
she would have been too mad to ever let me take you fishing again!"

From his point of view he had parked me on the rock and there
I should have stayed like a good puppy, so he was busy casting out
his line and reeling it in when he caught a glimpse of something red
out in the waves. He glanced back to the rock where I was no longer
parked. Then he dropped his rod and floundered over the rocks and
down to the water's edge where a big wave broke and he reached in
and pulled me out. It was like Mama Yemanja said to him: "Here's
your kid back; take better care of her next time!"

Years later when I went to a Bembe put on by the Umbanda
house, the Mama Renee' told me that Yemanja was surely my
Mama, but that Elegua was my Papa because his colors are red and
black and his animal is the rooster. He is the communicator and it
was He who got my dad's attention by showing him the red overalls
with the rooster patch. I survived to tell the tale, but my dad lost his
best rod and reel trying to save me.

There were several other incidents like this. When I was about
six my dad had put up a huge old army surplus canvas tent in our
backyard so that us kids could use it like a playhouse. It had a long
rope tied into a loop hanging down from the center pole where it was
used to hang up stuff. We were playing cowboys and rustlers and
decided to hang the rustlers. We took the rope and jury rigged it into
a noose then we took turns being the rustlers and getting hung. A
kid would put their neck in the noose and pretend to strangle and die

and then they would take off the noose and it was the next kid's turn. Soon it was lunch time and the other kids heard their moms calling, so they went home and I was left alone and never got my turn as a rustler.

But I was an only child and used to playing imaginary games by myself; so I tried to get the noose but it was too high up. I went over and got a box to stand on, put the noose around my neck and then fell off the box. I was just barely able to touch the ground on my tip-toes which kept me from breaking my neck or strangling immediately. But I couldn't reach the knot to untie the noose or release the pressure enough to get my head out of it. If I stayed on my tip-toes I could still barely breathe, but my legs got tired and I was getting dizzy from the lack of oxygen. Meanwhile, my mother was just about to take a nice long bubble bath, which she loved to do. She would spend an hour or more just relaxing in the warm scented water; sometimes she would sing popular songs like "Love Me Tender." She had just shut the hot water off and started to get in the tub when she stopped… "I haven't seen the kid for awhile, I better go and check."

So my mom found me in the tent with the noose around my neck; she panicked and ran to get the neighbor who cut me down. At first she thought the older kids had tried to kill me, but when I could get my voice back again I explained that I was the one who had done it. She looked at me really funny, "Honey are you sad or something? Do you think you want to die?"

I was completely nonplussed, "No Mama, I was just taking my turn to be the Rustler."

"Honey, I'm afraid someday your imagination is going to be the death of you…or me." She never told my dad what happened because she was afraid that he would spank me. I often wonder what might have happened to me if they had ever actually compared notes about my various escapades.

NARRATOR: She began learning about, and loving, dinosaurs at an early age, just like Tim Zell had.

MG: When I was in the first grade, I discovered a Little Golden Book called *From Then to Now*. It was a child-size bite of the evolutionary history of Earth, which was pretty wonderful in and of itself; but the real thrill for me was that it introduced me to Dinosaurs! They were my first great passion. I checked out all the books in the library about dinosaurs and learned all their complicated Greek names and proudly mispronounced them to any and all who would listen to me rattle on about them. Like so many dino-brats, I was the amazement of my relatives. I was also the instrument of bringing dinosaurs to the attention of my classmates and inadvertently becoming the most popular girl with all the boys. They called me "Dianasaur."

I did a book report on dinosaurs and brought my collection of dino toy models. Not only did I get an A on the report, but dinosaurs became an instant hit with the other kids, mostly boys for some odd reason. So for many months at recess we would troop off to a pleasant grassy area on the playground and reenact dino lifestyles and dino battles. I could roar and stamp with the best of them but I was not real keen on the pushing and shoving part (no fair using hands to hit with) so I quickly established my credentials as the expert and intermediary. I insisted, for instance, that you could not stage a battle with an Allosaurus vs. a Tyrannosaurus Rex because they were from entirely different epochs; Allosaurs were Jurassic and T-Rex was Cretaceous; they were separated by millions of years. Not to mention that anyone stupid enough to want to be the Allosaur would totally get creamed!

I was cut to the heart when Disney's movie "Fantasia" featured a primeval battle to the music of Stravinsky's "Rites of Spring." On one level I was thrilled that they had dinos at all, but to my utter chagrin they had the notorious Cretaceous T-Rex battling a Jurassic Stegosaurus to the bitter and bloody end. I thought Disney should have known better and tried harder to be accurate. They could have used an Allosaur and then the poor outgunned Stego would have had a fighting chance. And since Stegosaurs were my personal favorite dino, it seemed like a particularly cruel trick. I always cried when I saw that massive spiked tail thrash out its last despairing thump. I had lots of fierce arguments with my buddies over that episode. Even years later I had to play the sequence for Oberon so he could count the toes on the carnosaur and see for himself what an anachronism it was.

OZ: It turned out that the carnosaur depicted in *Fantasia* really did have three fingers on its little front limbs, which I maintained made it an Allosaur, as T-Rex had only two! So as a kid I had no trouble reconciling that scene. Still, I think MG was also right— from the overall proportions, the artists probably intended to depict a T-Rex, but they made a mistake in the number of fingers.

MG: I guess I was a pretty annoying know-it-all and eventually the boys went off to find other excuses for play fighting without some picky female referee. And I went back with the other girls to play at being horses or back to the library to learn about more cool critters. Hermione Granger would have understood me perfectly.

We had a pretty good life and we should have been relatively comfortable; but when I turned eight my father developed emphysema. He worked in the oil fields in an increasingly smog ridden city and smoked Kool cigarettes at a time when they advertised that Kool cigarettes were "Doctor recommended." Once he got sick, he could no longer work enough to make a living wage even though he tried. But he spent more and more time in the hospital until the doctors and hospitals ended up owning all his hard-earned money and property and we were forced to move into an 18-foot travel trailer and become Gypsies. He suffered from the stress of losing everything, the constant struggle to breathe, and all the steroids and other weirder drugs he was given (American doctors knew almost nothing about emphysema though the Brits had had it for years) while the doctors used him as a guinea pig. After a couple of years of this he went pretty crazy; he went from being a terrific dad to being perpetually ill, irritable and violently abusive.

Every Summer we would drive back to Mississippi to stay with our relatives there; this was when gas was 25¢ a gallon. A couple of times when my Dad got too weak to work and too debilitated by the smog to live in So. Cal, we would go back and stay for longer periods. When I was ten I went with my Dad by train from L.A. to New Orleans while my Mom stayed and sold the house and the car. He was so weak and thin that he had to be helped up onto the train and I had gone along with him to give him an epinephrine injection if he had a seizure and couldn't breathe. Both Polly and I learned to be his nurses pretty thoroughly by that time and eventually she went all the way and got her LVN license and took over working to support the Family. That time we stayed for a whole year and a half in Mississippi and I went to school there; I shunted around from one group of relatives to another in the summertime. I learned to milk cows, take care of 66,000 chickens and to harness a horse and plow a field. I learned to love the rural lifestyle, but I never fitted in with the people; I was picked on a lot and was always in trouble.

I had this major epiphany once in the chicken yard. My job was to go around every day and pick up all the dead bodies of the chickens that had killed each other and feed their bodies to the hogs. I got to where I could predict which chickens were going to be dead the next day. It wasn't really a psychic power, it was just the power of observation; the chickens that got killed were the ones that had any differences at all from all the other chickens. They would have tiny black spots on their wings or a slightly crooked beak or just a different way of holding their heads or walking. That's all it took and they were hog food. So one day I took a long, long look at all those white, white chickens henpecking each other to death and thought about myself in this white, white Southern society being henpecked as much as I was already and wondered about my future there. I have always learned a lot about the human race from watching the behavior of other animals.

The racism of Mississippi in the '50s and '60s was pretty much out there for everyone to see and most of my relatives acted like it was something that was natural and handed down from God as some sort of duty. If you spoke up you got knocked down and that was all there was to it. I got whippings regularly because I stood in the "colored line" at the Dairy Queen or drank from the "colored water fountain" or tried to give up my seat to an old black woman on the bus. I would also get in these huge theological arguments with my Grandfather. I read Darwin because I was a Dino-brat and I pretty much grew up with the notion of Evolution as a given. It was certainly taught in Calif. Schools and I had never really questioned it. I discovered that most of my relatives including my Mom believed that Evolution contradicted the Bible.

Surprisingly my Grandfather did not believe that at all because he did not believe in a literal translation of the Bible. He once told me: "The Bible, like all the other great sacred works of mankind, is a metaphor and anyone that believes in the literal truth of every single word of it is an ignorant idiot." He didn't see any problem with Evolution as a process of Creation at all. So we would have these discussions; the curmudgeonly old Southern Christian scholar and the impudent 11-year-old prodigy from La La Land.

Often the talks were really wonderful but they could turn ugly. He may not have believed in the literal truth of the Bible, but he believed some pretty wacky stuff. For instance he believed that African people were not human! I knew that was bullshit because I had Black friends back in California and they were just like me in every way that counted. But he honestly would argue with me that they were a lower sub-species of hominid. He would say that segregation was natural because Redbirds stayed with Redbirds and Blackbirds stayed with Blackbirds. I tried explaining to him that Redbirds and Blackbirds were different species and could not interbreed and different colored humans were more like different colored horses; white horses and black horses routinely interbred and so did people. At this point, the discussion went downhill rather violently and I was smacked again for "backtalk."

At that point in my life I still considered myself to be a Christian, but it was Granddaddy Moore who made the first real dent in my belief in the rightness of those teachings. It was around a discussion that I was having with him about my horse, who was 23 years old and didn't have many more years left. I said to Granddaddy: "I guess I will see him in Heaven someday."

He then informed me complete with cited scriptures that my horse would not be in Heaven because he did not have a soul; only humans had souls and went to Heaven. That rocked me back. Of course my horse had a soul! So I told him that if my horse wasn't going to Heaven then I didn't want to go either. He asked me if I was planning on going to Hell instead, but I said "no, I wasn't; I was going wherever the horses and other animals went." Oddly enough he didn't get mad at me this time; he just burst out laughing and called me "his little Heathen." Talk about prophetic words…

Horses were always one of the greatest inspirations and often the driving force in my life. One of my first words was "horsey," only I pronounced it "hokey." I spent most of my play time either rocking or bouncing on various wooden horses and later made up elaborate games about people and their horses: Cowboys and Rustlers, or Racehorses and Jockeys. The orchard lot next door became a pasture and the branches of the trees became imaginary horses. One tree in particular we called "the Raccoony Tree" and it was just the right height and with thick branches placed just so that about six kids could form a posse and gallop all over the wide open spaces of our imaginations calling out bits and pieces of the ongoing plot of long summer afternoons in the California sunshine. And when we got hungry we would just shinny up one of the other apricot or peach trees and bring down a handful of ripe fruit for our snacks.

I collected plastic model horses for my birthdays and at Christmas, and I created elaborate scenarios with them. My collection grew to around fifty, and then one momentous and tragic day they all got swept downstream in the Colorado River. I was heartbroken and the only way I could console myself was by imagining that downstream the horses would wash up on the Yavapai Indian Reservation and be found by some poor Indian girl.

Later on, I would read every book that Walter Farley ever wrote about *The Black Stallion* and his offspring, and saved up all my money to rent horses to ride at the Glenn Spiller's Riding—in those days it was $1.50 an hour. I didn't really start off by taking riding lessons; I just got up in the big old saddle and took off. We spent hours walking and cantering along the flood control dikes in the countryside of North Long Beach. It always felt like an instinct to me and riding Western was pretty much what everyone did there.

My parents could never afford to get me a horse of my own, but when I was in Mississippi I rode my cousin's horse bareback and old Prince Selum was my best friend even though he tried his darndest periodically to bolt and scrape me off on every tree and barn door that he could find. Once he scraped me under a tree branch but my long pony tail whipped around the branch and the horse went on but I got left behind hanging by my hair. My Grandfather saw me and laughed until I thought he would die. Luckily, I didn't break my neck. But there was never any offence taken either way between me and the horse, though I was pretty mad at Granddaddy until he stopped laughing and got the ladder to get me down.

I gradually got better at staying on, and one summer when I visited my Aunt in New Orleans I rented a horse at the Audubon Park stables and the only tack they had was English, so I said: "saddle up" and I got a few quick pointers from the stablehand. It was love at first ride! All that glorious day I was riding around the winding trails overhung with huge live oaks, draped with Spanish moss, and through lush the green landscape alive with birds and cicadas and dotted with little creeks and ponds with real alligators.

The English saddle let me sit in close contact with the horse (he was a blood bay with a wide white blaze named Winsome) and he was responsive to the reins so there was just an easygoing interaction. It left such a big impression on me (like most of my visits to New Orleans) that when I went back to California I decided to save up my money and take English riding lessons. I found a stable near where we moved to in Orange County and wheedled my Mom into taking me there on weekends and for the first time in my life I felt like I had found a place I belonged.

The place was called Los Cuervos and it was run by Lionel T. Harris, one of the most remarkable men I have ever had the privilege to know. He was a classic English riding Master with steel grey hair and twinkling blue eyes with a crisp accent and a no-nonsense manner. He had 50 horses of his own and boarded maybe 50 or more others. He usually had a gaggle of young girls tagging along after him, asking him a million questions, hanging on to his every word and eager to learn everything they could. He was a well spring of equine lore and taught us all patience and manners as well as cooperation and hard work. I cleaned stalls to help pay for my lessons and later graduated to cleaning tack, feeding and taking care of the horses and finally to assisting and teaching basic beginner lessons myself. I learned standard English equitation and then went on to Hunt Seat and to Jumping which was my great love.

And I finally got my own horse. His name was Sichon and he was a Thoroughbred Cross Country horse that had been a Steeple Chaser but was now retired. Like so many horses his owner was too busy and never rode him so he stood in his stall bored out of his mind with nothing to do. I made friends with him when I was making my rounds to feed and clean stalls for Mr. Harris. Shawney was a huge 17-hand bright bay horse with a narrow white blaze and hooves the size of soup plates. He was not the sharpest hoof knife in the tack room, but he was a sweet and loveable giant.

I fell in love for the first time with another being. He would listen to all my stories and I could lean on him while I brushed his coat and if I was sad he would rub his nose on my cheek and nibble my tears. Mr. Harris persuaded his owner to give him to me and I went about reconditioning him to become a show horse. It was a prodigious task because his strides were too long for jumping in show-sized arenas and he was pretty old to learn to collect himself and learn a whole new way of moving but I was determined, and he was willing to do what I asked him. At least he wasn't bored when I was around.

Again, I was lucky that I didn't get my neck broken because I was utterly fearless and didn't have much sense about what I could or couldn't do but I did have lots of good advice. We did pick up a couple of ribbons at small shows but what mattered the most was that I was immersed in a deep and meaningful relationship with a very special being that taught me to become empathic and listen with my heart; to give as well as to take in order to accomplish a mutual goal. I had a friend, a confidant and a protector.

From the time I was 12 until I was 16 I spent every minute I was not in school at the stable. Of course I had to get a part time job to help pay for board, feed and vet bills. Then Shawney got sick with a terrible disease called Lymphangitis and though we battled it together for a year and a half eventually it got so bad that he had to be put down. Of course it broke my heart, but I still stuck with horses and worked in a partnership deal with two women who used to go to race tracks and buy up retired racehorses to retrain for saddle and show horses. I bought a beautiful blood bay thoroughbred named Polished Flame from Caliente Racetrack and retrained him for show.

But by that time, I had my own car and had to spend more and more time working to pay for insurance and going to school so I had less time to spend at the stables…it was the old story again. Not enough money, not enough time. Unless you are willing to devote your entire life to nothing else, horses are a rich person's game. But even after I sold my horses and my life took me in other directions, I never forgot the lessons I learned from them and horses will always be part of the Mystery deep in my heart. I walk by them now in the nearby pasture and bring offerings of carrots and apples. In my dreams I still follow the jingling of the bridle reins, the bells and the call of the horns as I follow Rhiannon on the Fairy Rade.

Going from California to Mississippi back and forth like a ping pong ball had a strange effect on my upbringing. Luckily I was a

Gemini which helped for being in two places at once, but it did make me more than a little schitzy. For one thing I was always "the new kid" wherever we went, and the culture shock was enough to give anyone psychic whiplash. I just got used to never fitting in anywhere and developed coping mechanisms. I was always outgoing and I made friends pretty quickly—but I made enemies pretty quickly too. So I learned to tell stories to entertain other folks and keep them from picking on me. I would tell the people in Mississippi tall tales about those nutty Californians and tell the folks in California wild stories about those crazy folks in Mississippi.

I was a voracious reader and no matter what town we travelled to, if we stayed more than two days, I would beg to go to the library. It was my haven and my sanctuary. I would weave the stories I read into the tales I told and that is how I learned to teach people—by telling stories and anecdotes. The downside of all this was that I learned early on that in order to keep from being picked on or whipped by my Dad, or getting into trouble about stuff, I had to lie. So when I told stories I often embroidered them significantly; there were fantasy tales that I would tell as if they happened to me. My Mom and Grandma used to use the term "story-telling" as a euphemism for lying. So it all sort of got blurred together in my mind. I learned to tell stories to get attention and to distract people from being angry with me. I learned to tell them in odd ways because I never knew what I was going to get in trouble for, since every place I went to the cultural norms were different. This behavior in both the positive and negative ways would play a very large role in my life.

Actually, for the most part, I did have a happy childhood. I got to travel around and have adventures. One thing that was very good about my Dad, even when he was sick, was that he was interested in Natural History. When we were on the road he was usually up for taking a route that included places like the Grand Canyon or Carlsbad Caverns, with side excursions to Indian ruins or Meteor Crater; that way I got a very hands-on education. I have always felt strongly that I was a child of Nature. I could always talk to animals and hear their voices in my mind. I loved all kinds of animals, not just the cute cuddly ones. I used to drive my parents and relatives wild because I loved snakes so much and had no fear of them. My ophidiophobic uncle almost killed me with a hammer, because I brought him this little garter snake that I caught.

I frequently had dreams that would come to be true and sadly learned not to talk about them to other people. That was the first time people called me a Witch. I could feel spirits speaking in the wind and every time I would smell burning leaves in Autumn or fresh cut grass in Spring I would get a frisson of delight and the hairs on my neck would stand up and shiver. I would spend hours looking at the face of the moon and seeing the large, round and slightly sad eyes of the Lady (it never looked like the man in the moon to me).

One of the liminal moments of my life, which sums up this special relationship I have always felt with Nature, comes from the time when we lived near Parker, Arizona on the banks of the Colorado River. There we would experience these fantastic desert thunderstorms with huge lightning bolts that I loved to watch. There were two bridges over the river right near us. One was a gigantic, old-fashioned, metal railroad trestle, and the other was a broad modern concrete freeway bridge. My mom was always afraid of storms so she would go hide in the trailer, but I would sneak out and go down to the freeway bridge and sit on a rock all cozy and safe under the concrete bridge where I could watch the lightning strike the railroad trestle, over and over again. I would get high on the ions and ozone in the air and dance around and laugh and sing wordless chants, screaming back at the lightning and the thunder like some wild thing. I always felt supremely alive and at one with everything when these sorts of events happened to me.

And in this, as in most ways, I was very different from my parents and my other relatives—I always felt like a Changeling. I could remember pieces of my past lives and I loved to go out in the darkness and sing to the moon. In terms of religion or spirituality, I took what was available, which was mostly Christianity of one sort or another, but it never quite fit me. It was like borrowing someone else's clothes—they bulged in places I didn't, and vice versa. So I mostly grew up in my Mom's church, the Pentecostal Assemblies of God. They practiced an ecstatic for of Christianity, with Baptism of the Holy Spirit, speaking in tongues and dancing in the Spirit. I was fully involved in it and deeply immersed in the emotional gestalt of the experience. When the Holy Spirit was with me I always felt a strong uplifting feminine presence but I never really talked about that part of it to anyone.

All the aspects of that brand of religion are male: God the Father, the Son and the Holy Spirit, even the Angels are portrayed as masculine. It is a religion that is all about men and run entirely by men; but its adherents are 85% or more women. But it was what I knew, and I got along without asking too many awkward questions until one day I went to the pastor and said: "Look, I'm concerned because my father beats my mom and me. Where is God's will in this? What recourse do we have?"

Back then, there weren't any battered women's shelters and later on, I went to a psychiatrist to try to get family counseling help, but he had told my parents that I was crazy and needed electroshock therapy. So when I went to our pastor, he told me that it was the woman's duty to surrender to the will of her husband, and that if my dad killed my mom or I, we would get crowns in heaven someday! He said that my duty was to be obedient and not rock the boat, and that really tore the mask for me. After that all the bits and pieces that never quite fit started coming faster into a rushing torrent of questions and doubt. All this was right about the time of my puberty.

POLLY MOORE: Jesus says to love your companion—this is to the husband— "You have to love your companion like you love me." And if you really have that nature of Jesus, and that husband offers that wife that sweet nature, the fruits of the spirit as the Bible says— love, peace, joy and all that—then that wife is just going to be thrilled to death to fall in that shadow. Because then you're going to get all that love that everybody is looking for.

MG: I loved my mom so much, but I couldn't stand it that she was like a doormat. Whatever my dad did was okay with her—I guess it had to be, because periodically he would beat her and threaten to kill us both. That kind of behavior shaped me but I never gave in; it never broke me. She was always terrified, but I just got angry and would argue right back at him, trying to engage him in debate and showing him proof when I was right about something and he was wrong. I guess I was a smart-aleck kid who acted like I was his equal and he hated that—so we would get into these huge fights. Also, I would jump between him and my mom when he was hitting or kicking her. I can remember a time when he was threatening to kill me and I tried to bite his hand. He looked down into my eyes blazing back at him and I guess he must have seen a piece of his own fighting spirit reflected there and he couldn't bring himself to snuff that out.

Paradoxically, I never stopped loving my father; I know I must have loved him as much as I hated him. My father was my window and door into the natural world—he was sort of a Deistic Naturalist who loved Nature and introduced me to Her wonders. In spite of his craziness, he imparted that gift to me. My mother gave me deep love and appreciation for the spiritual world. She was an incredibly nurturing, loving parent. She taught me by example about unconditional love and a reverence for life. Hers grew out of devout Christianity, and though I took it in a different direction, we still shared in common a belief in the transformational power of unconditional love, a reverence for life, and a commitment to spiritual practice.

What I did not get from my mother was her fear. She led a fear-driven life from the time she was a child—even her faith was rooted in a fear of God and hell—but I rejected that whole fear component. Perhaps her love gave me the strength to do that, but I think that it probably saved my life, because if I had reacted to my Dad's threats with fear instead of the anger he recognized in himself, he might have killed me. I took away a lesson in survival: to not back down, to stick up for what you believe in and to be strong and not let yourself be intimidated by someone who is trying to bully you.

Little Diane in 1952.

Me and Mama, 1959.

Daddy and me, Mississippi, 1959.

Me on Prince. Forest, Miss. 1959.

My little trailer home, 1960.
L-R: Polly, Uncle Dudy, James,
Aunt Francis, me.

Morning Glory; High School
Drama Queen, 1966.

Me, Gary & Rainbow
on Oregon beach, 1971.

My perfectly normal Family...not!
L-R back: Polly, Gary, me
Front: Rainbow, James. 1971.

CHAPTER 13: Good Morning Glory (1961-1973)

G: WHEN I WAS ABOUT 13, I HAD AN opportunity to visit my aunt and my cousins again in New Orleans and attend Mardi Gras. I glimpsed another entire universe. It was so exciting I was overwhelmed, and I felt my spirit leaping up and exclaiming, "Wow—that's what I want! Somehow that is my religion!"

That's where I met Bacchus. He tapped me on the shoulder and said: "Girl, follow me!" And I did. After that revelation I knew that I was not suited to be a Christian.

POLLY: When she got old enough to know what she wanted, it never did bother me anymore. She's just as sweet as ever and I love her just as much as I ever did. I still had to accept the fact that she had her right, her prerogatives, to choose whatever she wanted. Of course I still always pray for her and for every one of her friends that they will be safe.

MG: Right about that same time I discovered the works of Ayn Rand. I read everything she wrote and was really into Objectivism for about a year. But I had always been psychic, and there was no place in her universe for mysticism. So I began a conscious, deliberate religious search. I studied a little bit about Zen Buddhism, Islamic Sufism and Yoga philosophy which eventually led me to a Hindu temple where I first heard about Goddesses in the world today. And I was amazed and awed: "Wow, what an idea! You mean there are living Goddesses in the universe still?"

I had read lots of Greek mythology as a kid—I was originally named for the Moon Goddess Diana, and that was fascinating. Learning about Lakshmi and Kali Ma and the power of Shakti was such an awakening. But when I started studying the actual practices I found myself dealing with the same old bugaboos of celibacy, sexism and obedience to male dominion. So I came to the sad conclusion that that just wasn't quite it either.

Next I moved into more magickal realms. I read *Lord of the Rings* and for awhile, I wanted to be an Elf more than anything else in the world. I guess on some level I always will… But I read other fantasy stories, classical fairy tales, Romance literature like William Morris's *The Wood Between the Worlds,* Celtic lore like *The Mabinogion* and the *Tain bo Cuilange;* I read *The White Goddess* by Robert Graves as well as the series of *Teachings of Don Juan* by Carlos Castaneda.

Somewhere along the line I got hold of a book called *Diary of a Witch,* by Sybil Leek. I was probably about 17, and it all just clicked into place. The book told how the "Old Religion" had been suppressed by Christianity; it described a Horned God like Pan or Cernunnos and His consort, the Goddess of many names. It all woke this deep feeling of recognition inside me. Like all the other bits and pieces I had been striving for were clues to this divine puzzle, and when it fitted together it all made perfect sense: a true revelation!

I realized that I was a Witch in this life and had been a Witch in other lives before. Unfortunately, her book also said if you're not born a hereditary English Witch, you don't get to be one at all. I thought: "What do you mean—that's what I am!" I felt I'd been offered this perfect gift, and then it had been snatched away. But I was not going to let what one person said about how one became a Witch stand in my way.

That same summer—my junior year of high school in 1965—I discovered LSD. I had a friend, Jimmy Spheeris, who was a folk singer, and he introduced me to the whole folk singing circuit in the Los Angeles area and along the Pacific Coast. Places like the Ash Grove, the Prison of Socrates, and the Cosmos featured local talent like Jackson Browne and Hoyt Axton in hootenanny style shows— along with rare concerts by the super stars like Joan Baez, Richard and Mimi Farina, Judy Collins, Buffy St. Marie and so on. He turned me on to the music of Dylan and also, eventually, to groups like The Mothers of Invention and The Fugs. We travelled around together (I had a car; he had a guitar) and we went to all these clubs and wild parties and had a truly wonderful time expanding our consciousnesses. He turned me on to Big Sur and the Laguna Beach artist scene as well. Jim was one of the truly germinal influences in my young life, and he remains one of the all-time greatest singer/songwriters that most people have never heard of. We were never boyfriend/girlfriend; we were just really good friends and having the time of our lives trembling on the brink of the remarkable cultural renaissance that would be the Summer of Love and the Sixties.

Of course, it wasn't all play for me. I still went to school and remarkably I managed to get pretty good grades even though I didn't study very hard. I guess it was because I was always fascinated by learning things. I was blessed by being in a good school with excellent teachers. I took 3½ years of Latin, four years of English and Composition, lots and lots of Literature, Biology, Physiology, Physical Sciences, World History, and of course my favorite, Drama. In Drama Club I found a social circle I could relate to; I was also involved in Speech Club and the Debate Society. I learned a lot of the best elements of creating a good ritual and about the Bacchic religious roots of the theatre from our Drama teacher. We were a pretty tight-knit bunch of theatre geeks who found a haven together against the storms of high school madness. The high point of my time there was getting the Best Actress award for my role in the Junior Class play: Moliere's *The Miser*.

I was also working part-time at a local hospital to pay for my car insurance, clothes and pocket money. I worked in the Laboratory and also did some emergency services work like EKG monitoring (before the days of the *Star Trek*-style monitors we now have) collecting specimens and phlebotomy. I did other assistant lab work as well as grungy jobs like washing test tubes and specimen jars. I spent time in the midst of life and death there, attending to people in crisis and also sometimes when they died. These experiences really made me want to understand the passages between the worlds.

I remember a watershed moment for me was when a woman came in to the ER with chest pains; she and I had the same doctor. He came into the room and was laughing with us as I took her EKG. It was supposed to be more of a precautionary test, and then suddenly her back arched upward and her eyes rolled back. I thought my machine had broken because the needles went haywire, but she had just suffered a massive myocardial infarction. We tried to save her—the doctor, the nurses, all the tools of the crash cart, they hit her five times with the defibrillator but it was just not going to make any difference.

Finally, there comes this nervous moment when everyone looks around sort of sheepishly at each other and shrugs. And then everyone looks at the doctor and he sighs and shakes his head and we all start packing up our gear while he has to go and tell this woman's husband the life-shattering news. The room emptied out and I was left alone with the woman, sort of lying like a broken doll on the gurney. One moment she and I had been laughing about some TV show and the next she was just lying there like a carved wax figure, her eyes still open staring into infinity. When I bent over her to disconnect the leads I stared into her eyes and sent out my thoughts to her as hard as I could: "Where are you now, and what is it like?"

I held very still and listened inward and I heard her voice say to me with this silvery little laugh: "Don't be in too much of a hurry, you'll find out everything soon enough." I thanked her and gently closed her eyes, then left with my machines and my questions.

Based on my reading, I decided that what I needed was an Initiation. So in the summer before my senior year, I conceived this whole story in my imagination about an English Witch that I had met in Venice (California, not Italy) who was teaching me about Witchcraft. I gave her a name: Vashti Esterath, and invented a lineage for her. I can still see her face in my mind's eye. Maybe I knew her from some past life, but in this one she was someone I dreamed about.

Then I took off for Big Sur for a month. First I lived off the land for a week, then I fasted and took a major LSD trip. At Lime Kiln Creek, I climbed up the side of a big rock by a waterfall and dove into the pool of water. The person who dove off that waterfall was a girl named Diane, but the person who climbed out of that pool was a woman named Morning Glory. That was my Initiation.

The next morning I awoke and three other Hippie-type folks were sitting around my sleeping bag and they had covered it with little field morning glory flowers while I slept. They all said: "Good morning glory!" and that is how I got my name. Oh, lots of people laugh because I am certainly not a morning person, far from it, but it was not the time of day that convinced me to take that name. Morning glory seeds contain trace amounts of lysergic acid and they are part of the ancient shamanic pharmacopeia; their bell-shaped flowers, like Datura, resemble the skirts of the Cretan Goddess. They are common and unassuming but hide a potent secret in their hearts. All of these are the reasons why I chose that name.

Why would I change from a perfect Witchy name like Diane? The answer is that I love the Goddess and I respect Her, but I did not presume to take Her name, especially after I came into my sexuality and began to follow the ways of Aphrodite. As a young girl Diana protected me, but in order to stay with Her as an adult I felt that I would need to give up my love of men. She can be very possessive, that Goddess, and I did not want to end up like Callisto or so many of Her maidens that strayed from Her side to follow the love of a man or a God. So whether it seems to fit or not, Morning Glory I became and Morning Glory I remain. Even if I mostly see the dawn these days about the time I am heading to bed. Hmmm... maybe I should have called myself Nightshade. Oh well, too late now!

After this experience I embroidered it and wove it into my story about Vashti the English Witch and how my Initiation had been under her tutelage so that I could convince others that my Initiation had been legitimate. Oh, what a tangled web we weave... But regardless of what stories I spun about it, I always felt in my heart of hearts that it was a legitimate Initiation. Of course it would have been wonderful to have had a teacher or a coven to have given me the gift of Initiation, but I am an only child and I learned early on that you make do with what you have. What could be more Witchy than that? So I might have managed to get myself a viable Initiation, but what I missed out on the most was the training. I never got to learn all the lore and magic spells, and potions and rites passed on from a living High Priestess. Once again, I just had to turn to the "do-it-yourself" tradition.

NARRATOR: Though the details of her story would come back to haunt her years later, Morning Glory was actually way ahead of her time: self-initiation rituals would become very popular in the decades that followed. And there were probably other Witches around then who had done the same thing, but back then everything was shrouded in secrecy, a lot of tall tales were told, and no one was recording any statistics. Indeed, even Gerald Gardner claimed to have been initiated by an old Witch that no one had ever met and, to this day, there is still speculation about who she was, what really happened, and if she even really existed.

CAROLYN WHITEHORN: I met Morning Glory in the Winter of 1967-'68. My ex-husband had initially met her, and said he was bringing this really interesting woman home for dinner. I was blown away because I had never met anybody that age who was that together or had that much inner power or strength. Over dinner she talked a little bit about being a Witch. She defined herself as a "Green Witch"—this was a new concept for everybody, and my oldest daughter was very interested in it. I don't know where they were living at the time, but they hung out in Laguna Beach some. We continued to see them.

During that period of time a lot of things were happening in my life. I had started making jewelry. A few months before I met MG my husband had quit his nice, straight paycheck-every-two-weeks job, and all of a sudden I'm trying to support a family of eight on hand-made jewelry that I was wholesaling to headshops and boutiques. And then Morning Glory came in, and put a little different mix into it too, because all of a sudden I was also doing Pagan jewelry and Goddess stuff. I ended up a few years later making jewelry and regalia for significant numbers of the Neo-Pagan community in Southern California. And I met them because I did stuff for Morning Glory and word passed on.

Then she and Gary got married and moved up to Oregon. Every time that MG was in Southern California she would drift into my store—by then I had a custom-designed-jewelry store—and stay anywhere from a couple of hours to a few days. She always felt like a major person in my life. She could walk into a room, not say a word, and everybody knew she was there. Their daughter shared a birthday with my youngest daughter. My daughter said that when she met Morning Glory, she knew what she wanted to be when she grew up. My daughter was actively involved with the Goddess before I was. She is now the high priestess for a coven in Santa Cruz. My daughter is also active with the SCA and other things like that.

NARRATOR: Morning Glory remained independent in all things, and even while she was still in high school and living at home she was working so that she could have a horse and her own car.

MG: I was still living off-and-on with my parents, but I also shared an apartment with a girlfriend from Drama Club who had graduated the year before me. I turned 18 on May 27, 1966, but I graduated in June. I moved out completely the day I turned 18, bought myself a seven-foot boa constrictor that I named Baby Doll, and for a year or so I pursued a career as a Laboratory Histologist for a private lab. That is a job that basically takes human tissue removed either in a surgery or autopsy and processes it so it can be microscopically examined by a Pathologist to determine disease status. It was challenging and interesting work that involved working with human body parts, chemistry, and learning dyes and staining techniques. Plus I was out of the high stress situations I encountered in the ER.

I have never been squeamish and grew up dealing with the realities of processing dead animals on the farm and dead humans in the hospital. Also, I have always had the "Addams Family" streak of morbid fascination with the gory side of life and death. I loved working with chemicals, color distinctions and biology and this gave me all that and then some. Of course, I had no concern at the time for all the toxic chemicals I was regularly exposed to, but nobody knew or cared in those days. The hours were rough for me because you had to be up and to work by 6:00am and in spite of my name I have always been basically nocturnal. But the folks at the lab where I trained were a congenial crew to work with and the pay was not bad for the time.

So, I worked and partied and went to Junior College for awhile, enjoying being a free bird entirely on my own, until my awareness of the political scene with the war in Vietnam and the repression here began to overwhelm my consciousness. More and more of my time was spent working at the Peace Center or going to Anti-War demonstrations or to Love-Ins, and it cut into my work and my regular life. The Psychedelic Sixties had arrived in full tilt! I got so frustrated with the poor level of education that was being handed out at the J.C. that I followed Tim Leary's suggestion: I turned on, tuned in, and dropped out. I guess it seemed like everything they were teaching me there I had already learned from much more gifted teachers in High School.

I decided that I needed to go on walkabout and took off for New Orleans. I visited my relatives there and ended up in Mississippi with my Grandmother where I quickly realized that my opinions on Civil Rights were going to get me shot. I was given to understand that I should take the first bus back to California before I ended up like the Freedom Riders who were being murdered left and right. So I decided to hitchhike back to California, but I got detained in Hot Coffee, Mississippi, where I barely missed being treated to some "good old boy" forced Southern Hospitality.

I was able to use my family connections to get out of there and my uncle wired me money for a bus ticket back to California. I bought a ticket to New Orleans and from there as far as Phoenix. But then I decided that since I was safely out of the South, I really wanted to hitch the rest of the way. So I headed off on the highway to Flagstaff and then across old Route 66 to revisit some of my old childhood haunts. The trip was fairly uneventful, though on the other side of the Grand Canyon I got picked up by a guy who wanted to play rough and I ended up having to grab my stuff and try to bail out of the car. He grabbed my hair and tried to stop me, so I stuck my pocketknife in his leg and rolled out the door when his foot came off the accelerator pedal and the car slowed down. I ran off into the twilight and hid in the sagebrush until the full moon came up, then I was able to flag another ride with a family this time. I got home and stayed with my folks until I got my car in the best possible shape and then I decided that it was time to follow my dream and move to Oregon and join a Commune.

I reclaimed my serpent from the friend who had taken care of her while I was gone. This time I did not plan to return and I wanted to get everything I needed to start a new life in a new place. A friend of mine from the Peace Center wanted to come along as far as San Francisco, so we headed North in the warm summer sunshine. There was an onramp near the gas station where I filled up (gas was now 70¢ a gallon) and my friend pointed out some hitchhikers on the ramp, so I pulled over and gave this guy a ride. I recognized him from the Peace Center and also from driving around and smoking pot in the back of his tricked-out old psychedelic panel truck. His name was Gary, and he said he was also headed for San Francisco and that he had just got kicked out of the military for being too weird.

Our first stop was Big Sur and I was planning on staying there for at least a month before I went any further north. I knew that I needed to touch the Earth and clear my head of all the bad vibes I had picked up travelling in the South and in the cities. When we got to Big Sur I offered to share my sleeping bag with Gary, because he had only brought a bedroll. But the deal was: if he wanted to do that, he had to help me keep my boa constrictor warm!

GARY FERNS: We met originally down in Orange County for a few months before we left for Oregon. I had just gotten thrown out of the Air Force and was sort of kicking around—a freewheelin' Hippie. I met Morning Glory at one of the local head shops in Santa Ana. She was "the snake chick," the one with the boa constrictor under the black light. We used to hang with the same people and go to the beach or concerts. She decided to move to Oregon. I was kind of bored when I heard about it and it sounded like it might be fun, so I decided to go along for the ride. We stopped at Big Sur and made this intense psychedelic connection and we decided we were married from that point on. We stayed at Big Sur for a week or so and then ambled on up the coast. Eventually, we arrived in Eugene and connected with this other family from Orange County that we knew from the Peace Center who had migrated there earlier.

NARRATOR: MG and Gary co-created a commune with their friends. Eventually they merged with another, larger group that had a communal-style farm and they all moved out to the country. Then MG and Gary decided to have a child together.

MG: After awhile on a farm out in Dexter, we co-created a commune called "Cat's Cradle" in Eugene, which was in a great part of town near this gorgeous old cemetery. We were pretty happy exploring the deeper meanings of life, listening to music and working on relationships and helping to take care of the kids that were in the commune with us. So we decided that we wanted to have a child together and we hitchhiked back to So. Cal. to get the rest of the stuff we had left behind when we went north. Gary had a panel truck that he had left down there, and we drove it back to Oregon. Our daughter was conceived in the back of that truck, while we were camping on Big River Beach in Mendocino.

GARY: It was a 1948 Chevy half-ton panel truck—one of the original psychedelic relics. We were on our way back to Oregon after spending Christmas with Morning Glory's folks down in Orange County. We stopped in Mendocino for the night and it was so cold there in February, that the only way to keep warm was by having sex. She had gone off the pill for quite a while at that point. It just kind of happened. That truck was still running up until the 1990s.

MG: About three months into my pregnancy, everybody in Cat's Cradle decided that they wanted to merge with a larger group that was called Crow Farm. That was my chance to actually live on a communal-style farm, so I was looking forward to it. We met the people and they seemed nice and interesting, but Gary was not so happy. At that point he wanted for the two of us to go off together, but I was always more into social experimentation. When it started out it was okay, but there were lots of weird drugs, pharmaceuticals and what-not that people were always doing as well as being extremely overcrowded. I didn't move to a farm to do drugs—I was pregnant! But we did have two lovely cows, Mousey and Sylvia, and a couple of pigs, Shagrat and Gorbag; and a pretty nice garden.

We made some good friends there and the kids were all great, but the interpersonal adult politics were pretty toxic. There were a lot of really obnoxious alpha male personality clashes. We felt crowded out and marginalized. One of the women there paid me the backhand compliment that: "I was too naïve to be unhappy." There was probably more truth than poetry in it at the time. I had hoped to find some other person there who might share my brand of spirituality, but that was just not happening. The best friends we had were the children and the animals.

CATHERINE C: They lived for a while at Crow Farm. The Crow Farmers reminded me of the conquering hordes coming over the hill in *Braveheart.* They were big, savage, robust folks, and not like your average early '70s Flower Children. They were meat-eating, rifle-toting, redneck Hippies (for lack of a better word). Crow Farm was a very rustic place.

MG: My daughter was born on Nov. 11, 1969. I had a home birth in town, in the back room of a friend's house. I had a 60-year old midwife who was an Osteopath who had delivered lots of babies, including the husband of the nurse who assisted us. We were just down the street from the hospital in case anything went wrong. I did not want to have to give birth in a hospital because in those days they would not let the father into the delivery room. That was a really big issue for us both! Like Cutter from *ElfQuest* said: "We started this together and we will finish it together." Both my parents and Gary's parents had come up for the birth, but I couldn't handle having my mom in the room for the birth because she was so nervous. I know she couldn't help it because she almost died in childbirth but I couldn't be relaxed with her there. So in the end it was just Gary, me, the midwife and the nurse.

I was convinced from all the books on natural childbirth I had read that my birth would be a snap. When I went into labor I thought there must be something really wrong because it hurt so bad. The women from the commune who had had several children said: "Don't worry honey, you're just in labor. We told you it was going to hurt, but you wouldn't believe us because you knew it all from books." I had back labor which lasted about 14 hours and there were times I thought I was going to die. I found out just how pampered and easy my life had been; anytime I really didn't want to do something I could usually figure out a way to get out of it. Childbirth is the end of that illusion entirely! From the moment it starts, the only way out of it is through it and out the other end. You can't fake it, or double-talk or lie your way around it or trade somebody else for your shift or any other thing. It is all about the Here and the immediate Now; it is the time when girls grow up and become women.

I know I actually got off pretty easy, and I really came to understand my mother's intensity when she talked about her 54 hours of labor with me. But it was all totally worth every minute of it. There were no complications at all and Gary was able to help and to be there as my supporter all the time. And finally there was the baby. She was this beautiful copper color like an Indian child; we named her Rainbow Galadriel. We stayed up all night long, so pumped-up on adrenalin after the birth, and just listened to the tiny little girl noises she made while she slept. Gary was such a great Papa.

After about four days of staying with our friends we had to go back to the Farm, and I really did not want to do that. It seemed so strange to me. I was so adamant about staying at Crow so the baby could be raised on a farm with other kids, but once she was born, wham! I just instinctively knew that it was not the right environment for my baby to grow up in. But I had made my life there and so we had to go back. It was hard for me to get up and walk around once I was back, and the house we shared was somewhat isolated from the rest of the Farm. There was a woman in the community there who had taken too many psychedelics and had snapped. She was convinced that because I was a Witch I was going to kill my baby, and so she kept trying to sneak into my room and take Rainbow while I was sleeping.

Right about that time there was an enormous amount of pressure put on Gary to go out and work with the men cutting Christmas trees as a way to raise money for the community. He didn't want to leave me and the situation kept getting crazier. Fortunately, my Mom and Dad came and stayed in their RV with me at the Farm and Polly would watch over me and the baby while I slept.

NARRATOR: The social experiment of a communal farm didn't work out the way they had hoped, so MG and Gary moved with their newborn baby back into Eugene. They eventually settled down in a loft-like space where they formed a new community that included their downstairs neighbors.

MG: But finally it just got to be too much. My dream of living and raising a child in a community had exploded and I realized I did not want my child exposed to this sort of risk. So we loaded everything into the Roach Coach and left, going back into Eugene and living in the room where Rainbow had been born. We were there for about six months. After that we moved back out to the country and lived in the little 18-foot trailer I had grown up in; my Dad had brought it along when they came up to visit.

It was a hard Winter; we had electricity but not running water. Still, we were young and strong and happy. It was certainly a challenge, but you can't moon around about how wonderful it is going back to the land to raise your kids the old-fashioned way and then whine about having to break the ice on the horse trough to get water to wash the diapers. Eventually, though, we did decide to move back into town, and we found a little place that was perfect for us, like a loft. The people downstairs were really nice, and we ended up creating a community of friends and it was wonderful.

CATHERINE C: A friend of mine told me that there was a Witch living upstairs from her. It was in spring of 1972. So I went up there to meet Morning Glory. She and I started talking, and I didn't come back downstairs for 48 hours. We stayed up night and day talking. She was fascinating and truly living a self-made life. That was a very valuable thing in 1972—my entire generation was really about re-defining life and not simply accepting the mantle of suburbia. We were very consciously trying to re-imagine our culture.

And here was someone who was living a life that was filled with commitment, integrity, and joy. She lived in an amazing little apartment with Gary, Rainbow, and an 8-foot boa constrictor named Baby Doll that they kept in a hollowed-out TV set. The place was painted the colors of peacock feathers. It was a sort of converted attic. Gary had a love for antiques, so they had Victorian-style furniture, which one could pick up at the time, and it was always filled with candles. They had a Hippie van called the Roach Coach and we had wonderful times driving over to the coast and the beach in that.

MG: I started writing for a local newspaper called *The Auger*. The name of my column was "Magick Words." And I was reading Tarot cards, teaching classes and giving little seminars for extracurricular clubs for High Schools and the College. I had lots of wonderful friends and Gary was a great guy, but more of a retiring Buddist-type spiritual person. He wasn't cut out to be a Priest to be the partner to my Priestess self; I just didn't have any magickal peers. I wanted to share my spiritual visions with the world, but there were no other Pagans or Witches there. I kept looking for other people to connect with; we even drove down to San Francisco looking for Witches, but we couldn't stay long enough to make any real connections. Everyone was really underground and secretive in those days.

At one point I tried to start a coven with some of the assortment of kids I had been teaching, but that didn't get off the ground. However, I did pick up a copy of Llewellyn's *Gnostica News* at a Psychic Bookstore there. I subscribed to *Gnostica* and finally heard about the Gnostic Aquarian Convention, to be held in Minneapolis over the Autumn Equinox weekend of 1973. Some of the people from Crow Farm that I had remained friends with were from Minneapolis, and they had given up on the commune and moved back there. So I decided that I was going to hitch-hike to Minneapolis, go to the Con, and finally meet some people like myself.

CATHERINE C: She functioned alone as a Pagan in Eugene. She would always get interviewed by the newspaper at Halloween, but there really wasn't much of a community of that sort there at the time. Still she seemed fine and happy—she wasn't always yearning and grumpy. Around the time of Elvis Presley's concert from Hawaii, Morning Glory heard that there was going to be a big festival in Minneapolis. She was desperate to go there. They didn't have any money, so I went to my father and I lied. I said I needed the money, I borrowed it from him, and I funded her trip. We sent her off with great love and encouragement, because she meant so much to all of us. She was an inspiration and a constant joy. And we knew that her religion was the foundation of that for her. So Gary and I did what we could. We sent her off. And she did not come back.

CHAPTER 14:
Cosmic Convergence
(1973-1974)

You shared your Vision with a crowd
I sat and listened mesmerized,
As what you stood for spoke so loud,
And what you dreamed shone in your eyes.

We took a walk and tried to talk,
But words weren't necessary then.
I'd do it all the same again;
I'd do it all the same again.
~ "Love of My Life," by Morning Glory Zell

Z: DURING THE LAST COUPLE OF YEARS, MY writings on TheaGenesis had been spreading throughout the community. It became a unifying mytheology. As Joseph Campbell later said in *The Power of Myth:* "The only myth that is going to be worth talking about in the immediate future is one that is talking about the planet." My articles from *Green Egg,* that I had expanded forth from the initial idea, had been reprinted in other places. The Llewellyn Publishing Company reprinted one in their publication, *Gnostica News.* And they also invited me to come and do presentations as a keynote speaker at the Gnostic Aquarian Convention in Minneapolis that was to occur on the Fall Equinox weekend of 1973. This was a big deal for me—my first major public speaking gig. A bunch of people wanted to come along, so we made plans to have a CAW table there.

Just before we left we had our Mabon celebration. Normally we would have held it on the Autumnal Equinox, but since we were going to be out of town then we held it a few days beforehand. Carolyn Clark, being our high priestess, conducted the ritual. She asked everybody to write down on a piece of paper what they would like to harvest for the year. We each had to think about what seeds we had sown, and what we would like to receive as our reward.

CAROLYN CLARK: During the time I was active I wrote and conducted many rituals—it was like being the conductor of an orchestra. I wrote them so that other people would be pulled into the action and not be spectators. That Mabon ritual was the first one I had done that involved that kind of requesting the Goddess through writing down our petitions and burning them. What I wrote down was that I wanted Tim to find his true soulmate so that together they could build the Church of All Worlds into a truly global organization.

OZ: I got my paper and pen and I started to write down, "Let me be reunited with Julie…" But something stayed my hand, and instead I wrote, "Let me be united with my true soulmate." I was shifting my thinking from my directing how I wanted things to be, to trusting the Goddess to know what was best for me. It was part of what had come from my months on my own thinking about things.

That went into the cauldron, and I didn't really think about it much more because then we were on our way. We packed up a van full of people and headed up to Minneapolis. When we got there we looked around and realized that it was not a gathering of our kind of people at all. They were into astrology, Tarot, crystals, reincarnation, and other New-Agey kind of stuff, but they weren't really Pagans in the religious or cultural sense. We're talking about people who, at that time, were featured in the *National Enquirer* and ran psychic hotlines.

Well, the other occasion for this was that Carl Weschke decided that they would also be having a gathering of Witches. So a lot of big-name people in the Witchy world had been invited. They had just gotten Isaac Bonewits on the staff of *Gnostica News* as their editor, so he was there. And they had brought in people like Ray Buckland and Margot Adler. And me, of course. The ulterior agenda for all this was to introduce a woman named "Lady Sheba." She had put together a grimoire, which, it later turned out, was essentially the Gardnerian *Book of Shadows* slightly altered. She was going to be presented to us as the new Witch Queen of America. Needless to say, that didn't go over very well among a bunch of radical anarcho-Pagans who had no use for British-style royalty in our movement!

OZ: While we were getting our table set up in the lobby, I looked around and coming in through the door I saw a gorgeous Hippie woman dressed in a flowing, beautiful San Francisco Gold Rush dress, all lavender, with creamy lace and long frilly sleeves. She had long dark hair and huge deer eyes and incredible breasts. That was more along the lines of what I had been hoping to find!

MG: I had lots of amazing adventures heading through the high plains in September; camping out in the snow at Yellowstone; sharing a tiny tent with the guy I was riding with and two other hitch-hikers. But we made it to Minneapolis and I got safely dropped off. When I got to the convention, I took a deep breath and looked around. It didn't seem like there was anyone there that looked at all like me. They were mostly older straight looking folks. I finally saw a bunch of folks with brightly-colored clothes, Renaissance-style tunics and cloaks at the Church of All Worlds booth. I asked this one long-haired fellow how to get to my first workshop and we exchanged some mutual excitement about the event and he gave me directions. After my workshop was done I returned to the CAW booth and hung out with the folks there; everyone kept telling me that I had to meet this guy who was with them because we were so much alike. He even had a snake.

OZ: Unfortunately I didn't have a chance to talk to her, because right at that time I was being hauled away to do interviews, and then I had workshops and a lunch engagement with a reporter from *Playboy* lined up. When I came back Orion was telling me, "Oh man, you have got to meet this woman! You and she have so many things in common." But by then she was gone. This kind of thing kept happening. She would come by the table when I was gone, and people would tell her about me. And then I'd come back and people would tell me about her.

This went back and forth until finally I came back to the table and she was there and we talked for a few minutes. We didn't have a chance to do much because I was just there to pick up some copies of *Green Egg* and head down to do the first of my TheaGenesis presentations. I told her I had to leave and she said, "Can I walk with you?"

I said, "Okay, but I've got to go do this workshop."

And she said, "Where is it?"

And I said, "It's downstairs."

She said, "I'm going downstairs to a workshop too, so I'll just go with you."

So we walked and continued talking. When we got down to the room, I walked up to the front and set the box of magazines down on the table. She sat down in the front row and that was the first time she realized that I was actually the speaker at the workshop she was going to.

There was a whole room full of people. I presented my "Thea-Genesis" paper. And at the end of the presentation they all came rushing up to talk to me. And Morning Glory was at the head of the line. She said, "We have to talk."

And I said, "Right." I grabbed her hand and we just walked out of that room leaving everyone else standing there watching us go.

MG: Eventually, when we did meet, it became a magickal melt-down. I hadn't really read his articles in *Gnostica News* before I came, but I realized that I had signed up for all of his lectures based on the titles he had created from popular rock songs; they were all about Nature and the Goddess. He gave this amazing lecture on The-aGenesis, which was the whole idea of the Goddess as an evolutionary force in nature, and how we were all part of that one consciousness. It was all the missing pieces of my own home-grown theology and answered all the biological and historical questions that had been plaguing me; wrapped it all up and tied it up with a neat bow and ribbon. I was completely blown away and so were most of the other people in the room.

OZ: I took her upstairs to a secluded bench behind some potted plants, and we sat down next together. As we turned to look at each other face-to face, suddenly, for both of us, the whole rest of the world just disappeared. For me, there was nothing else except her eyes, and I fell into them like diving into a deep pool. I felt we were completely and telepathically bonded, as if our souls had merged.

Suddenly our lives and our psyches poured into each other. It was love at first sight, but beyond anything that you read about. I heard the voice of the Goddess in the back of my head saying, "This is the one you asked for."

MG: I may seem like a pushy broad, but in many ways I am kind of shy; I'm especially nervous around people that I think are "famous" or more educated than I am. But I couldn't stop myself from going right up to the front of the room at the end of the lecture and telling this man: "I really need to talk to you!"

I had meant it in a sort of: "We should find time to have a conversation about this stuff" sort of way, but to my amazement he just took my hand and said: "You're right!" and walked me right out the door leaving all those other people behind with their mouths hanging open in astonishment. We went off to a little alcove behind some potted plants in the lobby and sat down and took a deep breath, turned to each other with a million things to say and found ourselves...speechless, timelessly falling into each others eyes, into each others memories, into each other's lives.

It was like when the Gelflings, Kira and Jen Dreamfasted together in the movie *The Dark Crystal* (which hadn't been made yet). We poured the essence of ourselves together in that moment and melded our thoughts and memories into a common pool. It was the most profoundly important magickal act that had every happened to either of us. We were so in love that we could hardly speak.

But I have always had the ability to step back from my feelings (it's a Gemini thing), so I paused and took a deep breath and said: "You know this is amazing and wonderful and I love you so much I can't even think straight. But I must think straight enough to be honest with you. I need you to understand that as much as I love you, I can never be in a monogamous relationship. It's just not in my nature and I don't want to deceive you. I want to be free to have other lovers and you're free to do that as well. I'll give you my whole heart and soul, but I cannot give you monogamy. There are other people in my life and there always will be other people. Yet what we have together is special and unique beyond any measure; nothing will ever take away from that."

And he looked back into my eyes and smiled like he had just found the Holy Grail.

OZ: I'd never had anybody present it to me as what they wanted. It had always been me saying that. Everything that we touched on was like that. We started coming up with every possible thing we could think of and every time we did we found a complete match. From that moment on we were totally inseparable. The whole rest of the weekend was like a dream. Everybody who had come up there with me was packed into one hotel room. (This was a custom I had picked up from going to science fiction conventions. We had all brought our sleeping bags with us.) The closet was just big enough for Morning Glory and I to lie down in, so that became our private space. Though I think we probably kept everyone else awake all night with the sounds we were making!

I saw your face once in my dream
A thousand miles and years away.
Then Fate began Her cosmic scheme
To bring me to your side that day.

I'd travel far, to where you are
Favorite Lover, my Best Friend!
I'd do it all the same again;
I'd do it all the same again.
        (~ "Love of My Life," by Morning Glory Zell)

MG: I have always been a "True Dreamer," that is from childhood I would have dreams that would come to be real. About two years before Gnosticon I had dreamed that I was going to meet a man who was going to be a teacher for me. The Goddess spoke to me and told me that I was to follow him and he would lead me into a completely new life. When I woke up, the dream was so vivid that I told Gary about it. So I went about my life, sort of looking for this person and wondering when I was going to meet him. I had memorized his features exactly in the dream by sort of freezing the action and had never forgotten them. When I met Tim I kept thinking, "this must be the guy in the dream, but there is something different about him; he doesn't look quite the same." I just couldn't put my finger on it.

And then I finally got a copy of the Gnosticon program book; I was flipping through it and I saw his picture. And it was literally like it was cut with scissors out of the dream. And I told him, "Wow, this picture doesn't really look that much like you."

And he said, "Yeah, it's an old picture, it was taken two years ago." WHAM! There it was. It was truly Destiny, in my face staring back at me. And there was no way I could deny it, explain it away with logic or escape from the inevitable reality of it. It was like the Gods said to me: "You have always asked for proof of real magick; you asked for a miracle, now here it is. Deal with it!"

Many people go through their whole lives begging for just one scrap of true magick and then rarely recognize it when it finally does arrive. But I was so blessed that I was not going to make that mistake; I was not going to lose this perfect shining Goddess-given gift. At that point I decided, "Okay, I have to accept that this is genuinely my Karmic fate. So now what am I going to do?

OZ: We became the darlings of the entire con. At the big banquet, they set up a special table just for speakers. Of course, I insisted that an extra place had to be set for Morning Glory! Right across from us was Isaac Bonewits, and he had two questions for us: "When are you going to get married? And can I perform the ceremony?" This was like 24 hours after we had met.

Well, we turned to each other and said, "Next year at the Spring gathering." Because they were going to be having an Aquarian Festival and Witchmoot on the 1974 Spring Equinox. "And yes, you can perform the ceremony." And that was that, we just acted totally on impulse, even though we knew there was a lot that had to be resolved before it could happen. I mean, she had a loving husband and daughter and a whole community of friends out in Eugene, Oregon.

MG: Much of our lives together have been about going with that cosmic impulse and doing the unthinkable because it is the right and perfect thing to do when you are in the moment.

Gary and I had always had an open marriage, but it's another thing to have two primary relationships over 2,000 miles apart. The whole drive back to St. Louis I was pretty much a basket case. I sat in the back seat weeping inconsolably. It was definitely a case of "be careful what you wish for"—it will come about, but at what cost? The price was my relationship with my husband and daughter and my wonderful community of friends in Eugene. I came to understand why the ancient Greeks feared the power of Aphrodite, the Goddess of Love; it was because Her gift was irresistible and caused lives to be torn apart and communities thrown into chaos.

CATHERINE: We all felt lost and betrayed. I was kind of beside myself and didn't know what to do. Along the way I found out what had happened. We would explain it to people that we knew by telling them that she went off to a Witches conference and fell in love with the head goblin.

MG: So, for two solid years I went back and forth from St. Louis, Missouri to Eugene, Oregon. I took being a commuting wife and mother to new heights of absurdity. But there was nothing else I could do; I couldn't be in two places at once. My heart was divided and when I was in St. Louis I desperately missed Gary, Rainbow and everyone in Eugene and when I was in Eugene I couldn't bear being away from Tim. I felt like the Little Mermaid. I had finally found my feet, but walking was an agony of a thousand cuts.

CATHERINE: When she came back to figure out what to do with her family she was quite sensitive to our feelings of loss. She came to see me and I said, "What happened? You owe me an explanation. You were physically gone and now it still doesn't feel like you're here." And I kept saying it over and over because I was so hurt.

And she kept saying to me, "I am here for you, and I am always connected to you."

And I said, "I don't believe you." And she put her hand on my arm and she literally sent an electrical shock into my body. It was the first time that I had ever felt her practice magic on me. But then we mended.

NARRATOR: Morning Glory and Tim had little time to prepare for their wedding. MG was traveling back and forth between Eugene and St Louis, where Tim was a very busy man. The Church of All Worlds had invested in a real printing press, and *Green Egg* had gone "semi-pro:" there were wrap-around covers, articles by people like

Robert Anton Wilson, and they were publishing a lot of advertising. So Tim Zell, as editor, publisher and typist, had to do what basically became his second full-time job. Though *Green Egg* was doing a fantastic job of connecting Pagans with each other and nurturing the growth of Earth based spirituality, it was not a financial success. Tim and everyone else who worked on it were doing it voluntarily.

And the relationship between Morning Glory and Tim was tumultuous from the start, and not helped by the environment she suddenly found herself in. It was difficult for her to trade the lifestyle and mild climate she was used to for harsh winters and a rough, inner-city neighborhood.

MG: I was totally unprepared for living in a hard, cold, big city. I had been living in Hippie communes and a liberal college town. Here I was in a situation where I was with the person I was supposed to be with and this church that I loved. But his whole universe was wrapped around this organization that was embedded in this really awful big city environment. Some people thought the city was great, but for me it was a nightmare. It wasn't safe to go out on the streets after dark. Two of the women in our community had been raped and brutally beaten. I grew to love most of the people in the church but they were all part of this toxic environment and some of them were not at all supportive of Tim and me. They saw me as a self-righteous interloper; and to be perfectly frank, they were pretty spot-on about the self-righteous part. I just didn't get how people could deal with the noise, the pollution and the violence; I was so homesick for Eugene that I was miserable and made other people around resent me.

NARRATOR: And from the moment that they had first met OZ and MG had had almost no privacy. Tim's house in St. Louis was a center of activity, and there were always people coming and going. That was the way he had lived his entire adult life. Finally, right before they were to be married in the spring of 1974, the couple had an opportunity to be alone together.

OZ: In the spring of 1974, MG and I were scheduled to be married. Just before the wedding some friends of ours who had a summer cabin in the Ozarks offered this to us for a weekend retreat to get ourselves together before the ceremony. Our lives were so busy that we had to take time out to do this. We went down there, and it was beautiful—spring was springing forth all over the place. Flowers were all in bloom. We made a little fire in the fireplace, and we tripped on acid. In the process of this we bonded in an amazing way.

Strongly in our minds at that time was the whole vision of the Awakening of Gaea, and the coalescence of planetary consciousness. We still hold that as a central myth in our lives and in our work. And one of the concerns that was going around among ourselves and our friends, who were also caught up in the Gaean mythos that we were developing at that time, was, "What happens when Gaea really does achieve consciousness? Do we all just get lost like drops of water in the ocean?"

Because we were so focused on this stuff (and our impending marriage) we became One. We were able to look out through each other's eyes, and completely be within each other. We had this epiphany that the emergence of planetary consciousness would not be one where we would be lost as individuals, like little drops of water being dropped into the ocean. But rather that our individual consciousnesses would expand into the larger awareness. So that rather than just seeing out of only one pair of eyes, we would see out of everyone's eyes. And everyone would have that same experience.

We found that, in our combined essence, our general magical capabilities were vastly expanded as well. We were sitting in a clearing in the middle of the woods. At one point we reached out to the sky and called out. And a hawk started circling around above us. We reached up and looked out of the eyes of the hawk, and we were able to look down and see ourselves and the forest all around us. We reached out and called butterflies. And swarms of butterflies came flying in from all over the place and landing on us. We called the wind, and the wind started picking up and whistling through the trees. We kept on doing that 'til the intensity got to be almost like a tornado, so we had to stop and slow it down. The wind slowly receded back to normal.

We picked violets to make violet jam, and it was the only time in our life when we were in a place where there were enough wild violets to do that. At the end of this retreat, when it was time to return home, we felt, "Okay, we know who we are." It was one of the great romantic high points of our life. We were totally bonded—forever.

And on April 14, 1974, we were handfasted and legally married in a huge Pagan ceremony at the next Gnosticon in Minneapolis.

We took our vows to never part
We pledged for Life and then for more.
You kissed my lips and stole my heart
In front of people by the score.

In velvet green, our wedding scene
Was filled with portent now and then.
I'd do it all the same again;
I'd do it all the same again.
      (~ "Love of My Life," by Morning Glory Zell)

NARRATOR: The 1974 Spring Gnosticon, where the wedding was scheduled to take place, was also being promoted as a "Witchmoot" to establish a "Council of American Witches" (later changed to "American Council of Witches" when it was pointed out that the initial acronym, CAW, was the same as that of the Church of All Worlds). 73 initiated Witches of many different Traditions attended, unanimously ratifying a germinal document that came to be known as "The 13 Principles of Wiccan Belief." Decades later, this remains a cornerstone of the Craft—right up there with "The Wiccan Rede."

At the Witchmoot Carl Weschke introduced an unknown author named "Lady Sheba." Llewellyn having just published her grimoire, *Lady Sheba's Book of Shadows,* Carl presented her as the new "Witch Queen of America." Needless to say, that didn't go over very well with all the other Witches who showed up!

The war in Vietnam had ended the previous year, and activists were turning their attention to other issues. The idea of Witchcraft had caught on in the growing feminist movement as a form of female empowerment—being a Witch was becoming a way of making a political statement. This bunch of radical anarcho-Pagans had no use for British-style royalty, and certainly weren't interested in having anyone as their Queen!

But the real center of attention for the weekend was on April 14, when Morning Glory and Tim were handfasted and legally married in a huge public Pagan ceremony.

MG: It was the very first public Pagan wedding ever; we wrote and created the entire ritual ourselves and it was really stressful. Partly because I was trying to handle things at a convention that was hundreds of miles away from St Louis, which is where I was living, plus I was still going back and forth to Eugene. I'd brought Rainbow to live with us for a while and she was only four years old and was very confused about the changes in our lives. Then at the Con we had to set up a CAW booth, plus we were both keynote speakers. I wrote an article and did a talk about my own understanding of what Witchcraft was, as a form of European shamanism. (This was a very controversial idea at the time. But I had just read Mircea Eliade's book on shamanism and done a lot of other research.)

And it turned out that the date that we had picked, unbeknownst to us, was Easter Sunday. Just try and find flowers or a wedding cake on Easter Sunday! Plus I had friends flying in from all over the country. (Unfortunately I couldn't afford to fly in my parents.) The wedding went off pretty much without too many hitches. Tim and I both had tears streaming down our faces but our voices were still strong enough that you could hear the words of our vows. We got all the way through it, and it was wonderful.

OZ: The story and photos appeared on the front page of the local paper, and they upstaged the Pope's Easter message to the world. Bryan was the ring bearer, and even my father attended it. Rainbow wore this little pink faerie gown and was the flower girl. She was given a basket of petals to scatter on the pathway for us to walk on. Not having any experience, or been given any instruction, she picked the petals out of the basket one at a time and very carefully placed them on the carpet. Margot Adler sang Gwydion's Beltaine Wedding song. Isaac and Carolyn performed the ceremony. Both of them had long hair down to their waist, and in the process of leaning over the altar both of them set their hair on fire with the candles. That was very impressive and everybody applauded.

DON WILDGRUBE: The handfasting took place with Carolyn Clark as HPs and Isaac Bonewits as HP, and yes, they did catch their hair on fire from the candles. Carol Barbier (who was the model for Tim's Diana poster) and I were the "Merry Maid and the Merry

Man." We drew the circle! Tim and MG basked in the glow of the press, being written up in a couple of Minneapolis newspapers, as well as *Gnostica News.* One of the major projects that came out of the Witchmoot that weekend was the "13 Principles of Wiccan Belief." They were originally drafted mainly by Tim, Carl and Isaac, then there was a big meeting with input from many others throughout the Craft Community. The Principles were finally adopted and are now a part of Neo-Pagan/Wiccan lore.

OZ: At the dinner after the wedding, my dad sat with Morning Glory, the kids and I. At one point I went off to the restroom and one of the other people at the table asked my father how he felt coming to this thing and seeing that his son was such a prominent figure in the Pagan community. He said, "I feel like I've given birth to the anti-Christ." But he told me he thought it was a very nice ceremony.
    And then Morning Glory ended up getting quite ill.

MG: At the time I had a condition called abdominal epilepsy. And it was a seizure disorder that affected my stomach, bowels and uterus—all my plumbing. So I would lose urinary control and bowel control and start vomiting. I had that disorder from the time I was a teenager. I had always had problems that were sort of like that from childhood, but it got worse when I hit puberty. I was on Dilantin, but I did not like to take it. That really screws up your red cells, and it has a lot of negative mental side-effects also. I had heard about new research about alpha and theta waves, and that you could reprogram your brain out into a healthier pattern of rhythms and prevent seizures pattern from re-occurring. When I told the neurologists they didn't want to have to deal with it. They told me to take my medicine and not argue.
    It just so happened that when Oberon and I got together, he had a biofeedback headset. So I was in the middle of the process of learning this new technique, and I had also chosen, foolishly, this time to get the meds out of my system. So when you load all the stress of the wedding weekend on top of it—plus Oberon and I had done some deep inner work and he had this whole vision that when we got together something really significant was going to happen. And we didn't know exactly what it was going to be.

Remember that this was a time when all this apocalyptic stuff was going down. The cold war and the Viet Nam war were still going on, and there was all this talk about WWIII. So there was a lot of psychic stress around it, and all these factors rolled into a ball.

After the ceremony and dinner were over, we went back to the hotel suite. It was time for the consummation of the wedding. And I felt the beginning precursor wave of a seizure. And I thought, "Omigod, what am I going to do?" So at that point I took aside some of women that were part of our intimate circle and already in our room and I said, "I need you take over for me, and be my proxy. Are any of you willing to help me with this?"

There were three women who happily volunteered and were in bed with Oberon, and I so I lay down there next to them. I used the energy that was generated by them all to block the seizure and stop it from happening. So towards the end I was able to be a part of it. And that was my wedding night!

OZ: Morning Glory and I had spent months creating the ritual. We published it in *Green Egg* and it became the template for Pagan handfasting and wedding ceremonies throughout the community. Decades later we would encounter Pagan groups who pulled out their ancient, passed-down-through-the-ancestral-lines, *Book of Shadows*—only to find that it was *our* ceremony they were using! In a sense our romance had an enormous impact in the larger Pagan community. After that we were constantly approached to perform handfastings for people. I think people kinda hoped the magick would rub off.

Tim & Morning Glory
Handfasting, April 14, 1974

Tim & Morning Glory wedding
newspaper photo, April 14, 1974.

CHAPTER 15:
The St Louis Nest
(1974-1975)

We merged our minds and hearts as One
We worked to heal the Planet's Soul.
We laughed and played and had our fun
We struggled always for our Goal.

In joy and lust, in Perfect Trust
We talked of how things might have been...
I'd do it all the same again;
I'd do it all the same again.
~ "Love of My Life," by Morning Glory Zell

Z: AFTER THE WEDDING RAINBOW CAME back to St Louis to live with us for awhile. Morning Glory and I gave each other snakes as wedding presents. I gave her a baby male Burmese python which she named Ananta, and she gave me a baby female boa constrictor I named Tanith. They grew up together. We joined the Herpetology Society at the St Louis Zoo, and I did artwork for their little newsletter. Morning Glory also did some nude modeling for a local photo studio—and I still find those photos inspiring these 35 years later!

One of the most memorable Nest meetings for me was held at a huge Victorian communal house where Michael Hurley and Orion were living at the time. This happened shortly after Morning Glory arrived, and I believe Julie was also there. I had just that day received two remarkable things in the mail. One was a giant poster called "The Evolution Mandala" by Dion Wright, the original of which had been painted in a corncrib in Woodstock, NY in 1965-'66. The other was a reel-to-reel tape of Margot Adler's first broadcast of "Pagan Press Review" on her NPR radio show, "All Things Considered."

Unfortunately, the bare wooden floor of the old house jabbed an enormous splinter into my bare foot. As Julie and MG both struggled to remove the splinter, others put up the poster and played Margot's tape. I sat on the floor totally engrossed in the Evolution Mandala, an amazing artistic visualization of the entirety of evolution on Earth from a single original cell, while Margot's lovely siren voice sang some of Gwydion's songs and read long passages from my "Thea-Genesis" article in *Green Egg*. The tears streaming down my face were from more than the splinter! Today, these 35 years later, the Evolution Mandala—now in a suitably ornate frame—still claims a central place in my home, as it has in every home I have lived in since it first arrived.

Like Julie, Morning Glory was fond of putting up little signs around the house. One on her bedroom door said: "If I'm not in accepting what I can't change, I'm out changing what I can't accept."

MG: OZ would go off to work at 6:AM and I would go back to sleep and then get up later and clean and cook and deal with Rainbow or work on the *Green Egg*. I am not a morning person, in spite of my name, and I was not really used to living in the city. When OZ left in the mornings he often did not bother to lock the front door, which in retrospect was a pretty dumb thing because of the neighborhood we lived in. So one morning after I had kissed him goodbye and he had left for work, I returned to bed and had just started to doze off when I heard the Indian bells attached to the front door jingling. I thought OZ had forgotten something and returned so I dragged myself out of bed and went out to see what he might need.

I was surprised to discover, not Oberon, but instead a young black neighbor kid about 12 or so holding a sheaf of newspapers in his hand. I stared at him and he stared at me (I was naked). He muttered something about "Do you want to buy a newspaper?"

I looked at the papers in his hand and they were a bunch of junk mailers, I told him very irritably: "Hell no! You don't just walk into people's houses without being invited. Get out of my house this very instant!" And I pushed him out the door. I went back in to bed and once again had just started to drift off to sleep when I heard footsteps in the hallway. This time I sat bolt upright and I was scared; whoever it was must have come in through one of the windows. What if it wasn't the little kid, what if he had just been a scout and he had an older brother or even a gang? But when I get scared I usually get mad and the more I thought about it the madder I got, so I picked up OZ's athame off the altar in the bedroom.

I still was drowsy and wasn't thinking very straight so I didn't bother to put any clothes on; I just picked up this big old curved iron Filipino headhunting blade and headed out into the hall. And there I came face-to-face with…the same slightly overweight dopey little kid who was standing wide-eyed beside our snake cage. Then he turned and saw me standing there with this huge knife. His eyebrows went clear up to his hairline and at that moment we were both thinking the same words: "Oh shit!" but for completely different reasons. I guess he figured he would just sneak back into the Hippie house and snag some loot while I was still asleep and then here comes the crazy naked white bitch with a big old mutha of a knife that was gonna carve his black ass like a turkey. He had probably heard all kinds of rumors about us being devil worshippers and so on. The house décor and the snakes certainly added to the ambiance.

For my part, I was cussing myself for giving into paranoia and picking up a knife which had upped the ante in this confrontation. I figured that I could wrestle this kid into the bathroom, lock the door and call the cops, but I couldn't wrestle him safely with a knife in my hand. I didn't want to hurt him; after all he was just a kid. But he would probably have no compunction of using the knife on me or of just trying to get it away from me, in the process of which somebody would get hurt. I frantically tried to think of some way to ditch the knife, but I couldn't see any way to get rid of it without him being able to pick it up. So I decided to just wave it around as a threat, keep my distance and try to chase him into the bathroom.

I headed for him and he took off running through the hallway into the living room and then dashed into the kitchen where he looked frantically around for a weapon of his own and then dove into the kitchen sink full of dirty dishes for a protruding handle and pulled out triumphantly and brandished at me….a cheese slicer! I stood in the kitchen doorway and watched the look on his face as he saw me cracking up in hysterical laughter. He turned his head and looked at what he held in his hand, sort of did a double take, threw the cheese slicer in my general direction and ran. He dashed back to the dining room window he had crawled in through and was halfway out of it when I grabbed his legs. I thought: "If I can just get one of his shoes off, I can take it around the neighborhood until I find Cinderfella's mama and then he will be in really deep doodoo." But he managed to wriggle one foot out of my grip and kick my other hand smashing it against the sill hard enough to make me let go.

I laughed for hours afterwards though, and especially when I told the story to OZ that evening. I held out a vain hope that I had at least traumatized the little brat enough that he would reconsider a career in housebreaking, but OZ said that he had probably retold the story to his buddies (leaving out the cheese slicer) and made out how brave and tough he was to have tangled single handedly with a crazy naked witch woman and survived to tell the tale.

Of course it would have been a different story if I had managed to get his shoe. Still, I can't help but think how many times people must find themselves in what they think is a high drama, only to see it become low farce.

OZ: Over the following months Morning Glory continued her studies towards ordination as a priestess in CAW. We counted all the previous stuff she had done before, so she moved ahead pretty quickly and ended up being approved for ordination in nine months.

At Lughnasadh, on the first of August, MG was scheduled to be ordained. The festivals at that point had been moved from the quarry to other lands that people had. Several of the folks in our community were working with other people or knew people with rural land, so we found ourselves with access to new places. One that we went to for a while was land that had a cave, a pond and a marsh. In preparation for the festival, Michael Hurley's wife, who had a kid Rainbow's age, said she was going to be going back to that farm where we had held previous events and spend some time out there, and she invited Rainbow to come along. We said Okay—we knew her, we knew her kids. Rainbow really wanted to go, and we thought that would be a lot of fun for her.

MG: The following weekend we went out to the place where we were having the ordination ceremony. Gary, who had come all the way from Oregon to be at my ceremony, went with us to the site of the gathering and Orion drove to the farm to pick up Rainbow. When he got there with her it was a shock. Her hair, which had never been cut in her life and had been down her back, had been cut short. He told us a horror story: she and all the other kids there had been dosed with LSD. This guru had shown up on the scene, and unbeknownst to any of us the women we knew had become his followers. He was calling for people to bring their kids so that he could begin a new order and purify the kids with drugs. The guy's name was Gridley Wright. He believed that all children belonged to him, and that they should all be dosed with acid, and that the fathers should all bow out or acknowledge him as the alpha male, and the women should all be subservient to him. He had all the women shave their heads. I had no idea of any of this. The woman whom I had trusted had been a strong feminist. But she had joined that cult. She had shaved her head and gave my daughter as well as her son over to the cult.

GALE SALVADOR: At first I was happy to be there. It was fun. There were other kids, and it was a communal, collective feel, but very rugged as well. The house was stripped down to a bare floor and cots. We were there for a few days and then it changed. I went for a walk one day and all of the foliage started dying. I kept walking and I ended up down at the river. I was really afraid. There was another little girl who was laughing and having a good time. Then I started hallucinating even heavier. Giant anchors started falling out of the sky and into the water. Later I was on a blanket with a woman who was supposed to be my caregiver, and Gridley was on a blanket next to us. I think he was giving us the acid in Kool-Aid. He said, "Do you want to come with me?" And I said, "No, I don't like you. You're a bad person." Then the whole earth cracked open on both sides of us. I said, "I want my mom, I'm scared." And he told me that my parents were dead and that I belonged to God.

OZ: There was no way out of this for her—she was trapped out in the country with this guy and we had no idea that this was happening. There were people there that knew us, had our phone number and saw what was happening and looked the other way and didn't call us.

MG: When Orion brought Rainbow to me and told the story, Gary and I went off with her alone in the woods and we just held her and told her she was safe now and we weren't going to let those people ever come near her again. I was in a quandary because on one hand I just wanted to take my child and leave but on the other, I did want to complete the Ordination Ritual that I had worked so hard for. So I asked Rainbow if she wanted to leave right now or stay for the ceremony and by that time she was starting to have a good time with us and some of the other kids so she said that she wanted to stay.

And that was my final ordeal before I went through my ordination ceremony, the symbolic ordeals that were part of the ritual were just that: symbolic. The real ordeal had torn my soul into pieces and I was furious at myself and at the universe but most of all at this Gridley-monster and the women I had trusted. I took deep breaths and got myself centered and then made myself get through the ceremony, but then we packed up and left. We went back to the farm and confronted the guy.

OZ: I was absolutely livid. He had two biker guys who were his guards. I went into complete overdrive, in full warrior mode. At that time I had the ability to morph into incredibly fast, reflexive moves. I could snatch bats, butterflies, and hummingbirds out of the air, and catch striking snakes behind their heads. So as I charged in I took two guns away from two different guys—a rifle, which I broke over my knee and threw into the swamp, and a flare pistol, which I tossed to MG. Once these guys had been disarmed, Gary was able to hold them at bay. I landed on Gridley, slammed him to the ground, and sat on his chest while I pummeled him furiously.

MG: I was haunted for years because Oberon took the guns away from two of the bikers, and I had the pistol and held it at this guy's head, and I could have pulled the trigger. I stopped and I didn't do it, because I knew that if I did that I would go to prison, and my daughter wouldn't have a mother. At that point I backed away and instead I called a curse down on his head—I asked the Mother Goddess to take him down for what he had done in his arrogance and madness. You have to understand that our attitude about psychedelics was that these were sacred medicines, they were magical allies. No one should ever be forced or tricked into taking them and to do this to a child was the ultimate betrayal of trust and profanation of the sacraments.

OZ: We tried to file charges against him and got nowhere with that. You would think that the Child Protection Agency or the police would want to do something. But they just figured that we were a bunch of Hippies, and we had left our kids with him, so we had no case. We were quite astonished by that. One cop actually said that they could prosecute us for trespassing and assault!

GALE SALVADOR: After that I was really depressed. A lot of my parent's friends told me that I was never the same after that, that I wasn't the same happy-go-lucky kid. My innocence was gone.

My dad took me back to Oregon. We hitchhiked back together. I hated hitchhiking. It used to terrify me. I felt insecure about the whole process.

MG: Years later we heard that Gridley Wright had fled the country and gone to India with his followers. When they were in India he declared that none of them would be allowed to have any vaccinations or Western medicine. And they were in a primitive commune. The children all got cholera and died. A father who had been tracking him down got there a week after they buried his children. When he found out what happened he pulled out a big knife, carved Gridley up (22 stab wounds, the report said…), and left him. And because of the orders Gridley had given, his followers let him die slowly and painfully of septic poisoning. So it was Kali who took him in India, but it was at the hands of Shiva, the avenging father.

OZ: The 1974 World Science Fiction Convention was in Washington, DC. We drove out to attend, and we won the prize in the costume contest as "Most Primal." We came as Peter Stag and the High Priestess of the Goddess Columbia from Philip Jose Farmer's novel *Flesh,* which was one of the very first science fiction books to really get into old-style Pagan sexuality.

We returned to Minneapolis at Mabon for the fifth Gnostic Aquarian Festival. We shared water with Robert Anton Wilson, who became a water brother and regular contributor to *Green Egg.*

ROBERT ANTON WILSON: Tim and Morning Glory, prime movers in the Church of All Worlds—the first religion in history to be admittedly based on a work of fiction; their theology is lifted verbatim from R.A. Heinlein's imaginary Martian religion in *Stranger in a Strange Land*—gave a seminar called "Omega" based on the evolutionary theories of the Jesuit paleontologist Teilhard de Chardin.

Synchronistically, they illustrated this presentation with an "Evolutionary Mandala" which I had previously seen in *Psychedelic Review* magazine when Tim Leary was editor. This amazing painting looks like an ordinary Tibetan Buddhist mandala of concentric circles at first sight; look closer and it shows representatives of all major species and families of earth-life (fish, insect, dinosaur, birds, reptiles, dogs, etc. etc. etc.) radiating out from a central DNA spiral.

"All life is One," Tim proclaimed. "This is no longer mysticism, but hard scientific fact. There is One Mind on this planet, the DNA computer . . ."

"And each individual mind can re-link itself to that One Mind at any time . . ." Morning Glory said.

"And when all minds learn to do that, we reach the Omega point, the planetary awakening foretold in all mythology," Tim went on.

Tim and Morning Glory have a great presentation there; the alternative back-and-forth delivery gives a quasi-ritual effect and emphasizes the real link between DNA science and traditional religious concepts.   (~Robert Anton Wilson, *Starseed Signals*, Page 229)

BRYAN ZELL: I always looked forward to going to science fiction conventions. But dad would not want to baby-sit for me. Dad always wore a snake around his neck, so if I was looking for him I'd just ask people if they'd seen a guy with a snake. It was easy to find him. I'd spend most of my time exploring the hotel or in the theater where they showed movies round the clock.

There was one convention that I went to with Rainbow, and she was a great asset. People always felt sorry for her. We would ask for money and they would give it to us.

GALE SALVADOR: Bryan and I were on our own. He was more of a guardian than my parents were. There was no supervision. We were running amok in the hotel. We'd go into the bar and eat maraschino cherries out of people's cocktails that they had left behind on the tables. MG and OZ were very young, and their idea of parenting was just, "let them do what they want to do." There wasn't much as far as guidelines, rules, boundaries or limitations, none of that.

MG: In retrospect, bringing my daughter to live with us in St Louis was the biggest mistake I ever made in my life. There were a series of tragedies that happened when she was staying with us, such as the whole Gridley Wright thing. Partly that was because I was a new parent and my approach to child rearing was to shower my child with everything I ever wanted when *I* was a child, which was lots of freedom and adventures. I didn't understand until years later that you have to give a child what *they* want to have, not what *you* want to give them. In Rainbow's case what she wanted was security and that has never been important to me, so it wasn't even on my radar.

Also, my attentions were on my brand-new relationship with Tim, and another significant part of my failure there was because I was totally unprepared for living in a hard, cold, big city. I had been living in Hippie communes and a liberal college town. Here I was in a situation where I was with the person I was supposed to be with and this church that I loved. But his whole universe was wrapped around this organization that was embedded in this really awful big city environment. Some people thought the city was great, but for me it was a nightmare. It wasn't safe to go out on the streets after dark. Two of the women in our community had been raped and brutally beaten. I grew to love most of the people in the church but they were all part of this toxic environment and there were quite a few of them who were not at all supportive of Tim and me. They saw me as a self-righteous interloper and to be perfectly frank, they were pretty spot on about the self-righteous part. I just didn't get how people could deal with the noise, the pollution and the violence; I was so homesick for Eugene that I was miserable and made other people around resent me. That kind of attitude thing is contagious.

My experiences in St Louis were not all negative. It is important to remember and celebrate the good times; too often we let our memories only focus on the negative. It was wonderful meeting all the people, making new friends and learning about the hodgepodge of bio-theology, science fiction mythos, complex ritual creation, family celebrations, Cheez-Its eating, magazine printing, bad pun telling traditions that formed the Church of All Worlds in those days. Nest meetings were homey and down to earth, but since they changed with whoever was in charge of it that week, you got a large of variety of experiences, a real communal spiritual smorgasbord. A Nest meeting could be anything from an all-out formal Wiccan style Circle to a Tantric group meditation, or a trip to the zoo. It was and is a marvelously flexible way of worshipping and when it is really practiced becomes the backbone of a strong spiritual community.

I remember with especial fondness the Circles that we would have with Carolyn Clark and the Coven of Gwynvedd at this spot that was a tangle of wild undeveloped property adjacent to and behind an old Orthodox Jewish Cemetery. It was very secluded area with a large bower of berry vines and honeysuckle far away from any houses so we would not be disturbing anyone. But even though we were neatly tucked away and out of sight, the neighborhood dogs always seemed to know that there were Witches about and would set up a howl. Of course we always met at the full moon so the dogs would be howling anyway. At first we were annoyed but then we realized it was evidence of Hecate's presence in the Circle and would always start to laugh when the dogs would go off.

Two other ritual experiences stick in my mind. The first one was a fantastic ritual that Candy and Allan Cambell and I created for Samhain one year. Candy was one of the most supremely gifted poets I have ever had the privilege to have known, and this ritual was an exquisite little masterpiece. Its theme was an archetypal decent into the underworld; that was the year that Samuel Noah Kramer and Diane Wolkstein published their translation and recreation of the Sumerian Inanna Cycle and we were very inspired by it. So we wanted to create something similar to Inanna's Descent but with a more Celtic/Universal feel to it. Part of the Mystery is that the Goddess on Her quest for Her lost Lover interacts with people in the audience, asking them questions and they give Her answers in the form of short poetic clues to His whereabouts. Everyone loved it and over the years OZ and I have used it, retooled and recycled it numerous times because it was so simple yet effective. It was such a blessing to finally be able to work together in a magickal community; it was certainly what I went in search of when I left Eugene.

The other ritual was a Yule ritual that Tim and I wrote that same year and we performed it at Don and Aileen Wildgrube's home. It was done in the style of a little children's story about what happens to various beings when the Winter comes. The Goddess is the Grandmother Crone and various creatures come to Her for "Shelter from the Storm." It starts off very simple with various critters, but it ends up with the Mother Goddess as a battered housewife and Jesus Christ as a despairing revolutionary. It was a Passion Play with a real psychic twist and a powerful message and we ended the ritual by playing the song of that same title by Bob Dylan.

I remember fondly that my part in the ritual was not a Goddess or a Priestess but instead I got to play a possum. That was very special for me because I had just discovered that Possum was my totem animal. About six months before this, Tim and I were returning from a meeting and we saw this critter amble out in the road in front of us. Tim pulled the car over, got out and ran after it. He caught it, picking it up by the tail and brought it back. It was a possum and she had a pouch full of babies. We took her home and kept her until her little ones were old enough to leave the pouch, and then we began to domesticate them and make pets out of them.

Baby possums make wonderful pets. They will eat literally anything, but they especially love junk food. And you can carry them in a pouch and they won't poop until you take them out and set them down to do their business. I fell in love with them. They are covered with soft pale fur, with wobbly pink noses and beady little dark eyes. Their naked tales are like a handle to pick them up by and when they are little, they really can hang by them for a bit. They are not bright at all but they are very sweet, sort of like having a retarded cat.

I took one of the babies for myself, named her my dangling Participle and gave the others to friends. We took the mama possum back out to the wild zone where she would have lots of berries and bugs to eat but be relatively safe from dogs and released her. The nice thing about possums is that if you can't care for them anymore or they get lost it's not a tragedy because their feral instincts are so hardwired that they revert to being wild in a matter of days.

Participle stayed with us and I made myself a possum costume for the Yule pageant and Participle got to be in the ceremony riding on my back. We always used to make jokes about how CAW was the first interspecies church. I started having dreams about Possum and began receiving wisdom messages from that Totem, so I guess it was a match. My Choctaw ancestors had lots of stories about how Possum brought fire and how Possum was a trickster sort of like Brer Rabbit, so I suppose there was a link there somewhere in my blood just waiting for the touch of the right pink wobbly nose.

Tim & Morning Glory with Tanith & Ananta, Feb. 1974.

Tim & Morning Glory
Feb. 1974.

The incomparable Morning Glory—
1974.

OZ & MG as Peter Stag & Virginia, Discon, Sept. 1974; "Most Primal."

PART FIVE:

Journey to the West

CHAPTER 14: Mitosis (1975-1976)

~ "Love of My Life," by Morning Glory Zell

OZ: AFTER THE POPULARITY OF THESE BIG seasonal celebrations we got lots of new members. Once again, the Nest soon became too big to continue to meet at my house. So Don Wildgrube and Tom Williams started taking turns holding Nest meetings at their places. A gradual mitosis happened and we ended up with two Nests. Don's Overland Nest was largely an entry level group, with classes and teachings. The group that met at Tom's was the Dog Star Nest—the joke was that we were the Sirius group. That was mainly for inner circle people who had been around for a long time. We tried to schedule things in a way that they didn't conflict with each other so some people could go to both. But there still arose a certain inevitable tension.

DON WILDGRUBE: I took over the central Nest. We would have an open house every Tuesday. Then on Friday or Saturday we would get together for our Nest meetings. The open house was for anybody that wanted to show up- that way we could weed out the people that we wouldn't invite back for the weekend meeting. For example, on guy was there and we were talking about nudity, because at our Nest meetings most people were nude. And this guy said, "If I have a problem with nudity, I'll just make loincloths for everybody."

OZ: Some of these tensions broke out in conflicts where the newer people wanted to be included in everything the inner circle groups were doing. There were accusations, not entirely unjustified, of elitism. It is an inevitable problem with democratic-style groups because of the illusion of equality. But there can never be true equality because there will always be people whose commitments are longer or stronger and that doesn't stack up with someone who just arrived ten minutes ago. But there is no way to measure "commitment;" there are no set of scales that you can weigh one person's level of commitment against another. A new convert can have the same emotional fervor of an old-timer.

Most of our generation has been in rebellion against hierarchy and yet organizations need a structure to survive. Vertebrates need a backbone to stand up. But Pagans, being humans, are social animals and respond to dominance hierarchy on a very deep level. They don't want to acknowledge that anyone is a leader, and yet they get very restless and upset if they don't get clear direction from the people they are expecting to lead them. In other words: if they don't feel that their leaders are leading them, they get frustrated and turn on them. It has happened all throughout the Movement; it's called "Founder's Syndrome."

I have never felt comfortable being a guru-type guy, but I can't deny that I seem to be a natural leader. We need to have leaders who care about the people they are involved with and not just out to feather their own nests…no pun intended. When I started the CAW, it was to have a community of peers, not a group of followers. But we set up the organization with a structure that would lead people further and deeper into it if they were willing to make the commitment. Anyway, when the Nests split up things started getting edgy.

MG: One night I went to a Laundromat and I took my snake with me—a six-foot Burmese python named Ananta. It was cold out, so he was tucked inside my clothes. While I was in the parking lot two carloads of inner-city teenage boys pulled up, jumped out of the cars and started heading my way and talking trash to me. I could see my death looking at me, and every single pore in my body just squirted adrenaline. When that happened Ananta smelled my fear, came out of my clothes like he was shot from a gun, and started making these loud hissing sounds. The kids jumped back into their cars and rolled out of there. I got back in the car, locked the doors and held Ananta and said, "Thank you, thank you, thank you. You saved my life." I came back from that experience and I told Tim what had happened, and he didn't really get it. He understood that I had been in danger, but I don't think it totally sunk in.

Around the same time I knew that my daughter had been picked on by the neighborhood kids, which was part of the reason for letting her go off to the farm to get away from that scene, but it just seemed to go from bad to worse. So I had to send my child away, back home to Eugene with Gary where she would be safe. I couldn't protect her in this city and I began to feel that I couldn't protect myself either.

Then I had this episode at the Laundromat and that was the final straw. At that point I told Oberon, "I love you, but I can't live in this environment. I'm going. I've given you two years of my life, but I can't do this anymore. You can come and join me, but I know you have a whole life here. You have to choose. If you choose to stay here, I can't live here." It was the hardest decision I ever made. To my everlasting joy, he decided that he loved me more than anything else and agreed to go with me to Oregon.

OZ: I agreed to it. At that point I would have agreed to anything to stay with her. I started telling people what was going to happen. This produced a reaction against her. When she had first arrived in St Louis, Morning Glory had been welcomed and embraced. And she had made an effort to connect with people in the Church. She understood the value of the bonds that form between lovers and the levels of trust that occur. There is a certain loyalty and commitment you have to people you have slept with that you don't have with other people. But when it became clear that she was going to take me away from them, it created a backlash. This crystallized in the "Denny's West Nest," a group of younger members of the Overland Nest who would adjourn to Denny's after the Nest meetings, where they would commandeer the large circular booth with a big round table at the far corner of the restaurant. They eventually produced a long "Resolution" consisting of numerous points of complaint about

Morning Glory. There was even some talk of "impeaching" her over the Gridley Wright affair. We were both devastated by this.

CAROLYN CLARK: The people who liked Morning Glory liked her so well that it got to the point that the Zells had to ask us not to come over to the house so often, because they wanted to spend some time together. But there were people who were not at all welcoming. Most people like things to stay the same. I'm kind of that way myself. A little bit of change is fine, but let the seasons roll as they've always done since the beginning of time.

MG: It was hard on OZ. He was working full time, publishing the magazine and running the Church. Even at that time I was quite amazed by the lack of respect he was routinely given by other members of the organization. Maybe I just didn't understand their personal style or their interpersonal history but it seemed as though he was constantly fighting an uphill battle with these people who claimed to love him so much.

OZ: I have never wanted to join a cult, so I certainly didn't want to create one! I have never understood their appeal to so many people—especially in the '60s. I have always been profoundly suspicious of gurus and cult leaders (reinforced by the Gridley Wright experience!), finding the entire concept deeply distasteful. It seemed the antithesis of the CAW's "Thou art God/dess" principle of immanent Divinity.

So in order to deflect the sort of worshipful attitude among cult followers that puts their leaders on a pedestal, I deliberately adopted a self-denigrating attitude of being sorta the "class clown." Hell, I was only in my late 20s and early 30s during that period; what right did I have to be trying to tell others what to do, how to live their lives, who to sleep with, how to cut their hair, what colors to wear, etc.? Instead, I did a lot of goofy stuff that really pushed the boundaries of absurdity, and invited others to join in.

In the words of Ken Kesey, I took on the role of the "bull-goose loony." I would always climb to the top of the tallest tree, or jump off the highest rock into the water. One time we all went down to a wonderful natural water-park in the Missouri Ozarks called Johnson

Shut-Ins, where water had cut channels and bowls through the rock that were great fun to play in. There was a very high cliff overlooking a deep pool, and some people were jumping and diving off it. So naturally I had to climb up and do the same. Tom Williams accompanied me, and just as I was about to take a run for it, he said, "No, let me go first. My mother is always telling me that if that Tim Zell jumped off a 50-foot cliff, I'd follow. So this time I want to dive first, and you can follow!" So he did, and I stood at the edge of the cliff watching as his dive slowly rotated into a perfect back-flop, hitting the water with a mighty "thwack!" As he painfully dragged himself out onto a flat rock, gasping like a beached whale, I decided to jump rather than dive.

There were many wonderful people and dear friends in our Nest, and we were very close—many of us lovers. There were several Jewish boys who came to us from Epstein Hebrew Academy: Steve Frischer, Kenny Cohen, Moritz Farbstein…and Jacques Ferache ("the strapping young man"). Denny Sargent, who later went to Japan for five years and wrote wonderful articles on Shinto for *Green Egg* in the 1990's. There were George and Marge Steitz, and their teenage daughter Terry. They held many meetings at their home, some based on a book called *Conduct Your Own Awareness Sessions* by Christopher Hills and Robert B. Stone (Signet, 1970). There was a kid named Kirby who dated Terry. Carolyn Clark, our first Priestess. Don Wildgrube (who succeeded me after my seven years as High Priest) and his wife Alene. Dan Ummel, who came to us when he was 18. He went to Morticians school at Forest Park Community College, and worked as a mortician after he graduated.

STEVE FRISCHER: I read *Stranger in a Strange Land* when I was 13. A fellow science fiction fan gave me Tim Zell's address two years later. From the time I got there I was more or less treated as myself and not a kid. That would be a lot more trouble nowadays—everybody is a lot more paranoid. But this was the early seventies, and the counter-culture, and people were more willing to give kids a chance to be involved.

For me it was the best childhood anybody could imagine growing up in. We got together every Saturday night, and that was the place to be—it was our social life. For a guy who grew up in the suburbs it was an eye-opening mix of people and ideas. We talked radical religion and philosophy all night. My first few years I'd go to a talk about something I'd never heard of. Then I'd go home and read books about it. And I'd go back the next week and talk about something else. That went on for two years before I finally began catching up with people.

In 1973, when I was 17, I hitch-hiked around the country for the month of August. I went through the letters section of the *Green Egg* and found people along my hitchhiking path who looked like they'd be interesting to meet. I wrote to them asking if I could come stay for a few days. I stayed a week with Robert Anton Wilson—I was just one of a bunch of kids that were staying with him.

Carolyn Clark was one of the smartest women I've ever known. She was blond and tall and had legs that went on forever. If you wanted to hang around smart women and educated women, you'd get your share of them in the CAW!

OZ: There was Ed Short—a lanky giant of a guy with a soft Southern drawl, who took over running the big Multilith press after we moved it into Don's basement. John "Tiny" McClimans, the first person to join CAW in 1967—and his mate, Heather. Tom Williams, who had the only color TV for watching "Star Trek." Bill Morris (later Orion Stormcrow), my "kid brother," with whom I would often spar Karate-style. Ed Whitehead, who created our first newsstand magazine, *The Pagan!* Ravi and Toni Kristen, who had arranged for CAW's incorporation. Nan Schwartz, an Atlan lover. Wayne Ochs, an honorary member of the Hell's Angels, and his wife, Peggy. Melvin Thomas, a hip black guy who lived at our Kingsbury Temple for awhile. Michael Hurley, who joined the Army and went to Vietnam, where he became GE's war correspondent (and later spent time in Antarctica!).

There was this laid-back kid named Spencer Knapp, who looked just like Krishna with his long black hair and smooth face. He'd go along with any crazy thing I came up with. He would lie down with a watermelon on his belly, and I would cut it in half in a single blow with the coven sword that Margot Adler had given me. I was really well-coordinated, so there were never any mishaps. One time, Spencer broke up the circle when he handed the chalice to Carolyn and said, "Don't spit in the cup!" instead of the traditional response—a phrase which we still use in his memory. There was Steve Picker and his wife Candice. And Steve Egbert, this kid with big eyes and a bigger smile, who lived for awhile in our basement, and ran the printing press.

DON WILDGRUBE: Tim and Morning Glory had been out to California, hitchhiking across the country. Steve Egbert was staying at Tim's house, supposedly watching over the animals. Some of the animals were OK, but a small screech owl that Tim had rescued from my chimney was left in the bathroom and died from lack of food. Instead of burying the bird, Steve left it in the bathroom to decay. When Tim and MG came home, they were exhausted and were about to go immediately to bed. About that time Steve announced that they shouldn't go to bed without changing the sheets and disinfecting the mattress. The bed was full of crabs! Steve did nothing about it so MG had to do the pesticide, scalding washing, and clean up the dead bird and all. They were not happy campers.

OZ: There was "Old" Charlie Leach, a "mad scientist" and John Bircher, who had invented the portable barbeque grill, and was our oldest member, being 30 years older than me to the day (we shared the same birthday). There were Candy and Alan Campbell, she being an exotic Middle Eastern Baladi dancer and a truly brilliant poet (writing under the name of Oothoon), and he working on a tugboat on the Mississippi River. There was the lovely Pendragon—a sculptor and artist for whom I modeled and vice versa, and whom I drew as Lilith on the cover of *Green Egg* #74. Stella and Lou Cotton, a retired Air Force Captain, with their horse ranch over in Illinois. Tom and Fredda Kullman, with their connection to the land where we held festivals. Wooster Lambert, who inherited land in Kentucky or Tennessee that he hoped CAW could use someday. Terry Casper and his wife Carol, who had the most exotic pheromones. Singing Flower. And many others over the years. I still think of them fondly, and the fun, magick, and adventures we shared. One of my favorite songs is still John Denver's "Poems, Prayers, and Promises," which we often played at our Nest meetings.

PENDRAGON: Tim asked me to model for a drawing he wanted to do for a *Green Egg* cover. I said, "Sure I will." He did the most marvelous drawing of me, with bits of costume and jewelry that were totally imaginary. It reminded me to some degree of some of the illustrations of Frank Frazetta. I was delighted. I had just lost a very wished-for boyfriend, and to see myself as this bat-winged strong woman made me feel much better. Tim Zell loves women. He genuinely loves women. Very few men do. That's apparent in his behavior and his fascination with conversation and talking to people. And also in how he draws, and how he represents people.

So I landed on the Halloween issue. After I saw it, I thought, "Wow, that woman looks wonderful and powerful." I decided to buy one and send it to the house of the guy that had dumped me some months earlier. I thought it would be such fun for him to open his mail and see it. I felt like, "Look at this—I'm doing fine"

Tim had this one pair of jeans that he seemed to wear all the time. They were completely disreputable even in the phase of the '70s which was Hippiedom in Missouri. (We didn't get the '60s in Missouri till the '70s.) As Tim's jeans disintegrated—I don't think there was much left of the original fabric—he had patches put on them. And there were embroideries, and there were handmade things, and I believe they had all been applied by prior women. They all represented either lovers, female friends, or maybe acquaintances that looked at the pants and said, "Oh my god, you're hanging out of those!" This wasn't "Gee, his knees are out." This was, "Oh, the world is soon going to know you much better than you may want them to." That pair of jeans was somewhere between a patchwork quilt done by god knows how many women—working separately, mind you, and in a linear way—and something like the Bayeux Tapestry, that tells a long, long story.

One year, when I was living at my mother's house, my mom was having Thanksgiving dinner. And I asked if I could invite Tim and Morning Glory. I had thought, "I don't know how my mother is going to respond to them." They were not like lizards on a leaf, changing depending on who was around. They were themselves. But their selves were interesting enough to get along with a really wide variety of people.

They came. And the conversation was nice, and she liked them both. And Tim was wearing the jeans. My mother was very proper in many ways, very much a lady. She saw his jeans and said, "I can help you with those." She put something on them. Not that night, but she added something to them in order to keep them together. She was stabilizing the fragility.

Morning Glory and I are exactly one month apart in age. And I always admired her. She was so sure, certain, and strong. She had so many hugely varied experiences. But she wasn't a braggart. These little snippet stories she told were really introduced as part of a larger conversation. It wasn't as though she were holding court. She seemed older because of her vast store of experiences. And I admired her for having the courage to have done so many things. Maybe a lot of them were just total folly, but to me at the time it was like looking at somebody who had lived many more years than I had, even though we were the same age.

We were girlfriends, and did a lot of just plain girlfriend things together. I genuinely liked her. I probably spent more time with MG than I did with Tim. I was in school then, and I was always the first one there and the last one to leave. I was in the studios seven days a week. I really focused on my art. But sometimes I really needed a short break. I had found that there was a piano bar that had free food from 4 to 6 in the afternoon. And a friend of mine was playing piano and singing. I told Morning Glory about it and we went several times, just to sit and listen to the music and eat the food.

Morning Glory had, at some point, little classes in the afternoon for a few women. She had some of us come over in the afternoon if we wanted to know more about hands-on, practical things like making incense. It was about different aspects of the Craft. There was no one else really doing that.

And I just loved Rainbow. On one of her trips back from Oregon MG brought Rainbow with her. In an odd way, she's had an impact on my life. I wasn't much interested in children. My mind was on my school and my art. I was blossoming into levels I had never dreamed of. I had discovered self-discipline, focus, and obsession, all of which are necessary to do anything with a natural gift. Without those things a natural gift is kind of useless. I didn't dislike children, but I was not fantasizing about motherhood at the time.

When I met Rainbow I think that she was 4½. She was pre-school age, but not by much. She had just been removed from the home that she knew, and she was in this quite different environment. I talked to her a little bit, and she was very bright and not pretentious.

She was very real and genuine. I remember thinking at the time that she was very unique child. I felt differently about her. When Tim and Morning Glory got married and went off on a honeymoon they asked me to keep Rainbow for a week. I was in school, and I worked at a daycare center. So I realized it would work out perfectly. I could take her to work with me.

So I did. I looked after the pre-schoolers. I remember them asking me, "Is that your little girl?" So I said yes, because it was simpler. She blended in with the children. The week we were together I realized, with a bit of a shock—that it was fine with me to have her with me. It felt right. If Morning Glory had said, "I'm leaving for a couple of years, can you keep her?" I wouldn't have hesitated. I thought it was as though she had always been mine. It was there and it was real. And she liked me back. She was so right for me that later when I married and I had children, I told my kids stories about Tim and Morning Glory and Rainbow. Oddly enough, one of my daughters, when she was pregnant and about to have the baby, said "I want to name her Rainbow." So she did, but spelled the name differently—Rainbeau.

OZ: The first summer that Morning Glory was with us, Ed Short introduced us to a wonderfully magickal place on the Missouri River, called Pelican Island. In the summer, it was connected to the mainland by a sandbar, so we could walk out and explore it. Sometimes we would camp out there, around a little fire. It was very spooky at night, with fog rolling in, and the mournful sounds of foghorns from passing riverboats. One summer day, walking through a marsh on the land side, we came upon a sapling tree that was twisted into a snaky spiral by a vine growing around it. A perfect Wizard's staff! I was just examining how to cut it away below ground and preserve the rootball for a top, when Ed whipped out his machete and whacked it off just above ground level. I have had the staff ever since; I named it Pathfinder and it has become quite well-known throughout the magickal community, but I've always regretted losing the rootball.

One time when Morning Glory and I were walking through the woods out there, we were joined by a man and his young son, also out for a hike. Suddenly our reverie was interrupted by the raucous roar of a dirt bike coming down the path from behind us. It was one of those annoying, destructive machines that was chewing up the trails and eroding the landscape. We could see the damage in the soft earth all around us. As it passed, MG slammed a whammy at it, and its motor abruptly cut out. The man and his son were suitably impressed. As we walked on by the rider, who was trying to get his bike started again, MG smiled sweetly and said to him, "Some of us enjoy the solitude of these woods. You could try walking; it's quieter and doesn't wreck the place."

There was a little private Science Museum in Clayton, a suburb of St Louis, with a pair of the life-size Sinclair dinosaurs out front: a triceratops facing off with an erect tail-dragging T-rex. The grounds of the museum were an arboretum of exotic trees imported from all over the world. One of these was an immense Linden tree, with long thick branches reaching down to the ground. It was a favorite climbing tree for grownups as well as kids, and Bryan loved to go there with us. We called it "the Grandmother Tree."

Another great attraction in St Louis was the Climatron, an enormous geodesic dome designed by Buckminster Fuller and built in 1960. Inside was a climate-controlled multi-level rain forest, complete with a waterfall, pool, exotic birds (including a roseate spoonbill), iguanas, and turtles. On the commentary accompanying the DVD release of the 1972 sci-fi classic movie *Silent Running*, Director Douglas Trumbull stated that the geodesic domes containing the last forests of Earth's future on the giant space ark *Valley Forge* were based on the St Louis Climatron.

BRYAN ZELL: The Climatron was a beautiful place to go to. My favorite part of it was the desert. I always thought it was interesting the plants that could survive without the jungle. And the giant Victoria water lilies in the lake that you could walk on.

We also went to a lot of the museums in St Louis. They were part of the World's fair of 1904. The first time I ever went to a museum was seeing the museums in St Louis. I remember the knights in shining armor, and all kinds of great shit like that. It expanded my consciousness. That was a good idea. If I ever had a kid, I'd do the same. I'd do it every day. I go to cities when I go on vacations, and I go to the museums. I go to every one of 'em.

NARRATOR: There was nothing else happening anywhere else in the world that was quite like the scene in St Louis (and there still isn't today). Writer Margot Adler was doing research for what would become her book *Drawing Down the Moon,* and visited the Nest to check the facts in person. The cutting-edge style of journalism at that moment was called "gonzo," which meant that the reporter became a part of the action that they were writing about. When Hunter S. Thompson was working on his ground-breaking book about the Hell's Angels, he got on a motorcycle and rode with them. So when Margot checked out the CAW, she didn't just watch and take notes.

MARGOT ADLER: CAW and the Zells were very into sexual experimentation. When I went to interview them in the fall of 1975, I spent a week living and sharing their life with them. I remember going to a CAW Halloween party in St Louis. I remember being very aware that there was a lot of sex going on, people pairing up and going into corners and stuff like that. I will confess that I was fairly prudish and I found myself very uncomfortable. I was single, and at that point my response was to take the one person there that I really liked and disappear with him into a bedroom so I didn't have to deal with the all the other stuff that was going on.

At the same time, truth be told, I thought Tim and Morning Glory were beautiful, loving people: loving towards each other and towards me. I thought, "This is definitely not what I normally do, and I am not really comfortable, but I'm just going to throw myself into this and see what a threesome is like." I'm not a very sexual person. At this point, I've been living in a monogamous relationship for 33 years. So this was definitely not typical for me. But I remember they had a mirror on the ceiling of their bedroom. I would look up and feel that we were all in some renaissance painting.

When I returned home I was very freaked out. I felt that I would have gone completely crazy if I'd lived their life for more than a week. It wasn't only the sex; there was a level of intensity that was hard to deal with. So, I went to a psychologist and said, "I don't know what I'm feeling about this. Should I have felt more comfortable? Is there something wrong with me?"

And she said, "You know, there are some people who are champion skiers. And there are some people who are champion tennis players. And these two people were champions at sex. And that doesn't have to be who you are." And I laughed with relief. So I ended up thinking: they were really good at sex, and incredibly open, warm, loving and inviting. It was easy to get swept into their lives. But for me what was most important was realizing that their life was not my life. I had to make my peace with who I was.

MG: At the time I just thought everybody was like that. It's not that I thought everybody was like me, but I thought that most Pagans took this kind of Hippie/poly/sexuality thing as a matter of course. After all it was straight out of *Stranger in a Strange Land* and *Island* by Aldous Huxley. I guess because I was a Hippie Witch and Priestess of Aphrodite, I didn't see why we shouldn't be living the way the people were in the books. That was where I was coming from.

I didn't think about other people having—I hesitate to use the word "hang-ups," so we'll just say inhibitions about it. Because I just didn't have any inhibitions. A lot of the sexual adventures that I had around that time were kind of all joy and enthusiasm, and "welcome to my bed," and "welcome to my life," and "we're all gonna be lovers and friends and it's gonna be a wonderful world." And I didn't realize that some people weren't comfortable with that. It never would have occurred to me in a million years. Probably the Crow Farmer who said that I was too naïve to be unhappy got it pretty close. I am one of those rare and very fortunate women, in that I was never molested as a child or ever raped. So sex was always this warm and beautiful thing to share with friends. Perhaps I was a *Quadishtu,* a temple prostitute, in a previous life.

OZ: In *Stranger in a Strange Land,* p. 278, Mr. Heinlein had noted: "Foster had in common with every great religious leader of that planet two traits: he had an extremely magnetic personality, and sexually he did not fall near the human norm. On Earth, great religious leaders were always either celibate or the antithesis. Foster was not celibate." And neither was I. And then Heinlein goes on to say: "Nor were his wives and priestesses…" And so it was with us, not that we were Fosterites. Sex is such a wonderful, glorious, beautiful thing ("a great goodness," as Michael says in SISL)—why wouldn't anyone try to experience as much of it as they can, with as many different willing partners as possible? What's not to like?

DON WILDGRUBE: I got along with Morning Glory kind of tentatively. The biggest problem was that Tim always had his head in the clouds. He was, and is, a dreamer. If he were different he wouldn't be Tim.

Julie, and a lot of other people, always kept him in line. In fact it used to be that when you had an argument with Tim you could tell him to go screw off, and he'd accept that. And if you argued with him, he'd say, "Maybe you're right. Let me think about that."

When Morning Glory came on the scene she protected him. And she would not allow anyone to say nasty things to his face. We used to be able to be open with everybody. Morning Glory and I were really never very close after that.

NARRATOR: The Church continued to evolve. The individual members were also evolving, but not all at the same pace and in the same direction. MG tried her hardest to go with the flow, but, in spite of her best efforts, it didn't work out.

MG: There was a lot of politics and negative stuff that had me shaking my head in amazement. I have to say that I could be pretty arrogant and hard to get along with. I was the Hippie from Oregon, who was always saying conditions were so much better back there; I must have been insufferable about it. But in so many ways I really threw my heart into the community there, trying to reach out to everyone and be as inclusive as I could, working to come to terms with how to be a good person and how to give of myself. But I was really not cut out for big city life. I came to care passionately about CAW and I was treated pretty badly by a lot of people there. But over the years I've made peace with it and most of the hatchets have been buried and not in anyone's backs.

Ultimately, I think that what happened was that cosmic wheels were turning. Because it was inevitable that I was not going to stay, and that Tim was going to leave with me, because our love was that strong. So the Church felt like I was the usurper who was coming to take him away. Even though it was never my intention to hurt the Church, the combination of the physical circumstances of living in that city, plus the unfriendliness of many of the people in the organization towards me and the lack of support that we received as a couple led inexorably to a kind of self-fulfilling prophecy of Doom. I came to feel like the character "Morgaine" in C.J. Cherryh's *Gates of Ivrel* series, who inadvertently destroys worlds even as she tries to save them.

NARRATOR: At least one person that I interviewed said that there was talk about Morning Glory's relationship with the Church being comparable to the one that Yoko Ono had with the Beatles: Yoko got the blame for the band breaking up after she married John Lennon. (In this scenario Tim Zell and Tom Williams were considered to be the CAW equivalent of Lennon and McCartney.) But listening to the later Beatles recordings now it's clear that they were already in the process of going their separate ways before Yoko entered the picture – in fact it's amazing that they stayed together as long as they did.

The same might be said for what happened with Tim Zell and the Church of All Worlds. After all, this was a group of people that had partly modeled themselves after a starship crew that was on a five-year mission. More than five years passed since the Nest had gathered in front of a TV to watch *Star Trek* every week. It was, for Tim, time for his next mission: to explore strange new worlds, to seek out new life and new civilizations, and to boldly go where no one had gone before.

OZ: In June of 1975, MG and I made a trip to Fulton, Missouri, for my 10th college reunion at Westminster. None of the other Atlans showed up, or anyone else I'd known when I was there, so I didn't connect much with any other students. But I did get a chance to visit with Gale Fuller, and to introduce MG and him. One episode from that visit stands out: I thought I'd take MG to a pizza bar where some of the students used to hang out, in vain hope of meeting someone I knew. MG was wearing a slinky snakeskin-patterned dress, slit up the side, and looked quite impressive. And at the back of the restaurant a bunch of old fraternity guys and ladies were getting drunk at a table. One of the frat rats was wearing a pair of women's panties on his head, and he cracked in reference to me: "Man, he must be some kinda pussy to let his woman dress like that!"

Without missing a beat, my soulmate sweetly retorted: "If your dick was half as big as your mouth is, he'd still be twice the man you are!" All his buddies and the girls rounded on him with ridicule while he tried to puzzle it out. Don't mess with MG!

We were always looking for places to hold our Sabbat gatherings—especially in the summer. Through Don Wildgrube we met Herta Drnec, who owned a place of large open fields and a small creek. She called it "Pangaea." Our Litha festival there in 1975 brought Harold Moss all the way from Burbank, California.

OZ: November 30, 1975 was my 33rd birthday. 33 is a significant year in many men's lives. Both Jesus and Alexander the Great died at that age! On my birthday, I resigned from my job as Director of Social Services at the Chouteau Russell Center of the Human Development Corporation. They threw a big going-away party for me. After nine years on-and-off, I had been there longer than anybody.

But at that point I had had enough of that kind of work. I was working more and more with abused women through the family-counseling program. I would try to help them get out of the bad situation, and I had a huge emotional investment in that. Being a man, I felt a personal responsibility to redress the suffering they had experienced at the hands of other men. But invariably, after we had put all this energy and resources into getting these women away from the abusive bastards, they would go back to them. They'd be back in my office a month later covered with bruises again. And then one of them was murdered by her ex-husband whom she'd taken back. I didn't have any real training in how to deal with this. I just didn't understand why they did it. It cost me a lot emotionally, and when it was time to leave I didn't ever want to go back. I wanted something really different.

Now there are recovery programs and whole institutions set up to deal with these situations, but there wasn't any of that stuff at that time. In my entire background and years of study in college and special training seminars, I never got any information about abuse, childhood sexual molestation, alcoholism, drug addiction, or recovery programs. These topics that are a major concern today were never even mentioned. I was completely on my own and making it up as I went along, based on little more than my natural sense of compassion and love of women. Today most of the field of social psychology is about addiction therapy and abusive relationships, but at that time these situations were treated as individual anomalies, not as a widespread phenomenon or syndrome.

We started liquidating things. Most of my vast library I donated to the Church. I began training Tom Williams to be my successor as editor of the *Green Egg*. Gradually I turned it over to him, and by the time we left it was completely in his hands. In December of 1975 we rented out the Annandale house and moved out of it. For awhile we crashed with Tom and had our stuff in storage. Bryan continued to stay with Martha and go to school. He entirely cut himself off from us, refusing even to talk to us on the phone. This really hurt a lot, but it was his choice, and I had to accept it.

MG: I knew he was angry that we were leaving, but I also knew Bryan had come to like me and accept me and that he deeply loved his Dad. I guess that kind of confusion is just too painful for kids to go through without getting their heads messed up.

BRYAN: I purposely avoided my dad and stepmother during the time of transition when they were getting ready to move out to the West Coast in the school bus. Morning Glory would call and ask for me, and I would refuse to talk to her because I was afraid they were going to kidnap me.

MG: I was really bewildered when I heard about this because we never forced our kids to do anything; if anything we bent over backwards the other way and gave them too many choices, which created a different sort of confusion. But we usually let them decide about things that seriously affected their lives and tried to abide by their choices.

OZ: We bought a used 1954 Chevy school bus, but it was for an elementary school so it was fairly small—about 25 feet long. It had a five-foot nine-inch ceiling, and I'm 5' 10", so that made it difficult to walk around inside. We started fixing it up to put it on the road. Since it was already painted red, we named it "The Scarlet Succubus." It's one of those magickal things—you give a name to virtually everything that has any investment of energy. We refer to it as "animating inanimate objects." The bus had previously belonged to a fundamentalist church, so we left the name of the church painted on the side. It was a great disguise. Later, as we traveled, we were able to stay overnight in church parking lots, and nobody bothered us.

We had very dear friends and lovers, Lou and Stella Cotton, who were Atlans and Mensans. Lou was a retired Air Force Colonel, and they had recently bought a farm in Southern Illinois near Carbondale, to raise horses. As soon as we were able to we moved to their farm to work on the school bus. When we left to drive there it was late January, 1976, and it was the worst winter in that area's recorded history. As we drove up to their place we discovered that their entire home had burned to the ground just days before, and there were still-smoking ruins sticking out of the snow. Their insurance company had provided them with a trailer that they had moved into. And they had another little trailer that we stayed in.

And so there we were in that incredibly cold, bitter winter. Charlie Leach would come out on weekends. He and Morning Glory would work on the brakes and mechanical/electrical systems of the bus, and I would work on the interior cabinetry, carpeting, insulation, kitchen, appliances, etc. Lou had a huge barn of a woodshop, so I was able to design, cut and construct an elaborate RV-type interior for the bus. I made seats that converted into benches and beds, tables that would fold up and down, a 10-foot-long kitchen, a toilet, a closet, and a whole side for bookcases and animal cages. Charlie built us a combination 12-volt battery charger and inverter so we could plug in anywhere. We made it very comfortable. It took us months, during which time we were pretty much cut off from St Louis, as the only vehicle we had was the bus, and most of the time it wasn't ready to drive.

MG: My dad was a mechanic, so Charlie and I rebuilt the engine, the brakes, and the carburetor. That was one of the most wonderful times of my life. I helped take care of the horses. I also got to help Stella train one of her mares to jump. Stella was a fine woman: beautiful, smart and strong. She took me under her wing. We visited her riding master and I learned a lot about choosing horses for three-day eventing. They had a beautiful pond and I learned how to ice skate; I loved the silvery sound the large hoar-frost crystals made when it tinkled against your skates. Ice storms on the tree branches turned the entire farm into a magical frozen fairyland. Tim and I got a chance to intensively be together for the first time. The whole time I was in St Louis one of the frustrations was that there was always something else: job, church, kids, or other responsibilities that took away our opportunities to be together.

OZ: In addition to our two large snakes, we had a pet possum with us—she provided endless amusement since possums are naturally ludicrous creatures. MG named her Participle, because she could dangle by her tail. I've always collected critters. On one of our hiking trips after she'd first moved to St Louis, Morning Glory and I found a Missouri tarantula and brought it home as a pet. And we then bought a Mexican red-legged tarantula from a pet store. We kept them in clear boxes and fed them crickets. We kept box turtles in the basement, where their primary job was to eat cockroaches. So I built special sections into our bus for the possum, snakes, spiders, and a colony of rats that we raised to feed the snakes. It was a bizarre traveling menagerie.

The final piece that I built and installed was a little altar, with a mirrored back and a drop-down front that could close up for travel. As I was completing it, late at night in the shop, a male Luna moth came spiraling down from the darkness above, to land right at my feet, and die. I took it as a sign of approval from the Goddess, and installed it into the altar, behind the mirror.

Once the bus was running, we made several trips back to St Louis, crashing with Tom Williams, and watching *Monty Python* and *Mary Hartman, Mary Harman* on his color TV. Our Wiccan teacher, Debbie, had made a pilgrimage to the Yucatan, from which she brought back psilocybin mushroom spores. Tom prepared a suitable bed for them in a large aquarium, and implanted them. On our final visit, the entire tank was filled with mycelium, but no mushrooms. That night was a full moon, so Tom took the aquarium out to his back yard and set it in the center of our circle. In the morning, the tank was full of lush mushrooms! So that day we all had our first experience with magic mushrooms—which was truly amazing, involving a lot of telepathy. Like, you'd get up to go pee, and when you looked in the mirror, it was someone else's face whose eyes you were looking out of. In the middle of our trip, Orion came by, and asked what it was like. I started to describe it, but he interrupted me, saying, "Not you, OZ, I want an objective opinion."

At that point we all cracked up, shouting in unison, "There *is* no 'objective opinion!'"

That spring, shortly before we finished work on the bus, a friend named Art Rosenblum, founder and director of the Aquarian Research Foundation, invited me to join him in attending a major UFO conference in Flagstaff, AZ. We had only recently heard the Firesign Theatre's latest album, *Everything You Know is Wrong,* and now I got a full dose of what they were parodying. It was definitely an experience of high weirdness—much like a sci-fi con, except that these guys didn't see it as fiction! I had a blast—like visiting a strange alien tribe.

In June, 1976, we finally left for good. We came back to St Louis in the bus once it was all completely fixed up. I settled up with Martha. We got together and figured out what she would want for her equity in the house, which I then gave to her. Then I put the house into the name of the Church. The idea would be that after we left they would sell it, and then the money would go into the church we were going to set up in Oregon. It was supposed to be a transfer from one branch of the Church to another. We would then have a foundation for whatever we were going to do.

NARRATOR: From the beginnings of modern Paganism, and continuing on up to the present, there seems to have been an unwritten rule within the community that the "clergy," in whatever way the people involved care to define that term, are not to be paid. People in positions of service to their Pagan groups are more often than not expected to somehow take care of themselves and their own finances – even if what they're doing is full time work, and they have duties that would be properly compensated for in any other religion. There are those who have been performing services at births, weddings, funerals and other rites of passage for decades who now have no retirement funds, insurance or any place to live out their old age that is connected to the spirituality they've dedicated their lives to.

Which is not to say that they are not loved or in or other ways rewarded. People do these things voluntarily. But their lives can be tough. Tim Zell was not paid for his years of service in St Louis, and as we have seen, he in fact personally helped finance the Church and its publications. He made a lot of sacrifices, not thinking about what might happen to his own security. The decision to donate his house to the Church was just one more sacrifice, and not one that would work out as he hoped it would after he left St Louis.

MG: A number of people who loved him dearly tried to talk him out of this. They said, "This is your life savings. Suppose the Board of Directors changes, and they're not your friends? You could lose everything." Tiny McClimans was particularly opposed to it.

And Oberon was like, "No, no, that could never possibly happen. We're all in this together." Don was right about one aspect of him, he has always been this starry-eyed idealist, and many people in the Church tried to get him to wake up. But he has always been resistant to it. I was completely out of my depth in all of this kind of thing; I had never owned property and knew very little about business or finance at that time.

OZ: It seemed like a perfectly good plan. Money itself has never really been particularly important to me. Maybe it should have been more so. My sole income during that period was unemployment compensation. After paying off Martha, most of the money I'd saved went into the bus itself. It was a matter of completely cutting loose and casting myself into the unknown. I had no idea of what I would do to make a living once we got to the west coast.

On our last night in St Louis we stopped by our old house at 1621 Annandale St., parked the bus in the driveway and went to sleep. We were going to get up the next morning and leave. But it turned out there was still a warrant out for my arrest.

The first week when Morning Glory moved to St Louis, one night the police showed up at the doorstep and hauled me off to jail. That was not a good way to start things off. Orion, who was crashing with us at the time, had been working on his car and had a bunch of parts spread out in the driveway. He went into the house to make himself some lunch. When he came back he put the car back together, and we thought that was the end of it.

But I was under continual harassment by an ex-fraternity "brother" named Greg Sheehan who had become the city prosecutor for University City. He really hated me because I had rebelled against the fraternity system. I was the first brother in the entire history of that fraternity (Phi Kappa Psi) to deactivate. When he found out I was living in his town he kept having me arrested on one trumped-up charge after another. One time, when my iguana, Gryf, got loose, I was charged with "harboring a dangerous animal!" I'd go to court and the charges were always dismissed. I didn't even have to hire a lawyer. In this particular case I was accused of littering—in my own driveway! This one was also dismissed, but a lingering echo of it remained. Just as we were getting ready to leave we were told that they knew I was moving to Eugene, Oregon, and that Greg Sheehan had just gotten a job as the prosecuting attorney there, so there would be no escape from his persecution.

So there we were, sleeping in the bus, and there was a knock on the door.

MG: The police were beating on the door and trying to get in. They had another warrant for his arrest. The door was locked. We didn't have any curtains on the windows so they could look in. So we just pulled the covers over our heads and lay verrry still—because the monsters can't get you when you're under the covers! They finally gave up and went away. At that point we jumped up, put our clothes on, and hit the road for Oregon. Westward ho!

DON WILDGRUBE: A funny thing happened when Charlie and Tom cleaned out Tim's house to sell it. Things were going well until they found the old freezer in the basement and decided to carry it out from the basement steps outside to take it to the dump. Tom and Charlie were carrying the freezer up when the door opened. Unknown to them, Tim, as usual, had picked up road kill for the bones to make into skeletal forms. Well, the road kill was in the freezer for a couple of years. The problem is that someone turned off the freezer when Tim moved out. Tom said that this green stench came out from the freezer. They closed the door tight and tied it shut until it got to the dump.

CHAPTER 17:
Eugene, Oregon
(1976-1977)

We wandered West and made a Home
With Unicorns and baby deer;
When round the country I would roam,
I know I'd always find you near.

Adventures bold and Dreams we told;
We never knew just where or when.
I'd do that part the same again;
I'd do that part the same again.
~ "Love of My Life," by Morning Glory Zell

ARRATOR: BY 1976, WHEN THE ZELLS headed West in the Scarlet Succubus, a new age had dawned. Or, to be more precise, *the* New Age, which was a label used to describe all the spiritual/metaphysical/occult kind of activity that had sprouted up in the aftermath of the '60s. Hippies weren't a "counter-culture" anymore – their haircuts and clothes had generally either gone away or been absorbed by mainstream society. The Dionysian ecstasy that had started at the Woodstock festival had become a part of the corporate music machine in the '70s, and drugs and sexual freedom were there for anyone who wanted them, not just the young and rebellious. (And there was an even larger menu of drugs and sex to choose from!)

The draft and the war in Vietnam had both ended a few years earlier, right around when Nixon had left the Whitehouse in shame. A Democrat (and peanut farmer) named Jimmy Carter was elected President. Everything just seemed kind of mellow.

The '70s were nicknamed "The Me Decade" by journalist Tom Wolfe, and he was referring to the social change from political activism to personal growth. After working to do what they could for the world, people were starting to look at what they could do for themselves, and New Age activity was a part of that. Lots of different things were considered to be New Age, including stuff like pyramid power, astrology and Tarot readings. The New Age was open to the public and becoming very commercial and popular. Pagans were still mostly underground, but as a result of the New Age phenomenon they had access to more resources, and eventually, each other. The center of all this kind of activity was California, of course, and that was where the Zells stopped off on their way to Oregon.

OZ: We managed to escape St Louis, and headed southwest to see Lance and Larue, who were then living in Santa Fe. In San Jon, New Mexico, just out of the Texas Panhandle, our bus broke down with locked brakes. We called Lance and Larue, who drove to meet us, and took us home with them while the shop worked on the bus. This was the first time MG got to meet my first water-brother, and we all hit it off splendidly. After a few days, they drove us back to San Jon to get the now-repaired bus, and we continued on our way.

MG: Well actually it wasn't that easy. The rear end in the bus blew out, something to do with the dual wheels, a frozen spider gear and the differential, so we limped into this tiny town off the road, the kind that exists on what they can glean from travelers. The repair guys were not having any part of dealing with a woman mechanic so I couldn't check out what they were doing, but at least they let us stay in the bus while they fixed it. On the surface that seemed like a nice gesture but these guys lived and breathed the very essence of the Hippie-hating "good ole boys" and spent a fair amount of time trying to intimidate us: "Hey Honey, you wanna look at my guns, I'd just love to kill me a big old snake like that one you've got." So we were enormously relieved when Lance and LaRue rescued us and our critters from the clutches of the James Gang.

When we got back to collect our bus and were in the office paying the hideously inflated bill, I overheard a big rig driver blaze in and start cussing about how they had sold him diesel with water in it that wrecked his engine. We paid and left with a certain amount of misgivings, and sure enough when we drove off in our newly "repaired" bus we didn't get too far down the road until the rear brakes on one side started heating up and locking. We really did not want to go back to that place so we just kept going and dragged the one rear wheel all the way to California. When we got to my folks place, my Dad and I took the thing apart and those idiots either through malice or stupidity had rebuilt the brakes backwards! I suppose in this case the old adage must apply: "Never attribute to malice what can be adequately explained by stupidity."

But I guess the roadside scavengers got their Karma in full, because when we drove by the town several years later on our way back to St. Louis to get our stuff from storage, we saw that the place had completely burned to the ground! We never found out whether it was some irate trucker that hit them with a gas bomb or just a grease fire in the kitchen, but they would no longer ply their wicked trade on hapless folk. Oberon turned around and looked at me and just raised one eyebrow eloquently. This time I solemnly swear, I had nothing to do with it. I don't lay out those kinds of curses no matter how much I'm tempted. But I do admit that I felt sort of like Eleanor of Aquitaine when they asked if she had poisoned her husband's traitorous mistress: "Poisoned Rosalind? Oh no, not I. It's true I prayed that she would die, and laughed a little when she did, but I never poisoned her."

OZ: The first place we hit on the West Coast was Long Beach. I met some of the people that Morning Glory had known beforehand, including Carolyn Whitehorn and Sharon Devlin. We did a lot of fun stuff with Sharon and her daughter, Moira. We were in a unique position because we knew so many people through *Green Egg*. Everywhere we went we were invited to coven meetings and Circles of different traditions. We got to experience a lot of different kinds of rituals and magick that people did. We learned their ceremonies, chants and invocations. It's been an incredible gift of our life to get to know so many magickal people.

MG: It was great to do a Circle with Ed Fitch in Southern Cal. and then later on go up to Northern Cal. to do a Circle with Gwydion. It was so exciting to see Witches and Pagans everywhere I went, in places where you would never think to find them—even in Orange County where I went to High School. One evening my Dad came to pick us up from a full moon ritual and he was asked what he thought about having a daughter who was a Priestess and he said: "My old man was a preacher and as far as I can tell, she's just some other kind of preacher. Doesn't matter what kind, they're all the same to me." But my Mom was really happy to meet Oberon, since he was all I ever talked about from the day I met him.

OZ: We stayed briefly with Morning Glory's parents in their Open Road camper. It's amazing how roomy a little camper can be when it's filled with love. To me, it felt like being born into a new family, for I had never experienced such love and acceptance from my own parents as I did from hers. I could hardly believe how readily and completely I was adopted into the family. There was still work to be done on the bus, and her father, James, fixed the botch job that was done on it in San Jon.

We finally got up to Greenfield Ranch just in time for the 1976 Summer Solstice. I really wanted to show the place to Morning Glory. We stayed there for the Ranch Solstice party. It was an amazing transformative experience. There was a whole community there, and that was what our dream was. At that moment I decided that I wanted to live there. But first we had to go to Eugene, Oregon. That was where MG's community was.

ANODEA JUDITH: The whole Ranch got together on Summer Solstice. People swam in the pond and there was food and celebration.

MOTHERBEAR: I put on a play at the Solstice party. I wrote the script based on the book *James and the Giant Peach* by Roald Dahl, and I cast it from the Greenfield Ranch kids, including my daughter LaSara and a lot of her friends. Anodea painted a picture of the giant peach for us to use. Oberon said that when he saw the play, and saw the giant peach, that he actually saw the peach growing. Then he knew he was in the right place.

LASARA FIREFOX: My parents had a summer drama camp where kids came up from the city, stayed out on the land for ten days, and created a play and performed it for their parents and friends at the end of the time period. They did it for many years.

CERRIDWIN FALLINGSTAR: I first met the Zells in 1976. Alison Harlow held a big Summer Solstice festival at Coeden Brith. I saw Morning Glory dancing and was very attracted. After the festival there was an afterparty at Alison's in Palo Alto that some of us attended. I saw them there and went up to Alison, suggested that I was interested in them, and she said, "well, if you play your Tarot cards right, you could probably end up with them tonight."

So I approached Otter rather than Morning Glory, because I was a woman who had never been turned down by a guy. I felt confident, even though in some ways it was Morning Glory that I really had eyes for. But they were a package deal, and so were my husband and I at that time (he was not with me at that party.) The three of us did end up getting together and making love that night. When I went back to L.A, I told my husband about these fine people I had encountered. He met them later on, also liked them, and we embarked on about a five-year affair with them.

My husband and I would periodically go up north to visit them, and they would come down to L.A. to visit us. Sometimes we met in the middle at someone's house in the Bay Area. We did this several times a year. I became Gale's honorary aunt and Goddessmother. Even after I wasn't romantically involved with her mother and stepfather I continued to see her. They would send her down to spend time with us. Many years later when she got married I performed the wedding ceremony.

MG: I thought that Greenfield Ranch was really wonderful, but I was really looking forward to coming home to Eugene and seeing my friends and my family. We left the Ranch and said our Goodbyes and headed North up Hwy 101. I always love driving that stretch along the Highway from Ukiah to Crescent City. You go through the Redwoods and alongside the ocean; at one point there is a fresh water lagoon on one side of the road and the ocean on the other. It always feels like a pilgrimage somehow.

When we arrived in Eugene we were expected and were met, if not by a full brass band, at least by several instruments and a juggling troupe: my old friends, the Flying Karamazov Brothers all came pouring out of Lucy Lynch's house along with Catherine and helped us parallel park the bus. It was definitely the homecoming I had dreamed about for so long. It was great to finally see all my old friends and introduce them to OZ at last. However, time doesn't stand still and I could see that a lot had changed in the years I had been gone.

OZ: We continued on up to Eugene, arriving just in time for the Oregon Country Faire—the best Hippie Renaissance Festival in the country! Morning Glory had been attending this annually ever since 1969, when she first moved to Eugene with Gary. She had danced there with her boa constrictor, Baby Doll, performing as "The Sensuous Serpentina." She fell in with the amazing juggling troupe, The Flying Karamazov Brothers (FKB), and became best friends with their manager, Catherine Crowell. And there were also all the other performers and friends of the FKB. MG even knew Ken Kesey— "Bull Goose Looney" of the Merry Pranksters, and author of *One Flew Over the Cuckoo's Nest,* who had a dairy and sponsored annual "Poetry Hoo-Has" in Eugene. So she introduced me to all these wonderful people, and I really felt welcomed into the community.

At first we stayed in the parking lot of the apartment complex where Gary and Rainbow were living, but there really wasn't enough room there. We met Anna Korn and Susan Arrow who lived in an all-women communal house with a long driveway next to it. Morning Glory was well-known as the local Witch and teacher, and they wanted to learn from her, so they invited us to park the bus in their driveway. We moved in and Morning Glory began a training coven and started offering classes.

ANNA KORN: I was in graduate school in Biology in Eugene. Right after the Zells moved there they had put a notice up in a women's bookstore. I guess most of the people in Eugene weren't aware of the *Green Egg* at that point, but I knew what it was. I had never seen an issue, but I knew who they were. So I contacted them and invited them to my house for dinner. They came over in the Scarlet Succubus.

Later, when they moved into our household, they parked the bus alongside our house in the driveway, and ran an extension cord from the bus and through our bathroom window. They would use the phone and kick in for the electric bill. And so we just shared things. It was pretty much a collective household. If they got a phone call we would go to the bathroom, lean out the window and knock on the side of the bus. My roommates, even though they weren't all Pagans, felt that it was peculiar and interesting to have them around. Only one of my roommates had a car, so it wasn't a problem having the bus in our driveway. You could have street parking, and we rode bicycles. Eugene is a very bike-friendly place. They have bike trails everywhere.

The house was really small—it was originally some kind of farm outbuilding, like a shed that had been turned into a dwelling. The rest of the block had the regular suburban houses and their lots. But the interior of the block was attached to our house, and behind the house there was this gigantic grassy field. We had a huge vegetable garden there, and we created what the Zells called a Woodhenge—a magic circle that had standing logs marking the edges.

One of the first things they did, as I recall, is they got a teaching position in the extension courses of the local Lane Community College, where they taught a class called "Witchcraft, Shamanism and Pagan Religion" for three trimesters. It was really quite a good survey course. The students in the course would come to circles that we had, and formed the core group of a little group of Pagans in Eugene. We formed a coven called *Ithil Duath,* which is Elvish for "Moon Shadow."

MG: We celebrated full moons and attended a lecture as a field trip at Mother Kali's Bookstore with my old friend and fellow Goddess scholar Max Dashu. We made friends with some of the people in the Parapsychology Dept. at the college and took some of our class to see their Kirlian Camera where we could practice our breath work and aura projection lessons and see the immediate feedback through the camera. At one point OZ got visible sparks to shoot from his finger tip and caught it on film. We also put together a wonderful Mabon Ritual in the backyard of Anna and Susan's house. It was based on the John Barleycorn cycle and was enacted to the music of that wonderful old folk song.

I really was hoping that Gary, Oberon and my daughter could all become one family, but too much water had gone under the bridge at that point. Gary was living in an apartment and didn't want to give that up. We could never manage to get jobs. I tried, but I couldn't make my two universes come together.

ANNA KORN: I've known Gail since she was about three, and her name was Rainbow. She was living in Eugene with her father, Gary. At that point she was the poster child for the local Project Head Start program. It was a federally-funded pre-school program that was getting kids oriented to school and exposed to the concepts of numbers and letters, to get them prepared to go to grade school later on. They had posters that said "Enroll Your Kids in Project Head Start" in various places around Lane County, and Rainbow's picture was on the posters.

GAIL: In Eugene I stayed with them sometimes in the bus, but I went back and forth. It was a bus! That's not where you raise a kid. With my dad I had my own room. In the bus I had a bunk.

I would always have them drop me off blocks from school. I didn't want anyone to see them. But one time, though, my mom did come to my school on Halloween. She was all dressed up as a Witch. And she told a ghost story to the entire school. And everybody thought I was the coolest thing ever after that. Sometimes they would bring the snakes to school for show and tell, and then it came in handy to have the freaky, weird parents. This was in third grade.

For a little while as a pre-teen I did embrace the Witch spirituality. I guess I decided that a lot of people involved in that world are drama geeks, and I am not a drama geek. I don't have a theatrical side to my personality.

I'm a very pragmatic, practical person. I like my reality. My therapist says that your personality is completely formed by the time you are three. So basically I was scrambling for stability as a child, because I didn't have it at all. That is a lot of who I am. There was a long time that I was really a control freak, and that was because of how I grew up. And I had to unlearn a lot of that.

Oberon was a fun guy, like a kid himself. I used to love the way he cooked, because he fried everything. When you're a kid it doesn't get any better than that. But he went through this really weird George Orwellesque phase where he thought the world was going to end in 1982. We'd be staying up late listening to talk radio or something, and he'd be like, "Oh yeah, it's all gonna end in 1982."

He had me convinced for a little while that that was it, that I only had a few years left. This still pisses me off now, because I would never do that to my daughter. That weird phase he went through was so out of character for him, because usually, he sees things through rose-colored glasses to the point where it's ridiculous.

OZ: I got very caught up on a 1974 book called *The Jupiter Effect* by astronomer John Gribbin. He proposed that on March 10, 1982, a rare planetary alignment of Mercury, Venus, Earth, Mars, Jupiter, Saturn, and Pluto on the same side of the sun could trigger a series of geological events that might spawn devastating earthquakes and massive tidal waves. It was much like the current mythos around the year 2012, and I felt I needed to spread the word so that people would be prepared. But I deeply regret conveying these concerns to our kids, as it cast a Damoclean shadow over their lives for many years—much like the shadow of a seemingly inevitable nuclear apocalypse which had haunted my own youth. I learned a profound lesson from this: never promote a mythos that has no future, especially to the next generation!

OZ: In the winter of 1976-'77, the Eugene city prosecutor found us again and told us we couldn't park a bus in a residential neighborhood and we would have to move. MG had some other friends whom she had lived with when Rainbow was born and they owned Sundance, a local health food store that had a big space in the back yard. That kept us hidden for awhile.

MG: I contacted all the folks I knew and they put the word out. But we kept drawing blanks and we kept being pursued by our old Nemesis from St. Louis, the City Planning guy that hated Oberon. We kept getting tickets that would force us to move our bus from wherever we were staying. We had to leave Anna and Susan's house and then we moved behind Sundance, my friends' health food store where we worked as janitors and got to eat all the past-dated food. Our Possum, Participle, was ecstatic, but eventually the City located our bus again and we had to leave Sundance. I kept waiting for the breakthrough that just didn't seem to ever happen.

OZ: Participle continued to provide amusement to many. Sometimes Rainbow would take her home for a visit. One time a little boy was over at their apartment to play. He noticed the possum all curled up asleep on the bed, and frowning with great concern, he said: "Raibo, Raibo, someting wrong wit you cat's tail!"

But one night while we were parked at Sundance, Participle found a hole in the floorboards of the bus and disappeared. We never saw her after that, but for many months afterwards, people still reported encountering her around the dumpster at night.

MG: Then we had a phone conversation with our friend Alison Harlow who owned the property of Coeden Brith on Greenfield Ranch in California. Gwydion and Alison had had a falling out, and he had moved off the land that he and Alison had originally talked about becoming partners on. She was offering to let us live there for free in exchange for being caretakers! We were friends with both Alison and Gwydion, and we thought, "Well, maybe if we move down there we could kill two birds with one stone. We could raise Unicorns, and maybe we can manage to patch up the rift between Gwydion and Alison." We were very naive in those days about these kinds of things!

OZ: I started examining my life at that point. It was clear that I had passed a watershed. The life I had previously led was behind me now. I was on a threshold looking towards a new life. It seemed like it was a good time for a vision quest.

So in June of 1977, Morning Glory drove me out to a tiny undeveloped hot spring (MacReady Hot Springs) that was in a remote area of Oregon, on the border of a national forest. I waded across the river to the other side, where there was another small hot pool. There I spent two weeks in complete isolation from humanity and civilization. I wanted to spend the entire time eliminating artifacts as much as possible. I left my clothes with MG, as I wanted to do the whole thing naked. I had only a sleeping bag, a pocket knife, a Tarot deck, a notebook and a pen. And that was it. So it was a matter of fasting and surviving in the wilderness.

I completely avoided any human contact. If I saw any people coming I hid from them. I fasted, meditated, soaked in the hot water, and thought about stuff. I carved a goddess out of wood, built a stone circle, and made a lean-to shelter. I wrote in my journal. When I came out, two weeks later, I was transformed. I was now a mountain man, and ready to begin a new life homesteading in the woods. Morning Glory drove up to get me, and took me out for a really great dinner. Shortly after that we made the move to Greenfield.

Tom Williams had taken over as editor of *Green Egg,* but within a year he quit and moved out to California too, "following," he said, "in my Primate's knuckleprints." There was one more issue after he left, dated Yule, 1976. It was so bad that when they shipped it out to stores the stores returned them. GE's reputation plummeted and the zine went out of business. The whole CAW in the Midwest ended up crumbling in the next year or two. A couple of outlying Nests survived because they were family-based and continued to meet. But the foundational infrastructure of the central Church itself collapsed.

DON WILDGRUBE: When Tim, MG, Bill, Michael Hurley and Old Charlie, left for the west coast, the publication was turned over to Tom Williams. Issue 78 came out for Beltane, 1976, and was on time. The next issue, #79, Litha, also came out on time. But all this time our bills for the press, ink, paper and more were piling up.

Tom finally called me and announced that he was leaving St Louis and heading out to join the others. John Patrick was in town at that time (he had moved to Chicago). I had a large step van and we went over to Tom's house and took almost all of the office equipment, the files and stuff. When we went down his basement we saw a pallet piled with hundreds of back issues of the *Green Egg.* He said that the next day he was going to take them to the dump to get rid of them. Tiny and I carried all of the old *Green Eggs* and put them in my truck.

After Tom left, we had an emergency meeting to see what could be done to rescue the *Green Egg.* It was decided to hold off until the Yule issue to get a staff working since the old staff did not continue. It was decided that I publish the *Green Egg,* with help from Ron and Rose Palozola and others. I put out the Yule issue and mailed it out on time. After each publication, money came in through new subscriptions and donations. This happened again with the issue I put out (#80), but Tiny did something uncalled for, he paid our bills! After three or four months of non-publishing, the revenue just barely paid for what was owed. The *Green Egg* was no more.

We didn't know what to do. We had a board meeting and it was decided to get out of the printing business, sell the press and all, and see how much money we could get to continue on. So the press and the equipment was sold. There was some original art that was auctioned off, but the bulk of the office equipment, files, etc. remained. All the remaining back issues of GE got taken to the dump.

NARRATOR: The *Green Egg* continued to feature a large and diverse selection of letters in every issue, right up until the (somewhat bitter) end. When it finally folded there was no one magazine that came along to take its place and do everything that it had done, but there was a solid foundation for a community to grow on. Pagans around the globe now knew about each other, and they found other ways to stay in touch. Margot Adler says:

> By 1978…CAW's role as catalyst for the Neo-Pagan movement had ended, at least temporarily, with the death of *Green Egg*.
>
> How important *Green Egg* was to the Neo-Pagan community is a matter of controversy. There are many who welcomed its death with a sigh of relief. But others, including myself, believed that it was a key to the movement's vitality and that its death in 1976 was a blow from which the movement is only now recovering…
>
> It is popular today to talk about 'synergy'—a combination that has a greater effect than the simple addition of its components—and that perhaps best describes the effect of *Green Egg*. It connected all the evolving and emerging Goddess and nature religions into one phenomenon: the Neo-Pagan movement.
>
> ~Margot Adler, *Drawing Down the Moon,*
> Viking Press, 1979; p. 294-5

NARRATOR: In the later issues of *Green Egg* there were extensive calendar listings of upcoming regional and world science fiction conventions, with lots of information about activities at the cons and how to register in advance. (The 1976 Worldcon in Kansas City, where Robert Heinlein was the guest of honor, was heavily promoted.) But after GE folded another major changed happened: outdoor Pagan Festivals began happening regularly around the country,

and they continued to get bigger every year. Some of the early ones
included the Pagan Spirit Gathering in Wisconsin, and the Starwood
Festival in New York, both of which are still happening today and
are quite popular. Once Pagans had their own big public events, they
no longer needed to use science fiction conventions as places to
hook-up at. (Although some Pagans continued to go to cons if they
were science fiction fans, there wasn't as much midnight skinny-
dipping in the hotel swimming pools after that.)

Tim and Morning Glory Zell missed most of this, of course, because they had gone into the woods, from which they emerged only
occasionally for events on the West Coast.

MG at Rex Rotary press
printing *Green Egg,* 1974.

Tim's drawing of Pendragon on
cover of *Green Egg,* Samhain 1974.

Green Egg collating party, 1974.

MG, Polly, Tim & Rainbow—
Long Beach, CA, Sept. 1975.

Farewell to HDC after 10 years
(OZ on L); Nov. 30, 1975.

The Scarlet Succubus, Jan. 1976.

Tim & Mom in Scarlet Succubus,
Summer 1976.

MG & Participle the possum;
Feb. 1976.

Tim and Morning Glory with
snakes Tanith and Ananta.
Eugene, Oregon, Mabon 1976.

CHAPTER 18:
The Magick Land
(1977-1979)

We're gonna move to the country
With a half-a-dozen lovers
I'm gonna move to the country
Aw honey squeeze on over

We'll leave behind the city and with it our doubts
When we get to where we're going we'll hoot and shout
And we'll turn each other upside down
And shake the concrete out
When we move to the country....
~ "Move to the Country"
by Christopher Bingham of Gaia Consort

G: THE IDEA WAS THAT RAINBOW would come and live with us, and go back and forth to Gary's in Eugene. By that time she was nearly six, and I let her decide where she wanted to live. And she opted to stay with her father because he had electricity, running water, and television.

I wasn't eager to leave behind my daughter again. But I felt that since Oberon had moved away from St Louis to be with me, I had to move with him this time. I went ahead and caved in because I could not bear to be parted from Oberon. But I was pretty bitter, angry, and unhappy about it. I felt that he was making me chose between my child and him. I couldn't verbalize my anger, or entirely even bring it up into consciousness. But it was there. A million times a day all of our stresses of living in a school bus kept bringing these things up and out. We were both headstrong people, and we were always butting heads and constantly bickering. I can see that it wasn't a very appealing thing for a child to want to live in a school bus on raw unimproved land with no running water or electricity with two bickering adults. But at least Rainbow decided to come and visit us in the summer when school was out.

So on July 4, 1977, we arrived at Greenfield Ranch, posting our old "Did You Remember to Dress?" sign at the gate. We told Alison what we were going to do with Unicorns and got her involved in it. To this end, the three of us formed the Holy Order of Mother Earth (HOME) as a monastic order of stewardship and ritual, and chartered it as a subsidiary of the Church of All Worlds. I think at the time Alison kind of humored us and thought, "yeah, whatever." She probably didn't think that we could really pull it off. But Oberon and I both had the same kind of no-nonsense "let's get our hands involved in this" attitude that was needed.

ALISON HARLOW: The Zells and I were close friends. I loved them both very, very much. They were living on my land for free, but it was a benefit for me to have them there because they were taking care of things. Oberon had gotten his unicorn idea some years prior. It seemed like an interesting thing to try to do. Nobody else was doing it. I had to advance them the money to pay for the unicorns, but they did ultimately pay me back.

OZ: We pulled up to the parking spot on Coeden Brith and immediately shed all of our clothes. It was hotter than blazes. Ace showed up in a big pick-up truck and said, "Let's go up to the pond and take a dip." We got as far as the Ranch House and the fire alarm was going off. There we were, stark naked in the back of a pick-up truck, and the entire Ranch was mobilizing to go fight a forest fire!

We dashed into the Ranch House and managed to find something to put on in the free box of people's discarded clothes. We then joined in and spent the entire day and night fighting the fire. In the night roots underground were catching fire and glowing. You'd walk around the landscape and it was like "Dante's Inferno." Many people became hospitalized from breathing the smoke of burning poison oak. That was our first day in our new home!

After the fire we got to meet more of the people who were living there. We were told by several of them that we should connect with Anodea Judith, as she was another Pagan. Shortly thereafter, we resolved to look her up. Several folks who owned a parcel together had a dairy, and they called it the "Udder Truth." MG and I hiked on up there and there was a cow with human feet sticking out from under it. We looked over the top of the cow and there was a long-haired, blonde Hippie girl down there milking it.

ANODEA JUDITH: One morning I was milking a cow, up in the shed, and Oberon and Morning Glory came to visit, and they said, "Anodea, we have come for you." They took me up to their bus, and I think I came out three days later.

Not long after that when I went back to visit I saw them outside doing this little purging ceremony where they were kind of gently tapping each other's naked bodies with a branch of leaves. And I said, "Oberon, that's poison oak!"

And he said, "Oh really?" St Louis had poison ivy, not poison oak, so he didn't recognize it. They got the worst case of poison oak that I have ever seen. They were covered from head to toe. Talk about an initiation!

We became fast and furious friends. We really related on a metaphysical level. I was already doing rituals and things on my own before I met them, so things kind of linked right up. We started working together producing events, circles, and magical trainings. Before I met them I had mostly been doing rituals with women, because I hadn't known any men that were into it.

OZ: Our first Thanksgiving on the Ranch was quite an event, and it was covered by a documentary TV crew from Brussels (or someplace in Europe). They were pursuing a quest to discover and document "Where have all the Hippies gone?" And somehow they found us—we'd done exactly what we'd always said we wanted to do: move to the country with a buncha friends and start a community! I remember Sequoia riding in on the bottom of an overturned galvanized steel horse trough, carried like a coffin by several strong men, that was to be installed behind the Ranch House as our new hot tub. And of course, the groaning trestle tables laden with the most amazing food that all those great cooks could come up with! Really, this was everything I had dreamed and hoped for—and more.

Over subsequent years, another major annual event was inaugurated: the Harvest Party, often held in conjunction with Samhain, when everyone who was growing pipeweed brought samples to share and compare. Dana Crumb (ex-wife of the famous underground cartoonist R. Crumb) was a legendary gourmet cook, and she would prepare all this scrumptious food for our own version of a "Mendonesian Harvest Feast."

Our friend Charlie Leach from St Louis soon showed up in a huge tractor-trailer loaded with the band-saw, metal lathe, table saw, drill press, milling machines, and other equipment from his machine shop. He parked next to our bus and tried to operate a shop off a gasoline-powered generator. But that proved really awkward, so he soon found a large shop to rent down in the tiny town of Calpella, which became our first off-Ranch outpost for phones, showers, etc.

Charlie's major obsession there—and for the rest of his life—was trying to reconstruct a magnet-and-gravity-driven "perpetual motion machine" he called "Bessler's Wheel." In 1712, Johann Bessler (who went by the magical name "Orffyreus") exhibited a large enclosed wheel which continued rotating indefinitely with no evident outside connections. But he wanted to be paid for his invention, and no one would do so; so the secret of the actual mechanism died with him. But enough drawings, notes, and descriptions from others survive that Charlie thought he could replicate it. Alas, he never got any of his many models to work.

We hadn't been up on the Ranch for too long before Bill Morris (Orion Stormcrow) also moved there, followed soon by Michael (later Brendan) Hurley. In 1978 the three of us tried to grow a little dope garden, but we really didn't know what we were doing, and it was a pathetic failure. And the tiny amount we did manage to bring to full term got ripped off. After that year, of course, I was too busy with the Unicorn project to give it another try.

Michael liked to listen to late-night radio, and one day he told me that there was this local program called "Clergy Forum," which was inviting clergy members of various denominations to come on and discuss the issues of the day. Michael called them up and made arrangements for me to be on the show. Now the format was that there would be two clergy each show, with the host acting as moderator. After the first half hour, the phone lines would be opened for another half hour of call-in questions from listeners.

On the appointed evening, Morning Glory and I went down to the studio. We were introduced to the other minister, who was from the Evangelical Orthodox Reformed Church—a very fundamentalist church, about as opposite from the Church of All Worlds as could be imagined. As it turned out, the host was also a member of that same church, so it was clear from the outset that this was a setup, and I would be ganged up on. But I was confident of my ultimate advantage: I'd read their scriptures, and knew all about their religion; but they knew nothing of mine.

The other minister opened with: "As I sit here in my clerical garb representing 2,000 years of Christian tradition, I wonder what someone from a little upstart cult could possibly have to say to me."

I responded with, "Well, I would have worn my own clerical robes, representing 20,000 years of Pagan tradition, but the horns wouldn't fit through the door!" (a reference to a Buddhist joke...). And it went downhill from there. The host, of course, didn't actually moderate the debate that soon devolved into mere argument; rather, he unabashedly joined ranks with the minister against me. But I felt I held my own pretty well, having honed my skills over many years of visits from Yahveh's Witlesses. And I was really looking forward to the half-hour mark, and the phone-ins, as Michael had promised to be a caller.

However, at the end of the first half-hour, the host shut down the show, and refused to take any calls. Probably he realized I was no patsy, and feared that I might get in a few points with callers. As we all left the studio, the other minister turned to me with a hateful look and snarled, "I wish we could still burn people like you at the stake!"

Morning Glory, who had been waiting in the outer room, responded with: "And I wish you had said that on the air!"

Some of our closest Pagan friends on the Ranch in the early years were Bran and Moria Starbuck. Moria was (and is) a truly gifted graphic artist and sculptor, who turned me onto Sculpy™ (a kind of modeling material that could be baked hard in a regular oven) and thus helped launch my own eventually career in sculpting. They had moved up from Los Angeles shortly before we did, and settled on the parcel that had originally been "reserved" for Morning Glory and me. It was in part to accommodate them that Alison agreed to let us move onto her land instead.

Bran and Moria had appeared on national TV for a Hallowe'en special a couple of years before (we had seen the show, and it was quite good). When the show was re-run the following year, one of their neighbors recognized them. She belonged to a Fundamentalist Christian church, and she got the Pastor and the whole church all riled up about the Witches in their midst. Bran and Moria got rocks thrown through their windows with threatening notes and burning bags of shit left on their doorstep. Finally, they had too much. They sold their house and packed to move to Greenfield.

Now, right at the foot of the valley enclosing the 5,600-acres of Greenfield Ranch is a conical volcanic peak that everyone calls "Witch Mountain," after the Disney movie. The whole Ranch lies behind it. As Bran and Moria were packing up the last of their kitchen wares, they placed the final coffee cup face down on a piece of newspaper to wrap it. When they turned it over, they saw that the rim of the cup enclosed within its circle a movie ad proclaiming *Escape to Witch Mountain!* And that's just what they did.

We had many wonderful adventures with Bran and Moria. They recruited us into their little cottage industry of handmade pottery roach holders in the form of funny faces and cartoony critters, which they fired in their kiln. We'd go down to Fisherman's Wharf in San Francisco and sell these to the tourists, and also travel the back roads of California in their RV, going to places like Big Sur and little-known hot springs. Eventually they decided they didn't want to be involved with the larger Wiccan/Pagan community any more, so they gave us their original Mosian Books of Shadows and all their handmade magickal tools, which we still treasure.

The folks across the valley from us were Marilyn Motherbear and her family. Troll was her second husband. They became some of our closest friends. They were fundamental homesteaders. They built a huge, sprawling farm and a vast house that was always being worked on. They had a bunch of kids, and that's why she took the name "Motherbear."

Morning Glory and I became aunt and uncle to their kids—LaSara, Emrys, Yolkai, and Patience. We would spend some Thanksgivings and other holidays with them. It was quite a hike across the valley and up the ridge to get there from where we were. Getting around the Ranch was not always easy.

Marilyn started up the Ranch school along with Zephyr and some other folks, and I taught in it for a while. We had a CB radio network of people on the Ranch. In the evenings we would just leave our CBs on and anyone who wanted to could join in on the conversation. Sometimes people would read stories or poetry, or maybe play chess. It gave us a nice sense of having our friends around us. Motherbear got into reading chapters from *Dragonriders of Pern*, and Gwydion played chess with a friend across the valley. My CB handle was "High Buzzard" and MG's was "Ditch Witch."

MOTHERBEAR: A CB radio system was put into place. We were using it contact each other, because in the early days you could not always get across the creek. So there was a communication system set up through the CB radios. I had been reading one of Anne McCaffrey's *Dragonrider* books, and I took a name from that to use as my handle on the CB channel. So when Oberon heard me using that name he said, "So you must be a Pagan."

And I said, "What do you mean by that?" He said a Pagan is someone who loves the Earth, and I said, "Then I guess I am one."

I had to get over my Protestant upbringing. Once I found out what it was, I was there. Once Gwydion had settled Annwfn they invited us to come to the Sabbats and Esbats and we started to participate. I remember calling a Quarter one of the first times we participated. I had very little notion of what the formalities of a Pagan Circle-calling might be. So I called West with my then husband, Troll, by singing, "By the sea, by the sea, by the beautiful sea"—the song from the Depression.

LASARA FIREFOX: In those days, in the life that had been chosen by my parents, and by Oberon and Morning Glory, Anodea Judith and many other latter-day "pioneers," a visit to another's home meant a two-hour hike and often a two-day stay-over. Roads were not roads; they were logging tracks that were impassable for sometimes months at a time. Many of us had cars that were not always working, and even the best of what any of us could afford was not built for the terrain.

My family settled at the end of one such not-a-road, with a waterway that was somewhere between creek and river. When it was in its river phase, we were land-locked. The only way in or out was overland hiking to the one bridge that crossed the river.

On one such pilgrimage that Oberon and Morning Glory made to our home, I recall all us—Morning Glory, Oberon, my parents, three siblings, and myself—sitting very cozily in the Cook House, the central element of our homestead, around the beautiful, antique round table that served as our dining set. Though I was only four or five at the time, I still remember the fire burning warmly in the cooking stove and the soft quality of the natural candle and kerosene light. I remember the stories and songs, and Oberon washing the dishes after the large and hearty supper my family had prepared.

Visitors were a rare treat, and these visitors were a god/dess send after weeks of isolation.

OZ: One of the things Greenfield Ranch was famous for was rattlesnakes. Gwydion wanted to re-name the place "Rattlesnake Acres," because he felt that Greenfield sounded too attractive. One of his favorite songs that he used to sing at parties was "Paradise." There was a line in it about how if you call some place paradise, you can kiss it good-bye. The idea being that if you make it sound really attractive everyone wants to move there, and before long it is overcrowded and polluted. So Gwydion was always agitating to emphasize the less desirable aspects of country life. His very funny song, "Sometimes I Wonder," was sorta the definitive piece on the difficulties on homesteading on the Ranch! Eventually, he wrote his own "Greenfield Anthem," which concludes with the verse:

There's a lot of other places some folks would rather be,
But the dust and heat of an unpaved street are good enough for me.
Now the summers make it hard to take, and the winters may get cold,
But I'm glad to say that I'm here to stay, even when I'm growin' old!
                    ~ "Greenfield," by Gwydion Pendderwen

When we first moved to Greenfield there was a community work project to build a drivable bridge across the creek to the Ranch House. Bonnie Raitt's brother David organized it, everyone showed up to help out, and afterwards there was the usual big party. There were a lot of work parties like that—for road repairs, barn-raisings, house building, making ferro-cement water storage tanks, etc.

At this particular one, this big old rattlesnake showed up. People were all upset and worried about it. Well, I'm a snake handler and a "parseltongue." So I gathered everyone around, sat down and had a nice conversation with the snake. The snake was coiled up, scared, and rattling like crazy. But then as it realized that no one was going to try to hurt it, and that people were just there to admire it, it calmed down. People could see how beautiful it was. The Northern California rattlesnake is called *Crotalis Viridus,* which means "green rattlesnake." It has a bright green color to it, and the tail is dramatically banded in black and white.

After that, when anyone encountered a snake that was in some place that it shouldn't be, if they could get hold of me I would come and move it. I'd put it in a bucket, take it somewhere far away from people, and turn it loose. During the whole time we were there (and since) nobody was ever bitten by a rattlesnake. We just developed this nice relationship. We didn't hurt them, and they didn't hurt us.

I've always had a natural ability to deal with any kind of animal. I have no natural fear of anything. I have no phobias or anything like that. I study their habits and I observe them and I learn things. I can pretty much deal with any kind of animal without any problem. Once you understand them it's not hard. My first real Wizardly magick is what we now call brown magic or "Beast Mastery"—communicating and working with animals.

MG: Rainbow lived with us in the summertime. She had a bunk bed inside the vehicle, but she couldn't take the crowdedness so we built her a tree house fort outside to go to when she wanted to get away; we fixed it up with cushions, blankets and dishes so she could even spend the night there if she wanted to, but she was not too keen on sleeping alone in the woods. I never understood being scared in the woods because I loved it so much even when I was a little kid. I was always wandering off and getting lost because I didn't worry about that sort of thing. The forest always seemed like a safe haven to me, but I came to realize that's not how many folks think of it.

Rainbow spent summers with us and in the winter she would go live with Gary and go to school in Eugene. We developed this rhythm of the seasons, sort of like the story of Demeter and Persephone. I would go spend Christmas, birthdays and spring break with her in Eugene. After a year or two of that she did stay with us for one year and went to the Ranch school.

GAIL: When I went to visit them, I had to take the Greyhound bus by myself. I hated that stupid bus. I never had any bad experiences, but it just stunk. People could smoke cigarettes on the bus back then. And for some reason, the bus always left at 3 in the morning, so we had to get down there in the middle of the night.

MG: Rainbow would come down and visit and go back and forth. One of the sad things was that all the kids for her to play with were on the other side of the mountain. We did a lot of walking, and we had lots of animals. So she grew up with lots of animals as her friends. She picked out this wonderful kitten from a pet store in Ukiah and we brought her home. We named her Octobriana. She was a tortie-point Siamese with an orange and black face and startling blue eyes. We would take long walks in the woods with Rainbow, OZ and me with Octobriana following along with us—not like a dog but more on her own. When we finally got the goats it was one of my daughter's chores to help feed the babies and we both enjoyed giving them their bottles and watching the fierce but blissful way they would suck down the milk.

GAIL: I tried to go to school on the Ranch, but it was a Hippie school and it was not working for me. I had dyslexia, and I needed more than what was being provided.

MG: In spite of both the public schools and the private school that Gary sent her to, Rainbow was ten years old and she still could not read, so I finally put my foot down because I did not want to have an illiterate child who would suffer for it her whole life. So I told her that she was going to spend the next winter with us and we would make sure she learned to read. She didn't like it but it worked. There was no TV or Mall or other distractions through the long winter months of rain and the only other kids lived miles away on twisted muddy roads.

But what we were rich in was books, lots of books—and especially lots of comic books. OZ is a comics collector and he turned her onto *ElfQuest* comics by Wendy and Richard Pini, which was a turning point in her life in many ways. The pictures told the story but it made her want to learn to read the words and find out more. Then we would work with her sounding out the words until she got it and something clicked in her head and the words finally made sense. After that she never looked back and she started reading for pleasure, first comics then kid's books and finally full-length novels. She once told me years later that was the point at which she became a time-binding being; she learned to judge duration by the six-week intervals she had to wait for the next installment of *ElfQuest.*

KIRSTEN JOHNSEN: My parents moved to the Ranch when I was six and a half. That was in 1974. Sometime that summer a few families got together and began the Annie Greenfield School. I lived, and still do live, at Chicken Foot Forks, which is on what we call the Orr Springs side of the Ranch—the West entrance gate to Greenfield Ranch opens onto Orr Springs Road. They usually call the other side of the Ranch the Fetzer side, because that's where the access gate leads through the Fetzer property. Annwfn is very close to the Fetzer side. I didn't live too close to Coeden Brith, in terms of walking distance for a kid. So I wasn't really introduced to Otter and Morning Glory till later.

Rainbow would come to the school sometimes. My main first connection with them was because a few of the girls at the Ranch School got some idea in our heads that we all wanted to get pet rats. I think it was because Rainbow had a pet rat, and she brought it to school. We had a school that actually went on throughout the year. We never really had vacations because it was sort of this Hippie made-up school, and people would just show up and teach different classes. It was pretty loosely organized. It was basically a baby-sitting service for the parents as well. So we all went over to Otter and Morning Glory's and chose some little baby rats from their rat factory. This had this going on because they had snakes, and they were feeding the rats to the snakes. They had a crop of very beautiful golden rats. I remember specifically that I named mine Carmel.

When I was about 10, 11 or 12, I would go over and spend nights having campfire sleepovers with Rainbow at Coeden Brith with Otter and Morning Glory. One time Otter let me borrow his copy of *The Last Unicorn,* and that was one of the first personal connections that I had with him. Other than that they were just part of the menagerie of crazy characters on Greenfield Ranch. They were very glamorous—they would come to the Halloween parties all decked out with live tarantulas on their shoulders. Sometimes in the summertime they would bring their python to the pond. They'd say, "We're going to let the python swim." It was maybe ten feet long. So everybody got out of the water. When smaller snakes swim in a pond they make ripples. This python made waves! It was really beautiful to watch.

OZ: Ananta was quite a character for a snake, and he was very well-mannered. When he was swimming in the pond, some of the kids would sit in an inner tube and hold onto his tail, and he would pull them across the water. He was wild-caught as a baby, and always wanted to get out and explore. Tanith, our boa, was very different. She'd been born (yes, boas are born live, not hatched from eggs like pythons) and raised in captivity, and was much more socially-oriented. When we'd go picnicking with them, she would climb up on the table and hang out with us among the ketchup and mustard jars. But Ananta would go off looking for some place to climb, or hide. One time he disappeared from the bus. I slept out in the field to dream-fast with him, and got the impression of being high in a tree. So in the morning I searched the tops of all the trees in the neighborhood and finally found him way up in a big bay. I had to climb up and wrestle him down—all ten feet of him!

GAIL: Oberon and Morning Glory had a really intense relationship. They fought very intensely for years. The whole time they were on Greenfield they fought like cats and dogs. They had screaming matches that would go on for days. They moved to the woods because they thought it was going to be all groovy and harmonious, and all they did was try to kill each other

CERRIDWIN FALLINGSTAR: Otter and Morning Glory fought constantly. It was distressing to my husband and I to see them fighting, and they kept trying to pull us in. So we would talk to them and try to give them a different perspective, and then they would get back together and do it all over again. There was no commitment on their part to learn to be responsible with their emotions, to treat each other and their kid responsibly.

They never fought with us. But it became more difficult to be around. I think that part of it was that life on Greenfield was hard. They were living in a very small bus on a remote piece of land. I'm sure they got on each other's nerves, and that their circumstances were very challenging.

OZ: Bryan was still in St Louis. We weren't really in touch with him. That is one of the things I regret. During the final months in St Louis and while we were putting the bus together, we tried to phone him many times. But every time we were told that he didn't want to talk to us. So eventually we just gave up. I wasn't in contact with him for a number of years. After we moved to the Ranch, we didn't even have a phone. I could have written but I didn't. I kind of dropped off the map. Just disappearing was somehow part of the whole thing of going to live in the woods. And since *Green Egg* was no longer being published, I didn't have any way to keep in touch with all the people I used to know.

MARTHA: I think the worst thing Tim did in regards to Bryan was having nothing to do with him once he left St Louis. I don't know why he did that. He always loved Bryan so much when he was younger. It was like he just gave up that whole world when he moved out there. Bryan was upset. Tim never wrote to him or sent him any cards.

BRYAN: I didn't hear from my dad for years. I had no idea where he was or what he was doing. I believed that Dad didn't want to pay child support. My step-father wanted to have the law pursue him for that, but my mom refused. She didn't want that to happen.

But I don't think my dad should feel guilty about not being there. There were times I didn't want him to be there. I was afraid of change, and I needed some stability in my life. After knowing what he went through after leaving St Louis, I feel I made the right decision. So I forgive him for that. But I often wonder where I'd be now if I'd gone with him; that's something in the back of my mind.

I started talking with him again when I was around 15 or 16. He mailed me a book called *Drawing Down The Moon*.

Morning Glory Godiva
on Coeden Brith.

MG building Snow Mom
on Coeden Brith.

Tim the Mountain Man,
Greenfield Ranch, 1977.

Tim in his deerskin shaman's robe,
Coeden Brith, Litha 1976.

CHAPTER 19:
Stonehenge Eclipse
(1978-1979)

The prophecies will come,
When Shadow mates with Sun!
Be there; you know where.
Feb. 26, 1979

NARRATOR: THE ZELLS DIDN'T HAVE ANY money and had a hard time surviving on the Ranch, just as they had had in Eugene. They kept expecting that they'd get some cash from the sale of the house that had used to belong to Tim in St Louis, but there had been some major changes in the Church after they had left town. Tim's house was sold, but after paying off the remaining debt on the loan for it and other fees there was only about $2,000 left, and that was then controlled by a newly-elected CAW Board of Directors. Half of that money was used to pay off bills that had been accumulated by publishing *Green Egg,* and the rest was eventually sent to California.

MG: We thought we were in a claustrophobic situation in Eugene, but on Greenfield there was no place to go to get away. We were supposed to get the money from the sale of the house in St. Louis, but we didn't. We really wanted to build a temple on that land. Oberon drew up elaborate plans and we took various classes on building. But by the time we got some money, it wasn't enough to build with. We were finally able to pull together enough money to buy the basic frame of a yurt.

OZ: We didn't have any money, and we were desperately trying to just survive. Eventually the unemployment ran out, and we were barely hanging on by the skin of our teeth. I had never experienced that degree of poverty before, and I was ashamed to try and communicate with anyone back in St Louis—including Bryan. We made things to sell at arts and crafts shows, and we would go down to Fisherman's Wharf in San Francisco with our Ranch neighbors Bran and Moria and sell little sculptures that we created with them.

We had a couple of other Pagan friends in Sacramento—Mary and Willowoak. Along with Gwydion (who had previously worked for the IRS), they helped us to get the CAW incorporated in California, so we had the infrastructure in place. We received State incorporation on Sept. 14, 1978. And we were expecting the money from the sale of the house to be sent to us. We were going to use that to establish a West Coast presence. But it never came. We got nothing but the runaround every time we called, and this crippled our plans for CAW for the next few years.

Apparently what was happening was that there were a lot of arguments going on back in St Louis. This became a divisive issue that broke up the entire St Louis CAW. It should have given us the warning that we were not going to receive the kind of support and loyalty that we would have expected from a Church we had founded. People were moving in who had a different agenda, which did not include treating us right. That was hard to accept for many years.

MG: One of the most painful things in retrospect that I remember from that desperate time was how Tiny McClimans had tried to warn OZ about this very thing originally when he had wanted to put his house in the Church's name. But somehow his warning got twisted around so OZ came to believe that Tiny supported the Church's position when in fact Tiny had quit the Church over that very conflict. It became a terrible wound and a terrible estrangement. I remember hours of trekking through the rain to the Ranch House to use the phone to call St Louis. Long painful phone calls with no resolution, followed by the long trek back home to the bus with nothing but a can of soup left to eat for dinner. Fortunately, my daughter wasn't around during the worst of this period.

DON WILDGRUBE: After Tim and MG moved to California, and they had been there a year or so, they decided that they would sell their house and bring most of the money to Nemeton for Forever Forests and other such projects. The problem was that they were no longer the owners of the house. They got Charlie Leach to act as their sales agent. All went well until the title company looked at the deed and found that Charlie had no authority to sell the house. That fell to me as Secretary of the Board of the Church. The house was sold and the check made out to the Church of All Worlds came to me. I immediately deposited it. This is where it really got hairy. I had calls from Tim, from Gwydion and others cajoling me to threatening me that I should send them the money. I stated that I couldn't, that I was bound by the decision of the present Board of Directors.

The new Board of Directors consisted of myself, John (J.P.) McClimans, Larry Andersen of Milwaukee, Dick Sells (President) of Chattanooga, and others with input from Bryan (a lobbyist from Washington, and very paranoid about Church/Government stuff) and Lady Sintana of Atlanta. J.P. and myself were the only ones on the board who actually knew Tim and Morning Glory and they didn't sit too well in the eyes of those who didn't know them.

Now the house sold for $15,000 and Tim expected $15,000 to be sent to him. Unfortunately, the loan for the house, about $10,000, had to be paid off and other fees from the sale, water and sewage. We ended up with about $2,000. The Board had heated discussions about the money. J.P. and I wanted to send the money out west or at least most of it. Finally Dick Sells decreed that we could not mention CAW in reference to the California people. The discussion got so bad that J.P. walked out of the meeting with his immediate resignation. It was decided that half of the money would be sent to California and the other half to pay off what we owed for paper, ink, plates and other items that were in arrears. Half of the money was sent directly to Church of All Worlds, California, on a cashiers check drawn on the Church's account. I did that and I thought that it was less complicated than sending it to Forever Forests or what ever. I was threatened for not following the directions of the board, and Dick Sell resigned, leaving Larry and I to hold the bag. Larry was in Milwaukee but I was in St Louis and was a sitting duck.

Tim sent Charlie, Bill Morris and Michael Hurley, then from California, Carolyn Clark, and others to confront me for the money and have me thrown in jail for embezzling $15,000. After a really heated argument, trying to explain the situation, and showing them the papers from the Title Company, all the people finally left. Bill Morris came back a bit later and we talked like civil humans. I explained just what happened with the money, with the feelings of people and all.

I was so disgusted with the goings on, that I decided to pull away from CAW myself, and form a Church, the Earth Church of Amargi, based on early CAW ideas. (The ECA is no longer in existence. I turned it over to Wayne Ochs who let it lapse a couple of years later because of lack of interest.) In our by-laws we stated that the Church could own nothing, I had been really burned. I had gotten my incorporation as part payment on a carpet job that I did. I had carpeted an entire house for a lawyer who did it. In fact he owed me $400. I had the check and to show my good faith and to be rid of the crap, I gave the entire check to Bill Morris to give to Forever Forests or whatever. Tim was angry with me for quite some time, and in the first issue of the new *Green Egg* (*Green Egg: the Next Generation*), dated Beltane 1988, he told people in an article entitled "It was 20 years ago today" how I had sold the press and house and all, then used the money to form a competing Church.

I wrote him and explained again what had happened and told him to check with others who knew what was going on.

In the next issue of the *Green Egg,* Tim apologized and said, "Let's let sleeping gargoyles lie."

OZ: When we first came to California, for quite awhile our school bus was our only vehicle. When we went down to The City, we would have to drive the bus from Greenfield Ranch and find places to park it. One time we had to drive to San Francisco to get some help for Morning Glory's medical problems. Some of her closest friends, including one lover, were part of the Flying Karamazov Brothers juggling troupe. They were living down there in the Height/Ashbury in a second floor apartment above a kite shop, across from Golden Gate Park. They said that we could stay with them for a few days, and if we parked in front of their building we could run a cord from the bus up to their apartment for electricity.

Well, the problem was that our bus was 25 feet long, and it needed two parking places. It's hard enough to find one parking place in San Francisco, but to find two adjacent is impossible. But the first night we got there, just as we arrived, two cars pulled out of parking places at the same time, so we pulled in. The next day we drove around the city, and that evening the same thing happened with the parking places, and again the third evening. Later that night Morning Glory was up in the apartment and I was relaxing in the bus when I heard a knock on the door. I opened it, and there was an old black man with a bottle of wine and a bag of pipeweed. He said, "Behold, I come bearing gifts."

So I said, "Come on in." He introduced himself to me. His name was Ben, and he turned out to be the local Voodoo Houngan. He said he'd been watching us and seen what had happened with the parking spaces, and he'd never seen anything like that before. He had looked in the bus window and saw our shelves of books on magick, and decided that he needed to talk to us.

Old Ben and I had a great time. We talked about our different traditions and cultural backgrounds. In my life I've had the wonderful opportunity to sit down and get close with several traditional shamans, including Choctaw, Quechua, Mayan, Taino, Hawaiian, Chinese, Australian Aboriginal, Tunguska and Yoruba. There has been a common foundation—a great sense of humor, an understanding of the deeper stuff and connections to the Earth. The core of shamanic type stuff is universal, and that became the core of what I eventually brought into the *Grimoire*. Ben was one of the first people that I got on that level with. Finally Morning Glory came down and joined us and we continued on late into the night.

A lot of people in traditional practices don't tend to share their stuff. But there we were in the back of our school bus and there was nothing that we couldn't talk about. We totally dug it. It helped to infuse our own sense of magick.

In 1972, Gwydion and Alison had created a publishing organization called *Nemeton* (Welsh for sacred grove) which put out several issues of an excellent magazine by that name, as well as amassing a considerable networking file. Once the Church of All Worlds was established in California, Gwydion had Nemeton chartered as a CAW subsidiary, and turned its purpose to producing his songbooks and record albums to support Annwfn.

Starting in 1977, Gwydion began organizing an annual New Year's tree planting festival, for which he created a special branch of CAW, Forever Forests. Over the following years, hundreds of people came up to the Ranch each January to plant thousands of cedar, pine, Douglas fir, and redwoods on logged-over land on

Greenfield ranch and other places. This active combining of the spiritual with the ecological brought us into contact with Earth First!, where people from CAW and other Pagan Ranch folk like Sequoia, became an active presence in the early days and even during the Redwood Summer of 1990.

The winter of 1977-'78 was the founding time of the Covenant of the Goddess (CoG). Aiden Kelly, MG and I, and various other folks who were in the Bay Area Pagan Community decided it would be a good idea to form an alliance among the many groups. It would be an umbrella organization that would provide a legal structure for little groups that were not legally incorporating to join underneath it for legal protection.

Throughout my life I've been involved in every effort I could possibly get involved in to form associations and alliances to try to create a game that everybody could play in. I've always felt that there needed to be some place that all the different Pagan groups could come together. That has been a real challenge, and an ongoing thing. Most of these were short-lived. But the Covenant of the Goddess was destined to become a significant one.

This involved trips to different places. One of the first ones was down in LA. Allison and Gwydion went with us on our bus. One of the people down there was Poke Runyon. At one point Poke came up to me and said he wanted to make an apology for having been such an ass many years before when we were both involved with the Council of Themis. I accepted, and we smoked a peace pipe together. It was quite nice. We've gotten along ever since.

A few months later (Feb. '78) we were doing the same thing up in Seattle, continuing to recruit people for the Covenant of the Goddess. While we were up there Morning Glory got a call from her mom. Her dad had had a serious heart attack and was in the hospital and wasn't expected to live. She left and flew to LA. That left me all by myself on the Scarlet Succubus.

Part of my ongoing work has been the search for unknown critters. In the Pacific Northwest I was in the neighborhood of the Bigfoot mythos. I was reading a book on Bigfoot by Peter Berne who said his headquarters was on the Oregon/Washington border. I decided to go see him on the way back. We met in a restaurant and made a great connection. While I was there I was looking at postcards of things in the area, and one of them showed Stonehenge. It was restored—not the ruins that you normally see. I turned the card over and read that it was in Maryhill, Washington. I showed it to Peter and asked him where it was. He gave me directions—it was very close to where we were.

So I went to check it out. It was amazing—a full-scale concrete replica of Stonehenge as it had originally looked before it fell into ruins. It was out in the middle of nowhere. I was able to find out that it had been built by railroad executive Samuel Hill as a memorial for the people who had died in World War I. He had this notion, which was popular in those days, that Stonehenge had been built by the Druids as a temple where human sacrifices were conducted. Of course, that is not a true account of what happened at the original Stonehenge, but it gave him a justification to build it.

He picked the location because it was the only place in North America where two paths of solar eclipses would ever cross. They would form an "X marks the spot." The first crossing had been in 1921. And the next one was due in 1979, on February 26th!

The altar stone in the center of the ring of the Stonehenge had been laid into place for the eclipse in 1921. Subsequently everything else—trilithons, heelstone, menhirs, portal stones, and the great outer ring of lintel-capped stones—was built around it. It was all prepared for this coming eclipse—just a year away!

I was blown away by the whole idea. It occurred to me then that we ought to do something about it. This was going to be happening in less than a year. Shortly afterwards two events occurred. One was the Oregon Country Fair, which is the weekend before the 4th of July, followed by the Rainbow Family Gathering, which was happening in Oregon that year. I went back to Greenfield Ranch, and Morning Glory returned from Los Angeles. MG was sick with the flu and didn't feel like going to Oregon, so Rainbow and I hitchhiked up to Oregon together. We went to the Fair and were hanging out with the Flying Karamazov Brothers and their friends, many of whom were performers. I decided it would be a great time to trip. There was a huge tree with a multi-leveled tree house built in its branches, like the Elven flets of Tolkien's Lothlorien. I was up there for quite a while, and I had an amazing vision. I saw a black sun over a trilithon, and heard the words: "The prophecies will come when shadow mates with sun. Be there. You know where." This burned itself into my brain. I came down from this and started drawing pictures with the date and verse on it and putting them around places. Shortly after that Rainbow and I went to the Rainbow Gathering, and I handed out cards with the image and date on it

GAIL: Oberon took me to the Rainbow Family gathering. I was around seven or eight. I don't know what happened, but he ended up losing me. I was lost for days. I ended up staying with the Hare Krishnas, because they were feeding me and stuff. I watched this guy freak out on acid and kill himself. It was a weird weekend. Eventually I found him somehow. He was in a teepee somewhere, and I was like "ohmygod, where have you been?" He was fine with it, and I was pissed.

OZ: I have no justification or explanation for losing Rainbow at that gathering. I don't recall just how we got separated. I did have a campsite and kept checking back there for her—and at other campsites. But among tens of thousands of people, it wasn't easy to keep track of each other, and I failed to do so. Fortunately, there are many good people at these gatherings, and some of them took her in and looked after her until I found her again. Still, that was inexcusable, and she had every right to be pissed.

After the Rainbow Gathering, I continued to print up flyers and send them out to people. Of course, this was in the days before email. But it still got around a lot. We started making plans for going up to the Maryhill Stonehenge and doing a ceremony for the eclipse.

At that same time MG and I were on the land planning on raising Unicorns. We were building pens and barns and looking for suitable livestock and setting everything into place. During that time we were mostly engaged in that process. But we were also preparing for the eclipse ceremony. We contacted other Pagan leaders that we knew—mostly people from the newly-formed Covenant of the Goddess. The Stonehenge was on the property of the Maryhill Museum—we contacted them and got their permission. They were enthusiastic and cooperative in every way.

In November of 1978, MG and I drove our new pickup truck back to St Louis to collect some of our stuff that we'd had to leave in storage there because there'd been no room in our bus for it when we'd left. We had no room for all of it back at the Ranch, either, but Lance and Larue agreed to store some stuff at their place in Santa Fe until we could return for it. After we visited them, we continued on to the Grand Canyon, which I'd never seen. We got there in the evening, and there was no place to stay. So we bought a little tube tent and strung it between two trees and taped some plastic trashbags over the ends. We kept our snakes in mailbags when we travelled but we took them out and put them into our zipped-together sleeping bags with us to keep them warm and then we went to sleep.

In the morning, we awoke to discover that it had snowed in the night, and our tent was buried in snow! We dug ourselves out, and then had to pass the snakes one by one up through the snow tunnel we had dug to get them back into the bags inside the truck. They were both pretty unhappy about their first experience with snow. Nevertheless, we decided that it would be nice to have breakfast at the rustic Bright Angel Lodge and then hike down into the Canyon. But everyone who goes down into the Canyon has to sign up at the Ranger Station so they'll know that everyone got back out.

When we went to do so, and I gave our mailing address as "Redwood Valley, California," suddenly all eyes were on us. The date was Nov. 18, and it seemed that the news that day was all full of the horrible massacre of 918 people at the People's Temple settlement of Jonestown, in Guyana, South America! Since their church had previously been established in Redwood Valley, everyone wanted to know if we were connected to them. Of course, since they had all moved down to Guyana several years before we came to California, we didn't really know anything about those guys. For years it was sort of uncomfortable for us being a Church with a mailing address in Redwood Valley.

But we enjoyed a nice breakfast, and then hiked a little ways down into the Canyon. When we returned to the truck, we discovered that Ananta, our rambunctious Burmese python, had somehow worked his way out of the mailbag and had gotten completely entangled behind the instrument panel. MG had quite a job to cajole and extricate him!

MG: We continued on into Colorado to visit my cousin and his family who lived near the Ute Indian Reservation. It was after dark when we got lost along the way and stopped to ask for directions at the only light we could see from the road. It was down a driveway that led to a cabin in the woods. I got out to go up to the house and ask for directions. I knocked on the door and was alarmed to hear the barking of what sounded like several wolf packs together with the Hounds of the Baskervilles. The door was opened by a huge Ute Indian man and the dogs surged out in a snarling mass. Now, I love animals but I am not the Dog Whisperer; I have never lived with them and I don't speak their language. But I stood my ground and tried to ask the man if he knew where the road we were looking for was. He said he didn't know, and so I turned to go and one of the dogs slashed at my leg and tried to hamstring me. I dodged away and yelled at the guy to call off his dogs. He just laughed and shook his head and went back inside.

I managed to reach down and pick up a branch to brandish at the dogs and was able to limp back to the car backwards with blood streaming down my leg and the dogs stalking me until I reached the truck and got the door open. OZ wanted to go back to the house and have words with the guy about his dogs, but I told him to cut our losses and keep on driving while I rinsed off my wound and packed it with paper napkins. We finally located my cousin's house and were welcomed heartily and helped into the house where I could dress my wound properly. They were concerned that the local guy's dogs might not have been vaccinated for rabies because a lot of the local tribal folk didn't have the money for that sort of thing. This did not make me feel any better but I didn't feel like I wanted to interrupt our journey to go and have many long needles stuck in me for rabies treatments so I decided to take my chances.

Whenever we went anywhere, we would often pick up road-killed animals. Sometimes we could save a critter if it was only wounded, but if it was dead we would sometimes still try to take it and use it in some way. I guess we wanted to make its death seem less stupid and senseless that way. I would sing to the animal's spirit and to the Goddess that the spirit would be released and go back to Her to be given a better rebirth. Then we would skin the creature and process the hide and fur and use it to make costumes for rituals and use the skull and bones for spell-working.

We had developed a language steeped in black humor for spotting roadkills which allowed us to make the split second decision whether it was worth it to stop for the animal or keep on going. If it was a "smack rabbit," a "crush puppy," or a "flat cat" it was past the hope of help and was impossible to reclaim. But sometimes we got lucky. We rescued box turtles and patched them up with epoxy; or found screech owls that had flown down to catch a mouse breaking cover at the side of the road, were temporarily blinded by mud splattered from passing cars, and just needed to have their eyes rinsed out and set free. Sometimes we would find a freshly-killed hawk or squirrel that would make a nice pouch or a beautiful headdress.

On this journey we found a real prize: it was a skunk that had just had its head run over and was completely intact. It had died so quickly and so recently that it had not released its scent glands. Skunks have a lovely black and white pelt but mostly you can't get within 100 yards of a dead skunk because of the stench. This skunk was different; it hardly smelled at all, so we wrapped it in plastic, packed it in ice, and put it in the back of the truck. When we got to my cousins, after we had a nice visit, we asked them if we could go out into the back of their parcel away from everything and skin an animal we found on the road. My cousin sort of blinked once or twice and said: "What kind of animal?" Reluctantly I explained that it was a skunk, and to his everlasting credit he just blinked a couple more times and asked me if I wanted to borrow his knife.

OZ: The following February, up at Maryhill, the museum curators talked to the local media about the upcoming eclipse and the plans for a huge Pagan ritual there, and set up a press conference for a few days before the event. In addition to MG and me, our group included Anodea Judith, Isaac Bonewits, Stephen Abbot, Alison Harlow, Anna Korn, Tom Williams, Orion Stormcrow, Selene Kumin, Danaan, and many others. When we all got there we explained to the media what we were going to do. They said that we were crazy. It was the middle of winter, and in that part of the country you can rarely see the sky at that time of year because it's so rainy and cloudy all the time. So Isaac popped up and said, "We've got a bunch of weather workers with us. We'll just clear the clouds out of the way." We realized that we had to actually deliver on that!

On the day of the ritual, people started showing up. The museum put out portapotties. The police were there to direct traffic. More than 3,000 people drove up in cars and started setting up camp.

The night before the eclipse some folks built a fire in the middle of the Stonehenge circle. They began to play drums and dance. As people danced around the fire they cast shadows on the stones. The size of the shadows exactly matched the size of the stones. It was as if the stones had been built specifically to be screen backdrops for shadows of dancers. We recalled that one of the obscure and odd names of Stonehenge was "The Giants Dance." And that was what we were seeing—the stones themselves appeared to be dancing. The energy was incredible. At one point the energy was so intense we all lifted our hands up to the sky and screamed. There was a clear sky up above us, and nothing but stars. Not a cloud. We looked at each other and said, "Okay, we've done our work here.

We got up in the morning, put on our robes and got out of our tents. There was a procession in the morning mist that was over everything. The crowd parted as we approached the altar stone.

As the sun rose and the edge of it started being eaten away by the moon, we began chanting the most effective, universal weather chant: "Rain, rain, go away, come again some other day." And the clouds parted. The sky went completely clear. It was an utterly blue, clear sky. We looked off towards the distant horizon and we saw, heading towards us, the shadow of the moon rippling across the landscape. And then we were engulfed in shadow. The sky went completely black and stars came leaping out. All the birds that were flying squawked and dove for cover because they thought night had suddenly fallen. You could hear cows mooing and lowing as they went to lie down to sleep. There up in the sky above us was this great eye. Because when the surface of the sun was completely covered by the moon, what leaped out from behind it was the corona. It looks like the iris of a cosmic eye, with the pupil at the center of it. And we suddenly understood the image of the eye of God that you see on the back of a one dollar bill and in all kinds of Masonic and ancient Egyptian art. It's the image of a solar eclipse.

ANODEA JUDITH: We did a nature ritual inside the Stonehenge. It was early in the morning, and I played the Element of Air. What an eclipse is, is that the moon goes in front of the sun, that is what is literally happening. So for our ritual we had a woman carry a big Venus of Willendorf statue. She was playing the moon, and we had somebody playing the sun. So it was the Goddess coming in front of the sun, and the feminine kind of eclipsing the masculine and getting some notice. And I think at that time the feminine was really starting to come back alive. People were starting to rediscover the Goddess, and we were bringing notice in the world to the feminine. Not that the feminine is better than the masculine, but it had been so repressed and hadn't been seen. So for a short time it got to stand out in front of the masculine.

OZ: It was at that same time that the planet Pluto moved into the solar system, inside the orbit of Neptune. Normally it lies outside of it—it has this long elliptical orbit. For a 20-year period it would be inside the orbit of Neptune and therefore inside the solar system. That 20-year period would end in 1999, and on August 11, the last total eclipse of the sun in the millennium was due to fall over southern England, where there are numerous ancient stone circles. Stonehenge would be just outside of the range, but there were others inside it. So that was pretty exciting. We set the first piece of a 20-year working into place. And that 20-year working was the first beginning of an Awakening. What we wanted to do was infuse the shadows that moved across the face of the Earth with an energy field that would carry with it a sense of awakening among the people, which would eventually lead to a planetary Awakening.

After it was all over, we gathered up our stuff and people broke camp and headed off in their different directions. All the scientists had gone to the observatory up in Golden. That was the official place, where the main story was supposed to be. But up there you couldn't see anything. It was totally covered by clouds. That evening we went back to our hotel and turned on the news to see if it had anything to say about us. Walter Cronkite was hosting. He showed satellite photos of the shadow moving across the face of the Pacific Northwest. And there was nothing but solid clouds until it got to right where we were. And the clouds opened up like the iris of a camera for the length of the eclipse. And when the shadow moved on it closed again, then a little further down it opened up again at the Warm Springs Indian reservation in Idaho. Those were the only two places that the eclipse could be seen at all.

Commenting on this phenomenon, Walter Cronkite said, "While the Pagans and Druids claimed not to be seeking any converts, it seems to us that after this demonstration of their weather working skills, they may have won some among the members of the Meteorological Society." The next days we were in all the newspapers. They wrote about how the Druids cleared the sky so that the people could see it. And all the good photos came from Stonehenge.

The following day there were stories quoting the scientists as saying that we didn't actually clear the sky because that's not possible. They were just not going to let us have the credit.

MG: Right after the eclipse we had to go down to Berkeley to spend a few days with Isaac Bonewits. It was the beginning of March, 1979, and the weather was bitterly cold. We had our snakes, Ananta and Tanith, who needed to be taken care of, but Ananta weighed nearly 100 lbs. at this point and so this time we decided to leave them behind because we were hitchhiking down to the City. Oberon had made a box for them that they could be kept in. It had a shielded light bulb in it to keep them warm. But it had to be plugged in somewhere, so we took them and the box down to the auto shop where Orion was working, in the small nearby town of Calpella. All he had to do was keep them warm for a couple of days. And since it was really cold, we covered the box with a blanket.

We were in Berkeley with Isaac and Anodea, when Orion showed up on their doorstep. He said, "I hate to be the bearer of bad news, but your snakes are dead." Apparently just after we left there had been a heat wave. Nobody had thought about the snakes—out of sight, out of mind. Because of the temperature change they had baked to death in their box. We were totally stricken by this.

OZ: We returned to the Ranch and buried them next to where we were building the barn for the Unicorns. That was quite a blow. We were wondering what it all meant. We had just been through this incredible eclipse ritual, and then we had the backlash of losing the snakes that we had been so bonded with. And now we were about to embark on our venture with the Unicorn.

So we walked down to the stream that ran through the land. Called Eldritch Creek, it was one of those Northern California creeks that in the summertime is just kind of a loosely-connected sequence of stagnant puddles; but in the wintertime it becomes this raging torrent because of all the rain. We wanted to check on how the erosion control work we'd done during the summer was holding up. And most importantly, we needed to talk about our lives, and our plans for the future.

One of the things that I wanted to discuss with MG was my name. I'd been wrestling with this thing ever since I'd gone to Oregon. The guy who was the manager of the Flying Karamazov Brothers was named Tim Furst. Since Tim had been my name, and through previous years that had been the only name that I had had, it produced an interesting situation. You just don't have two people with the same first name in a bunch of Hippies, because they tend to use only one name. So when somebody said, "Tim," it got confusing as to who they meant. And then I moved to Greenfield Ranch, which had originally been bought by a guy named Tim Baker. And people were talking about him all the time. *He* was the "Tim," not me.

So I tried to look for some other identity. Many people who moved to Greenfield Ranch just took another name, a mystical or magical name. One that had occurred to me was "Atavar," which is like the reverse of an *avatar*. An avatar is a manifestation of a superior being, like a god in human form. But an *atavar* is kind of a throw-back, like Tarzan or Conan, a primeval "noble savage" sort of thing. I thought that was a cool name, kind of a play on words. But it was too obscure. Right about that time Ralph Bakshi's movie *Wizards* came out, and it featured this goofy little Wizard whose name was Avatar. This presented a problem, because people thought that was who I was trying to identify with; and moreover, that I couldn't spell it right. So they thought I was being pretentious and illiterate at the same time. So that didn't work very well.

Now, I am fundamentally an aquatic creature. I had grown up by a lake, and in my youth I spent much of my summers swimming—mostly underwater, popping up for air. I swim like an otter, and Morning Glory had taken to referring to me as an "Otter in the water." It had sort of become a nickname, but only in the context of swimming, and not a name that I had taken seriously. She suggested that I take that name, and I said it wasn't really dignified enough. If all went according to our plans, I said, in a year we were going to be out in the world with our Unicorns, and media people would be talking to us, and I would need to have a really cool name to go by. I needed something mystical and arcane—appropriate for a Wizard.

We were having this conversation on the high bank overlooking Eldritch Creek. Below us the stream was roaring by in full flood. Morning Glory said, "Why don't you ask the Goddess for a sign?"

So I said okay, and did this little invocation: "Oh great Goddess, Mother of all living, give me a sign for a name in which I may continue to do your work and be known in the world." At that exact moment—no sooner had the words left my lips—we looked down at a rock that was poking out of the stream. And a wild otter popped up out of the water. It was the first one I had ever seen. It climbed up onto the rock, looked right up at us, spun around in a little pirouette, and disappeared back into the foaming froth.

Morning Glory and I turned and looked at each other. I shrugged my shoulders and said, "I hear and I obey." So after that, whenever people asked about my name, "Otter," I would say truly that it was the name my Mother gave me.

Maryhill Stonehenge on day of
Solar Eclipse, Feb. 26, 1979.

Solar Eclipse at Maryhill Stonehenge,
Washington. Feb. 26, 1979.

Solar Eclipse ritual altar at Stonehenge, Feb. 26, 1979 (front row, L-R: Selene Kumin, Anodea Judith, Morning Glory, Isaac Bonewits, Tim Zell, Anna Korn)

Appendix A:
A Brief Chronology

1961 Tim Zell begins freshman year at Westminster College, Fulton, MO, where he meets Lance Christie and Martha McCance.

1962 Lance and Tim read *Stranger in a Strange Land* and share water (April 7), vowing to begin living according to concepts set forth therein. They form a water-brotherhood called "Atl" and begin publishing *The Atlan Torch.*

1963 Tim marries Martha (April), and they have a son, Bryan (Sept. 15).

1965 Tim graduates from Westminster with BA and Majors in Pre-Med, Psychology, Sociology & Anthropology; begins graduate school at Washington University in St Louis on USPS scholarship in Clinical Psychology; begins new Nest of CAW there.

1966 Tim quits graduate school, begins working for Human Development Corp as Head Start Counselor. *Star Trek* premiers on TV (Sept. 8).

1967 On Labor Day, Tim first goes public with Church of All Worlds, applies for incorporation. He begins using term "Pagan" as self-identification for this new religion. He completes Life Science College for a DD, becomes ordained as first Priest of CAW (Dec. 21).

1968 CAW receives MO corporate status on March 4; opens first coffee house/temple on Gaslight Square—the "Instead;" Tim begins publishing *Green Egg* (March 21). He also obtains a Teacher's Certificate and begins teaching public grade school. Temple closes in Sept.

1969 With Fred Adams of Feraferia and others, Tim co-founds the Council of Themis—the first Pagan ecumenical council. CAW Nest meetings held at homes on Friday nights, for *Star Trek.* Sci-fi Worldcon in St Louis (Labor Day)—Tim attends his first Worldcon, and meets many people (including John C. Sulak)…

1970 April: CAW opens a new storefront Temple on Kingsbury St. OZ does his first acid trip (at Solar Eclipse, March 7); he meets Julie (April 1); CAW major participant at first Earth Day (April 22). CAW gets its IRS 501(c)(3) (June 18). Tim begins Witchcraft training under Deborah Letter. On Sept. 6, Tim has major Vision of the Living Earth, which he writes up as "TheaGenesis." This is the first publication of what later becomes known as "The Gaea Thesis."

1971 Martha and Tim separate, later to divorce. Tim initiated into Craft by Deborah Letter. Julie, Bryan, and Tim travel to East Coast for sci-fi Noreascon (Labor Day). They win "Best Group" in costume contest as "Tom Bombadil, Goldberry and Frodo," along with Mark Whitroth as "Strider." They meet Susan Roberts, Ray Buckland, Leo Martello, Robert Rimmer, and many famous Witches. Tim begins correspondence with Robert Heinlein.

1972 Council of Themis dissolves due to internal dissension; Council of Earth Religions formed. Tim & Julie attend sci-fi WorldCon in Los Angeles; win Grand Prize in costume contest as "Cernunnos & Cerridwen." They meet many Califia Pagans, travel up to San Francisco and Greenfield Ranch to see the new land being bought into…

1973 Tim & Julie break up in Spring. Tim hitchhikes to Rainbow Family Gathering in Lander, WY. Gets arrested in Colo. for hitchhiking. Meets Bonnie Sherlock—receives 2nd degree Craft initiation. At Mabon Tim attends Gnostic Aquarian festival in Minneapolis, as a keynote speaker on TheaGenesis. There he meets and falls in love with Morning Glory. She moves in with him.

1974 Tim & MG are married in huge public Pagan handfasting in Minneapolis (April 14). Isaac Bonewits & Carolyn Clark officiate; Margot Adler sings Gwydion songs. Tim & MG attend sci-fi Worldcon in Wash. DC, win 1st prize in costume contest as "most primal."

1975 On 33rd birthday (Nov. 30), Tim quits his job, rents out the house (now put into name of CAW). Tim & MG buy and fix up an old red Chevvy school bus: "The Scarlet Succubus."

1976 Tim & MG leave for West Coast. After many adventures, they end up in Eugene, OR, where they teach classes on "Celtic Shamanism" at Lane Community college. Their research uncovers the lost secret of the Unicorn. Back in St Louis, GE folds. Soon, so does CAW.

1977 Tim & MG move onto 5,600-acre Greenfield Ranch as caretakers on Alison Harlow's 220-acre parcel, *Coeden Brith*. Their plan: to raise Unicorns! They transfer CAW HQ to CA, form Holy Order of Mother Earth (HOME) with Alison and begin land-based Pagan life,

1979 Total Eclipse of the Sun (Feb. 26) over full-scale Stonehenge replica in Washington state. Tim & MG officiate at rites, along with other Pagan luminaries. 3-4,000 people attend. They clear the clouds, get much media attention! Tim receives new name of "Otter," making his initials "OZ."

Appendix B:
The Scarlet Succubus

By Oberon

When John was putting this book together, he asked me to give more information on the design and building of the interior of the Scarlet Succubus, which he thought was fascinating. But the first edition had no room for this explanation, so here it is, in detail:

All the interior woodwork was a textured grey paneling, looking like the wood of an old oak barn, with walnut trim. The ceiling and floor were carpeted in a textured brown pile. Exposed walls of the bus were painted lime green. As you came in the front door, there were two bench seats behind the driver's seat, with a sliding door behind them. They had a double layer on the seat part, with a piano hinge along the front edge, so they could be folded out into two short beds, and another hinged piece on one side could be raised up between them to make one long bed. The 3-inch-thick lime-green Naugahyde seat and back cushions were also hinged, with snaps that fastened them in place. When the seats were made down into beds, the cushions would lay out flat to become a mattress. Under the shotgun seat was storage for tools, etc. Under the driver-side seat was the extra battery and inverter system that Charlie built for us. These compartments were accessed by lifting the seats (which were also hinged in back).

Between the front seats was a sliding door that gave access to the rest of the bus. The top of the bus was curved, so in order to place a track for the sliding doors, I had to cut a crescent-shaped section across the top, which made for a low doorway, upon which I and people around my height were always banging our foreheads. We called it "The Gerald Ford Memorial Arch."

Passing through the sliding door, on the left was a 2-foot wide lime-green Formica counter running the 10-foot length of the central room, and ending at a wall, behind which were the table and benches of our dining area and bedroom. I removed several of the windows on the sides of the bus and replaced them with insulated panels, so there were two windows on the left side of the "kitchen," with a blank wall between them. Under the Formica counter were, first, a 3-way refrigerator (AC, DC, propane), with a counter-to-ceiling cabinet above it. The back of the refrigerator could be accessed via a louvered panel on the outside of the bus, to ignite the pilot light or plug in an outside electric cord. To the right of the cabinet, under the window, was a sink, drawing water from a large tank under the counter that could be filled from outside. There was a propane flash heater for hot water.

To the right of the sink was about four feet of open countertop, with cabinets underneath and overhead. The overhead cabinets had sliding doors in tracks, and fluorescent lights underneath. The cabinets under the counter were only one foot deep; the back half was walled off to contain the water tank and a special metal-reinforced compartment for two propane tanks, with a large blow-out panel on the outside. At the far end of the counter, up against the wall, was a propane stove with a 4-burner range, and a window behind it. The right rear wheel well was under the stove. The fronts of the stove and refrigerator were both lime-green. And in the middle of the 6-foot wall between the windows was a little foot-square fold-down altar, with a mirror inside, faced with bark when it was closed.

The carpeted aisle down the center of the kitchen area was about 4 feet wide. The right side of the kitchen was a complex set of closets, bookcases, and animal cages, taking up another 4 feet in depth. First (behind the front seat) was a wide clothes closet, with a mirror on the inside of the door and a shelf at the top for hats, etc. The outside of the door was covered by a large poster of a comic book series called "Amethyst." Next was the chemical toilet, with a holding tank underneath. The outside of the toilet chamber door held a calendar. I left a window in the toilet chamber, glazing it with a kind of frost-like spray-on stuff. To the back left of the toilet chamber were 3-foot-wide, 3-foot-deep open shelves for towels, extra toilet paper, etc. On the kitchen side, the front of that same space was occupied by a 3-foot-wide, one-foot-deep bookcase, with our *Encyclopedia of Man, Myth and Magick,* the *Time-Life Science* and *Nature* books, and other books on history, nature, magick, etc. After the bookcase, the remaining portion of the wall held two large cabinets with hinged doors that opened down. These were about 3 feet wide, and one was for our colony of rats (snake food) in lab rat bins. The other cabinet we initially used to house our possum, Participle, but when she bailed in Eugene, we used the cabinet for papers and stuff.

Underneath the cabinets and bookcase ran a 6-foot-long snake cage, about a foot in height, and 4 feet deep. It had a drop-down door, half screened with ¼" mesh, with a sliding panel in the door that could be slid shut to hide the snakes (Tanith, the boa, got to be 6 feet; and Ananta, the Burmese python, grew to 10 feet). Under the snake cage was the left rear wheel well, which left an odd-shaped space around it which could be accessed through a trap door in the bottom of the snake cage, under the Astroturf carpet in the cage. This was our hidden stash spot where we kept anything we wanted to make sure that no one would ever get into.

Passing through the 3-foot-wide opening at the back of the kitchen area, you came into our dining and social area. On the left side were bench seats and a specially-designed double-hinged table with a lime-green

Formica top that could be set down onto molding at the fronts of the seats to make a full platform for a bed. When it was up as a table, it was supported by a single folding leg. There was room for four people to sit at the table. Like the ones in the front, the lime-green Naugahyde seat and back cushions were also hinged, with snaps that fastened them in place, and when they were laid down flat across the table, the whole space made a full-size double bed, which is where MG and I slept. Under the seats were storage compartments, accessed by lifting the seats. One of these contained all our magickal tools and items.

Across the 3-foot-wide aisle from the table and bench seats was a 6-foot-long sofa. Facing the sofa, the wall to the right was completely a bookcase for paperbacks (mostly fantasy and sci-fi). Just like the bench seats in the front of the bus, the seat of the sofa was double, with a piano hinge along the front, so that the seat could be lifted up and laid down to bridge the aisle, making a really huge bed. Moreover, the back of the sofa, which was angled enough to be comfortable in the down position, was also hinged along the top, with chains at the corners that could be hooked over ceiling hooks to hold the back either horizontal—for a bunk bed—or higher at a 45° angle. The underside of the sofa back held a full-length mirror. The sofa back had a snap-on lime-green Naugahyde cushion that became a mattress when it was in the bunk bed position. The seat of the sofa had a long hinged cushion, with the back folding up behind the sofa back when it was in the sofa position, or pulled out to cover the whole bed area when the seat was folded out into a bed. Under the sofa were several storage compartments, accessed by drop-down doors. These held boxes of stuff—mostly papers.

So we had several options for sleeping arrangements. We could just raise the back of the sofa, making two single bunk beds. We could open the sofa into a double bed. We could put the table down between the bench seats and make another double bed. Or we could do it all and have a gigantic family bed for four people (which we did upon occasion...) with an angled mirror above to make it all more interesting...

The back of the bus was curved, with a small back door in the center. I built cabinetry into the curve that provided a nightstand shelf and more bookcases at the back of the dining and sleeping area. I built overhead cabinets above the table and bench seats. And in the middle of the ceiling above the dining/sleeping area, I put in a domed skylight that also opened so you could stick your head out. I left all the windows in the dining/sleeping section, covering the side ones with a stained-glass design clear contact paper. And all the windows had curtains that could be pulled shut for privacy.

As to how I acquired my carpentry skills, well, I've always been good at making things. I'm a natural artist, and I can easily conceptualize from two to three dimensions, and design plans, blueprints, and cut-outs that will assemble into 3-D structures. See the cut-out paper models in the back of my *Companion for the Apprentice Wizard.*

I guess this started as a kid. I used to enjoy cutting out and assembling little cardboard animals printed on the backs of cereal boxes. I liked this so much that I started making my own, and for an art project in junior high, I made an entire cardboard "City of the Future" with futuristic sci-fi buildings, elevated roadways, and even little futuristic cars. I got into making wood and plastic models of planes, spaceships, and animals, and won prizes in model contests. And I spent countless hours assembling ever-more-complex puzzles in the days before television, when we'd lie around on the living room floor and listen to the radio while we put puzzles together. (I remember particularly enjoying episodes of "The Lone Ranger," "The Green Hornet," "Superman," and "The Shadow.")

In high school, I took wood shop, which taught me all the tools of woodworking and cabinetry, and how to use them. I also took mechanical drawing, learning how to diagram things I wanted to make. And finally, I took a class in architecture, learning building design and how to make blueprints. I drew blueprints and built a ¼":1' scale balsa-wood model of a circular dream house I designed. I used pinheads for cabinet door pulls, and nylon stockings for screen doors—it was that detailed. I had this for many years, all the way through college, but in 1965, sitting on top of all our worldly possessions in the back of our VW camper, it was eventually trashed by the cat we picked up on the way from Grand Lake, Colorado, to St Louis (where I was heading to graduate school at Washington University).

So I can pretty much get an idea in my head of something I'd like to build, and just do it. Sometimes I make diagrams, but often I just do it on the natch, making it up as I go along. I designed and built the cabinetry interior for the VW camper that Julie and I drove to the East Coast in 1971, but she rolled it on the way home and pretty much trashed it. After the Scarlet Succubus, I built two yurts at Greenfield for MG and me, and Diane & Zack, as well as our barns and stables for the Unicorns and goats. And I worked with others (such as Gwydion) on various house- and barn-building projects on the Ranch, as well as bridges, water tanks, stables, etc. I'd have built more if I'd ever had money…I designed a really nifty circular house I'd hoped to build on Coeden Brith, but we could never afford the materials. I still have the blueprints, though…

Appendix C: Index